ALWAYS USE PROTECTION
A TEEN'S GUIDE TO SAFE COMPUTING

ALWAYS USE PROTECTION
A TEEN'S GUIDE TO SAFE COMPUTING

Dan Appleman

Apress®

Always Use Protection: A Teen's Guide to Safe Computing

ISBN (pbk): 1-59059-326-X

Printed and bound in the United States of America 12345678910

Technical Reviewers: See Acknowledgments
Editorial Board: Steve Anglin, Dan Appleman, Gary Cornell, James Cox, Tony Davis,
    John Franklin, Chris Mills, Steven Rycroft, Dominic Shakeshaft, Julian Skinner, Jim Sumser,
    Karen Watterson, Gavin Wray, John Zukowski
Assistant Publisher: Grace Wong
Project Manager: Sofia Marchant
Copy Editor: Ami Knox
Production Manager: Kari Brooks
Production Editor: Ellie Fountain
Proofreader: Elizabeth Berry
Compositor: Gina Rexrode, Point n' Click Publishing, LLC
Illustrator: Kinetic Publishing Services, LLC
Indexer: Valerie Robbins
Interior and Cover Designer: Kurt Krames
Manufacturing Manager: Tom Debolski

Library of Congress Cataloging-in-Publication Data

Appleman, Daniel.
    Always use protection : a teen's guide to safe computing / Dan Appleman.
        p. cm.
    Includes index.
    ISBN 1-59059-326-X (soft cover : alk. paper)
    1. Computer security. I. Title: Teen's guide to safe computing. II. Title.
    QA76.9.A25A63 2004
    005.8--dc22

                                2004003941

Contents at a Glance

PART III
PROTECTING YOURSELF

PART VI
APPENDIXES

Contents in Depth

PART II
PROTECTING YOUR PRIVACY

PART III
PROTECTING YOURSELF

About the Author

Dan Appleman's career is typical of someone who, unable to choose what he wants to do for a living, decides to do everything. From founding a software company (Desaware), to cofounding a publishing company (Apress), to programming, to writing books (this is his seventh), he's a firm believer that the question "What do you want to be when you grow up?" can't and shouldn't be answered until you're at least 80 (so he has a way to go).

Meanwhile, he's also a consultant, public speaker, and columnist, and volunteers as a youth group advisor (which is how he knows the kinds of security issues teens actually face today).

Acknowledgments

I imagine this is how it feels to win an Oscar award, and have just 60 seconds to thank everyone involved in your project—hoping you won't miss anyone.

It takes a lot of people to put a book together. First, there's the great crew at Apress. On the editorial side, there's Gary Cornell, of course, and Grace Wong (working her usual magic), and Dominick Shakeshaft, who was especially helpful in encouraging me to go all out with this project. It's a thrill working again with Sofia Marchant, Ami Knox, and Kari Brooks, and for the first time with Ellie Fountain and Elizabeth Berry—thanks to them, this was by far the smoothest and highest quality experience I've had with a book. I'd also like to thank Doris Wong, Hollie Fischer, Julie Miller, Stephany Le, and Glyn Davies, whose input and support was and will continue to be invaluable. And kudos to Kurt Krames for his interior design and brilliant cover.

Many thanks to Roan Bear for her help designing the web site.

Thanks also to the crew at Desaware, especially Franky Wong, Karyn Duncan, Marian Kicklighter, and Stjepan Pejic, who kept the company running while I was off writing this book. Thanks to my family for keeping *me* running while I was off writing this book (especially my mom, whose food is both good and plentiful).

There is one group of people whom I simply cannot thank enough for their help. They are my reviewers—most of whom range in age from 13 to 19, who went over each chapter in detail as it was written. They contributed suggestions, corrected errors, and pointed out areas that were unclear. Their (sometimes brutal) comments often resulted in changes, ranging from minor rephrasing, to immediate deletion, to wholesale rewriting of entire sections of the book. And I'm especially grateful for the support they expressed along the way.

In alphabetical order (some last names withheld by request due to privacy issues):

Gabriel Appleman, Daniel B., Joseph B., Tal Bar-Or, Eran Ben-Zvi, Lucas Duncan, R. Kyle Forbes, Serban Giuroiu, Lior Gotesman, Itamar Haritan, Amir R., Gabriel Rocklin, Rachel Rocklin, and Liron Shapira.

Also thanks to Daniel, Boaz, Kendra, Gon, El-ad, Roi, and many others who offered feedback and suggestions at various times.

Thanks, Curtis, for the inspiration—even though you had to get hacked to make it happen.

And a special thanks to Jeff Haritan and the folks at the brainstorming meeting for the title. You were right (as usual).

Introduction

Does your computer sometimes crash for no reason—or act strangely? Are you seeing unexpected lag or sudden dropouts when playing online games? Has your Internet connection gotten slower? Are mysterious pop-up windows appearing at strange times? Have you discovered that someone has impersonated you on an instant messenger program without your knowledge? Are you OK with strangers (or friends or family members) knowing everything you do on your computer? Have you ever wondered which of those amazing e-mail offers are actually true?

This book was inspired by a call I recently received from my nephew. For some reason, his computer desktop was just vanishing at random times—usually a few minutes after turning on his system. It turned out his computer had been infected with a nasty program called a *computer virus*.

Now my nephew is smart. He knows not to download and run programs unless he knows where they come from. He knows what a virus is. Yet, to my surprise, he didn't have an up-to-date virus protection program on his computer.

The next week I helped a friend of his out whose computer was attacked by another program called a *Trojan*—I'll tell you more about that in the book.

It turns out that teens actually have more sophisticated security needs than most adults. It's not enough for you to know about firewalls—you need to know how to keep one up while playing online games. You're much more likely than most adults to be using Kazaa or other peer-to-peer file services, and you're much more likely to be downloading files. The kinds of identity theft you are likely to experience are very different from those experienced by your parents. And because in many families teens know more about computers than their parents, it can sometimes be difficult to find help when problems occur.

This book covers all of these issues and more. It's a book about computer security—the first one ever written for teens and young adults. It goes far beyond the usual "beware the dangers of chat rooms" warnings to teach you everything you need to know to protect your computer, your privacy, and yourself.

Even if you are a beginner now, by the time you finish this book, you'll know more about computer security than almost everyone you know. You'll know how to clean viruses off a system (and maybe even get paid for it). You'll learn how antivirus tools and firewalls work—**and how they can fail**! You'll know how to play online games without opening your system to attack by outsiders. You'll know how to surf the web and shop without leaving traces for advertisers (and others) to follow. You'll even know about cyberterrorism, and how you can help prevent it.

And best of all, you'll be able to help your friends and family members clean up and secure their systems. Because let's face it—they probably need all the help they can get.

What Isn't in This Book

No book can satisfy all the people all the time. And computer security is a vast subject, so some things will be left out, and others may disagree on what I've chosen to emphasize. So here's a bit about my philosophy in writing this book, and the things that I'm assuming as I write it:

- I'm going to assume that you know the basics about using your computer. I'm not going to waste your time with pages explaining what a computer is, how to use a web browser, or how to run a program from the Start menu. Most of you are already routinely using your computer for a variety of tasks. So if you're a real computer beginner, you might want to get a more introductory book before going for this one.

- There are so many different web pages, viruses, virus scanners, firewalls, routers, scams, versions of Windows and browsers, and so on, that detailed instructions on how to deal with each of them is impossible to include without turning this book into a massive encyclopedia. Not only that, but threats and technology evolve, so discussing particular viruses and scams and applications is pointless. Instead, I'm going to try to take you behind the scenes to understand the nature of the threats and how they work. That knowledge, with a bit of common sense, should be enough for you to apply the knowledge to your particular computer and environment.

- There are books out there for parents that teach them how to monitor their kids online. This isn't one of them. This book is written for you to help you take responsibility for protecting your own computer, privacy, and yourself.

- It is not for me to judge what kinds of web sites you visit or files you download. My job is to teach you how to protect yourself. The decision of what kinds of web sites are appropriate or inappropriate, what kinds of files you download, and so on is between you and your parents or teachers. Every family and community has their own standards, and I have no intention of trying to impose my values on you.

- This book only covers Windows. That's because most teens (like most everyone) use Windows desktops. However, the principles do apply to other operating systems as well, so much of the book will have value even if you aren't using Windows.

About Footnotes

You'll notice a lot of footnotes appear in this book. These aren't the "be sure you cite your sources" footnotes that your teachers force you to use in English or History (you know, the ones full of *ibid* and *opcit* and other fun Latin terms). I use footnotes for two things: First, if I use a term that I think most of you will understand, but that might confuse some readers, I'll use a footnote to clarify it. Second, I like to use footnotes for side stories and comments that are hopefully entertaining and humorous, but not really essential.

Those of you who understand the text and find my sense of humor to be incompatible with your own,[1] feel free to ignore the footnotes completely.

About AlwaysUseProtection.com

Almost every author of computer-related books provides a way for readers to obtain updates and corrections to their books—after all, things change rapidly in this field.

In this case, I wanted a way to not only offer updates and corrections, but also go into more detail on specific situations, and even answer reader questions. To my astonishment, the domain name AlwaysUseProtection.com was available, so that's where you can go to find not only updates, but also whatever else I feel like posting. My hope is the site will be useful, but I also plan to have fun with it.

---

[1] *Those of you without a sense of humor should definitely skip the footnotes.*

For My Readers Outside of the U.S.

The web is called the *World Wide Web* for a reason. It truly is international. Yet there are some areas where this book is unavoidably U.S.-centric. For example, any references to specific laws refer to U.S. laws.

It is my hope to include information for other countries on AlwaysUseProtection.com. But to do so, I need your help. If there is anything country specific that you would like to contribute, please submit it on the web site in the feedback section for the appropriate chapter.

Introduction for Parents

Some of you may be wondering, Where are all the horror stories and warnings about how to protect kids from sexual predators in chat rooms? What's all this talk about viruses and firewalls and protecting the computer? Surely that's not as important!

And you're right—protecting teens from online predators is important. And don't worry, there is a chapter on online behavior and privacy in the book. But online protection is a subject that is and has been widely spoken about. Most teens have heard about it. You've talked to your son or daughter about it, right?

None of the teens that I've dealt with have had a truly dangerous online experience. Yes, some of then have engaged in questionable discussions (meaning things you would probably disapprove of), but as often as not they were the ones lying about who they were, and they clearly understood that the people they were talking to were probably lying as well. They knew better than to give out personal information—it was just a game.

But most of them have suffered a computer security breach. I've helped many clean up after viruses and worms. I've seen numerous cases where a stolen password allowed someone to impersonate someone else, and have even seen friendships jeopardized in the process. I've seen teens have their machines hijacked by hackers and locked out of their own e-mail or instant message accounts.

It's not enough for teens to know not to give out their personal information online or arrange to meet with strangers. Teens today need to understand the fundamentals of computer security. They need to know how to protect their computers and their privacy. They need to know about programs they download that might spy on their activities. They need to know how to protect their passwords and why.

This book will teach your teens the most important things they need to know. It won't protect them from every possible threat, but it will protect them from the kinds of security issues that they are actually dealing with already on a routine basis. It will help them stay out of trouble, and help them fix problems once they occur.

Appendix C has more information to help you as parents. Meanwhile, you don't have to do a thing—besides getting your teens this book. It's designed to teach them to help themselves. Though in truth, unless you're already a security expert, it probably won't do you any harm to read it as well.

PROTECTING YOUR MACHINE

The minute you dial in to your Internet service provider or connect to a DSL or cable modem, you are casting your computer adrift in a sea of millions of other computers—all of which are sharing the world's largest computer network, the Internet. Most of those computers are cooperative and well behaved, but some are downright nasty. Only you can make sure your computer is ready for the experience.

Gremlins in Your Machine

- You notice that for some reason your computer seems slower than it used to be. You've tried using the Windows disk defragmenter utility,[1] but it didn't seem to help.

- Internet access seems increasingly unreliable—with slower browsing and increased lag and dropouts while playing online games.

- Some of the programs on your machine that used to work don't work anymore.

- The light on your disk drive flashes constantly, even when you aren't doing anything.

- Some web sites become inaccessible. Or typing in the name of a web site brings you to a completely different site.

- Files on your computer have mysteriously vanished.

- Your machine starts rebooting[2] occasionally without cause.

- Applications, including your desktop application, suddenly disappear.

- You start receiving e-mail reports from friends or automated reports from other computers claiming that you sent out a virus.

- Bizarre, even threatening, messages start appearing in chat windows, even when you aren't using an instant messaging service or visiting a chat site.

- Your computer suddenly fails to boot.

- Your hair grows three inches overnight, and you notice your friends holding their breath when they're within sniffing distance of you.

---

[1] A tool available on most Windows systems to make disk access more efficient. Go to your Start menu and select Accessories ➤ System Tools ➤ Disk Defragmenter to access this tool.

[2] Rebooting is the technical term for what happens when you have just finished writing a paper and have not yet saved your work, and suddenly the screen goes blank and your computer restarts as if you had just turned it on. Goodbye paper.

OK, I'm not going to be able to help you with that last one. You'll want to read "Basic Hygiene for Teens" or "How to Exorcise Demons in Three Easy Steps" if that's your problem. But if you're seeing any of the other symptoms, you may have a gremlin in your computer. A vicious little fictional creature whose sole purpose in life is to cause grief to you and to anything technological in your vicinity.[3]

What do fictional creatures have to do with computers? Well, it turns out that many of the terms I'll be using have roots in biology, history, and mythology—and for good cause. The software I'll be discussing behaves in many ways like the biological counterparts they're named after. And all of them, viruses, worms, bugs, etc., act just like a gremlin would could it actually sneak into your computer to raise havoc. I'll talk more about that later.

If you're seeing any of the symptoms I've listed (other than the last), or any other unexpected or surprising behavior, you might be a victim of a computer virus. Oh, and there's one other symptom that indicates you may have a virus:

Everything seems to be just fine.

That's right. Your computer may be infected and show no symptoms at all. In fact, it might not even be causing you any harm at all—it may be busy attacking someone else without your knowledge.

In this part of the book, you're going to learn all about the various types of viruses that can infest your computer, what they do, how they work, and how to prevent them and what to do to get rid of them if the worst happens.

Why Should You Care?

It's a funny thing—there are plenty of books and articles on computer security for businesses. And there is plenty of information for adults on how to protect their credit card and tax information. Yet there seems to be an unspoken assumption that these things aren't important for teens. It's not as if you have anything really important on your computers that you can't afford to lose, right? It's not as if you don't have plenty of extra time to reinstall software and try to restore your system. How important can your privacy be anyway? Who cares if your system goes down for a few days or weeks—you can write your homework by hand the way we used to when we were kids . . .

Well, I think that's total nonsense.[4]

Many of the teens I know have wasted hours and days dealing with viruses. It's caused them to lose homework, to miss important messages from friends (both e-mail and instant messages), to drop out on scheduled online games, and

---

[3] The term *gremlin* entered widespread use around the World War II period, as an imaginary creature that would cause mechanical failures in the airplanes of England's Royal Air Force.

[4] Writing a book for teens, I must of course be judicious in my choice of words. Please feel free to substitute the four-letter word or profanity of your choice for "nonsense."

to blow deals on eBay. They've brought on draconian restrictions by parents who themselves don't know how to prevent or clean up viruses. Life is frustrating enough without having to deal with unreliable computers. Computers are supposed to be tools to make life easier and more entertaining—not sources of frustration and extra work.

There are many personal reasons why you'll benefit from having a clean and secure system. But it turns out there are other reasons as well.

Just as viruses in nature try to spread from one person to the next, computer viruses try to spread themselves from one computer to another. When your computer becomes infected, it will try to infect others by a variety of methods (which you'll read about in the next two chapters). Your computer may also be hijacked to attack web sites.

So in protecting your own computer, you also protect those of your friends and neighbors, and in the event of cyberterrorism or cyberwar,[5] maybe even your country.

---

[5] *Two terms you'll learn about in the next chapter*

When Software Attacks: All About Viruses

Anytime you do something on your computer, whether it's browsing the web, chatting with a friend on an instant messaging service, writing a paper, or drawing a picture, you're running a program. In fact, the Windows environment itself—the desktop that allows you to view and select files or configure the system—is just a collection of programs.

A computer program is just a set of instructions to a computer. But programs take many forms. They can be *executable files* (files with the extension .exe), or *batch files* containing console[1] commands (files with the extension .bat). They can be scripts that control other programs—for example, a program built into a word processing document that automatically counts the number of words or creates an index, or a script that controls game play on a custom game map.

Once a program gets on your computer, it has access to pretty much all of the capabilities of your machine.[2] As long as the software does what you want and expect it to do, there's no problem. But what if the author of that program had other things in mind?

Evil Schemes

There's almost no limit to the kinds of nasty things viruses and other malicious programs can do. Here's a brief list of some of the kinds of threats that your computer faces if one of these programs is allowed to run on your system.

---

[1] A **console** is the window you see when you request the command prompt from the Start menu. It mimics an old-style DOS window where you type commands in without a graphical interface or mouse.

[2] There are exceptions to this, depending on the type of program or script, the language it was written in, and the configuration of the system. But it's best to work under the assumption that any program on your system can do anything the program's author wanted to do.

The Destroyers

These are programs that have one goal—to trash your system. Some of them do it quickly, by simply deleting your disk partition, boot sector, or reformatting your drive.[3] Some do it slowly, deleting or scrambling random files until your system won't run. Some only target your data—scrambling or destroying data files while leaving key system files in place.[4]

The Annoyances

These programs don't want to destroy your system, only your sanity and patience. They just like to get on your nerves. Maybe they'll periodically terminate your Internet connection or reboot your machine. Or throw garbage up on your screen or suddenly close programs. They might redirect your browser to different web sites, or sign you up to spam e-mail lists.

The Thieves

They say that information is one of the most valuable commodities, and these programs want to steal it from you. They want your passwords, your game CD-keys, and all the personal information they can get. Credit card numbers and tax information (with Social Security numbers) are favorites. They want to know what web sites you've browsed to and get copies of any e-mail you've sent or received. You'll read more about this kind of software in Part II of this book where I discuss privacy.

The Hijackers

These programs don't want to harm your computer at all. They want to take it over and put it to some other use. They might want to use your computer (along with thousands of others) to send corrupt network requests to a particular web site in order to overwhelm it and prevent others from accessing it (this is called a *Denial of Service*, or DoS, attack). They might want to turn your computer into an e-mail server that will allow them to use it to send out spam. They might hijack your hard drive to store pornography, pirate software, or other illegal content.[5]

---

[3] All things that will cause your computer to fail to start and probably lose all of your files

[4] Hint: The old excuse "The dog ate my homework" won't get you anywhere nowadays, but if you try "A virus ate my homework" you might just get an extension. Most of your teachers don't know much about computer security, and I promise by the time you're done with this book, you WILL know more about it than most of your teachers (actually, most adults, period).

[5] This alone is a good reason to take computer security seriously—do you really want to explain to your parents why the FBI is knocking on your door?

Viruses, Worms, and Trojans

Viruses, worms, and Trojans are different kinds of malicious programs. I'll tell you how they differ in a moment, but in truth, most people use the term *computer virus* to refer to all three types of program. So after this section, just assume that when I talk about viruses I'm referring to worms or Trojans as well.

Viruses

In biology, a virus is a submicroscopic piece of genetic material (RNA or DNA) surrounded by a coat of protein. It reproduces by attacking a cell and hijacking its internal structure to create more viruses. Once the cell has done its job, it self-destructs, leaving behind even more of the virus to go and invade other cells.

A computer virus does much the same thing to a computer program.

A computer program consists of a sequence of computer commands along with some data. Once loaded into memory, the program "runs," meaning that the computer executes the command sequences.

Figure 2-1 illustrates a normal program. Imagine that each square represents an instruction that the computer will execute. Each program has a starting point—the first instruction that runs when the program is loaded. So as the program runs, it will execute each instruction in turn, starting from the "starting point" and continuing to the end.

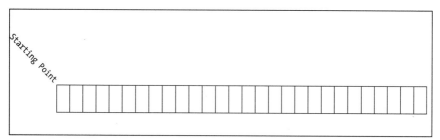

Figure 2-1 A "healthy" program

Figure 2-2 illustrates what happens when a virus infects a program. The virus literally modifies the program file on your disk. The gray squares represent instructions that the virus has added to the program. First, it adds additional code to the program, usually at the end of the program. The viral code is indicated by light gray squares. Next it changes the code at the starting location of the program to force the computer to run the viral code. The new code at the starting point includes an instruction to jump to the rest of the virus code (as indicated by the arrow).

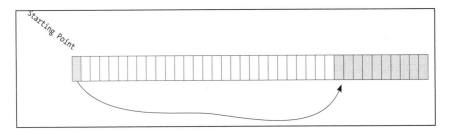

Figure 2-2 An "infected" program

If the virus is really smart, it might also execute the healthy code, in which case you may never know that the virus was running.

Viruses can do any of the things listed earlier in this chapter (and others I probably haven't even imagined), but there's one thing almost all of them do. They try to infect other files on your system or on your network.

Worms

Most of the time when people talk about viruses, they're actually talking about worms as well. A *worm* differs from a virus in that it doesn't infect other files. The worm is a standalone program—it works independently.

A virus runs whenever you execute an infected program. For example, if your paint program is infected, anytime you try to run it the virus will run. Worms can't use this particular trickery, but they have their own ways to get started.

- Most worms add themselves to the list of programs that should run automatically when your computer starts. In Appendix B of this book you'll learn more about self-starting programs.

- Worms also like to trick you into running them, claiming to be something they aren't. For example, a worm might claim to be a game, or a cool program sent by a friend. In Chapter 3, you'll learn all about how viruses and worms spread.

- Worms can also attack vulnerabilities in your system across a network or the Internet, even if you do absolutely nothing—quietly sneaking in without your knowledge.

Other than being standalone programs, worms are just like viruses, and do the same kinds of things once running on your system.

Trojans

Trojans are a kind of virus (actually, a worm most of the time). They're named after the Trojan horse.[6] That's the one where the ancient Greeks defeated Troy by pretending to give up, leaving behind a giant wooden horse in which they had hidden some soldiers. The celebrating Trojans brought the horse into their city, only to be defeated when the soldiers snuck out at night and let the Greek army into the city.

When a Trojan gets on your system, its goal is to allow outsiders into your system.

Recently, my nephew visited a friend, and found him struggling with his computer. Every time he connected to the Internet, he'd start getting pop-up window messages from someone. The messages demanded he give over his Warcraft and Frozen Throne CD-keys, or the blackmailer would delete files on his system. In fact, by the time I heard about it, the system had already suffered quite a bit of damage—not only did his Internet browser no longer work, but even basic programs like Notepad had been deleted.

You might be wondering, How did the attacker find the infected system when it connected to the Internet?

The answer is that he didn't. The Trojan knew its creator and would contact him every time the computer connected to the Internet. The attacker only needed to sit back and wait for the Trojans he sent out to call home and let him on to the infected systems. Some Trojans work this way, others simply instruct the computer to wait for instructions, configuring the computer to listen for future contact from the attacker—perhaps sending out an e-mail or other notification to the attacker so he can build a list of infected computers to contact at will.

That is perhaps the scariest thing about Trojans. An ordinary virus or worm is preprogrammed—it can only do what was designed into it originally. As terrible as those things may be, at least they can be identified and dealt with. A Trojan opens your computer to access by outsiders—real people—and there's no telling what they might do on your computer. They might do nothing more than keep watch on what you're doing; waiting for some interesting information they can steal or use to threaten you. You may not know anything is wrong.

Spyware and Adware

Spyware and *adware* are both terms for software that monitors what you do on your system (effectively spies on you) and does something with that information. They can range from extremely dangerous, to helpful—and in fact, in many cases they get installed on your system with your full permission. In fact,

---

[6] *Not some other type of Trojan*

one can argue that some of them don't qualify as viruses at all. Consider some of these variations:

- A keyboard monitor spyware program might watch every keystroke you type, waiting for cases where it can detect you typing in an account name and password. Once it has them, it might send the information out to someone who can then use them to impersonate you—hijacking your bank account, e-mail service, or other online service.

- A web page tracker might watch while you browse, and anytime you shop for something it might bring up a pop-up redirecting you to a different store, or swapping in an affiliate code[7] so someone else can make money off your purchases. Such a tracker might also check pricing for you and offer you a better deal than you were about to get.

- Some software, especially free software, includes advertising—thus the term *adware*. You accept the advertising in much the same way as you accept commercial television: the commercials pay for the content.

Is an adware program that you allow on your system a virus? Probably not. However, I'll be honest—I'm not a big fan of such software. First, you usually don't know everything they do. Sometimes that information is buried in the fine print—you know, the endless license agreements that you accept without reading.[8] Second, even beneficial adware might have side effects. It might interfere with other programs and will often slow down your system.

So I won't tell you that you should delete all adware from your system. But you should be aware of what adware is present on your system, and know how to remove it if you don't like it. As for malicious spyware, it's a virus, period.

 RULE OF THUMB If you install software, and can't easily figure out what it does or how to remove it, you should consider it a potential virus.

Adware and Lag

Spyware, adware, and P2P services such as Kazaa make use of the Internet. The thing to remember is that their use isn't limited to when you're actually doing something relating to the software. For example, you know that when you're downloading a file on Kazaa, or someone is uploading one from your system, Kazaa is making use of the Internet. But it turns out that Kazaa uses the

---

[7] *This is a code added to a web address to help web sites know who referred them to the site. Some web sites will pay money to sites that generate referrals that result in sales.*

[8] *Almost nobody reads those agreements before clicking "I Accept". You might try reading one sometime—the things you are agreeing to might astonish you.*

Internet even when no files are being transferred. When Kazaa is running, your computer is part of the P2P network, and your computer will periodically send out and receive information relating to searches and other maintenance operations. It will also periodically download and display advertisements if you're using the adware version. The same applies to other adware and spyware—you have no control over when they connect to the Internet to perform their operations, and how much data they are transferring.

When you're connected to the Internet, you have a certain amount of bandwidth available—this is the number of bytes per second that your Internet connection can handle. On a modem, you have up to 56 kilobits per second download and 28 kilobits per second upload. That translates into under 7 kilobytes per second download and half that on upload—not very fast.[9] Any data transferred by spyware and adware subtracts off the available bandwidth for other tasks. It can slow your Internet performance even on a fast DSL or cable line, and can make a dial-up modem connection virtually useless.

Each spyware or adware program on your system can take up some bandwidth—and it can definitely add up. Worse, it's not evenly distributed—a program may do nothing for an hour, and then try to tie up all your bandwidth for several minutes.

This "hidden" use of your Internet bandwidth can be fatal for online gaming, and is actually one of the common reasons for lag and for people being dropped from games. You can be in the middle of a Warcraft game when an adware program wakes up and starts several large transfers. Next thing you know, your screen freezes and you find yourself dropped from the game.

Viruses can have the same impact on bandwidth, but there are plenty of good reasons to get rid of viruses that have nothing to do with gaming. But adware is something you may allow on your system intentionally, and it's important you realize the side effects this may cause.

Why Do People Write Viruses?

Viruses cause a huge amount of harm. They cause individuals and corporations to lose critical data. They waste enormous amounts of time. They are expensive to deal with, both in prevention and in cleanup.

So it's worth taking a moment to consider why people write these things.

There is the stereotype of the nerdy teenager or college student who writes viruses just because they can. It's part of the "hacker" mythology—a way to prove one's technical prowess or just get some attention. And there is some truth to this stereotype. I should, however, note that the use of the word

---

[9] There are 8 bits in a byte, so a modem speed of 56 kilobits per second is about 7 kilobytes per second. In fact, you'll get less, because a 56k modem only gets at best 53k in practice.

hacker is really incorrect here. A classic hacker is someone who delights in solving tough technical problems. The kind of "hacker" who writes viruses is more correctly called a *cracker*. You may also hear the terms *white hat* and *black hat* to replace hacker, where a white hat is someone who uses their knowledge of computer security for good to protect people's systems and privacy, and a black hat is someone who is using their skills to cause harm.

Definitions notwithstanding, the term *hacker* is commonly used today to represent both white hats and black hats. So if, later in this book, I refer to a hacker attacking your system, you'll know I'm really referring to a black hat. Why? Because only a black hat would use their hacker skills to attack your system.

For those of you who are interested in going further into computer security or computer internals, it's a fascinating field. I would strongly encourage you to become a hacker in the classic sense—a white hat. Aside from the ethics of the matter, it's just as challenging, just as fun, and a whole lot less likely to land you in jail.

The Real Threat: Cyberwar

The media may play up the occasional teenage hacker who edits or spreads a virus, but that isn't where the real danger in the future lies. You may have already heard that more and more viruses are coming out of countries that aren't entirely friendly to Western ideals. As more and more of the free world's infrastructure and economy becomes dependent on the Internet, we become increasingly vulnerable to attack by terrorist organizations or unfriendly governments. The terms for this are *cyberwar* and *cyberterrorism*. (Perform an Internet search on these terms for further information—there are many sites that discuss the issue.)

Cyberwar typically refers to government-sponsored attacks. These can be attempts to hack into sensitive government installations to obtain secrets or interfere with government or military operations. Or attacks on banks to try to cripple the financial system.

Cyberterrorism typically refers to attacks made by nongovernmental groups. Occasionally you'll hear about acts of cyberterrorism—government or media web sites that are hacked into and modified for political purposes. One can make the argument that many viruses are, in fact, acts of cyberterrorism.

We don't actually know what a real cyberwar would look like. You can bet that most governments invest heavily on both offensive and defensive techniques. But considering how poorly we are handling viruses and privacy attacks in a time of relative peace, the thought of full-scale cyberwar is disturbing indeed.

An attacker doesn't have to actually break into a web site to bring it down. Even the largest web site can handle only a limited number of requests at a time. Let's say a bank's web site can handle 50,000 requests per second—a very significant number. Rather than attack the bank directly, a cyberattacker might distribute a worm that would quietly infect millions of computers. That worm might have a trigger date—as soon as that date arrives, every single infected computer tries to contact that bank's web site. Suddenly, the bank is receiving a million fake requests per second—far more than it can handle. Legitimate requests get crowded out by the fake requests—so people trying to contact the site see an error. This is called a Denial of Service attack.

Because Denial of Service attacks rely on hijacking as many computers as possible to perform an attack on a few sites, one can argue that protecting your own computer and making sure it can't be hijacked isn't just a matter of personal defense, but of national defense as well.

When Software Sneezes

Biological viruses infect people in several ways. Some travel through the air when you sneeze or cough. Others sit on a surface until you touch it, or touch someone who is sick. Yet others are transferred through close contact or cuts, wounds, or unsterile needles.

A virus can't hurt you until it gets inside of you, and so it is for computer viruses as well. They can't harm you until they find their way onto your computer. Unfortunately, computer viruses have just as many ways of spreading as biological viruses, maybe more.

Scientists couldn't learn how to prevent the spread of disease until they understood how viruses and bacteria spread.[10] So you too will need to learn something about how computer viruses spread, the subject of the next chapter, before you'll be able to deal with them effectively.

---

[10] For example, the reduction in worldwide cases of malaria didn't begin with vaccines or medication—it began with the discovery that malaria was spread by mosquitoes.

From Sneaks to Slammers: How Viruses Get on Your System

So far you've learned about the different kinds of viruses and the kinds of things they do. But before a virus can do anything, it has to be running on your computer—which means that it has to get onto your system in the first place. That's what this chapter is all about. I'll include some hints and previews on how to protect yourself in this chapter, but the focus will be on how the viruses spread—protection will be the focus of the six chapters that follow.

Dueling Perspectives

Sometimes it's important to look at a subject from two different points of view in order to really understand it. In this case, allow me to introduce two fictional guest authors to share their own perspectives.

Dr. T, the Engineer, Says . . .

As future computer engineers, we deal with the tangible and measurable. A bit of simple logic is all it takes for you to understand exactly how viruses spread, and consequently, how you can block them.

Viruses can enter your computer through two channels and two channels only:

- *Physical media:* That includes CDs, DVDs, floppy disks, and memory sticks (USB or other)

- *Your network:* That includes both direct network connections and e-mail

Let's take a quick look at each of these.

Floppies, CDs, DVDs, and Memory Sticks

As soon as you place a floppy disk, CD, or DVD in your system, the files it contains become available to your system. However, the presence of an infected file alone isn't enough to do damage—it has to execute. There are three ways files on one of these media can execute:

- It's possible for a virus to infect the boot sector of a CD, DVD, or floppy disk. The boot sector is the code that runs when you reboot or start your machine, and is responsible for loading the operating system. If it's infected, it can directly cause damage, or proceed to infect other files on the system. So you should always use caution booting from a floppy disk, CD, or DVD. Only do so if you know the media is safe, or has already been scanned for viruses. Also, be very careful not to accidentally leave potentially infected floppies in your system, since many systems will boot from a floppy disk by default if one is in the drive when the computer starts.

- CD and DVDs have the ability to run a program automatically when they are inserted. If the autorun program is infected, the CD or DVD can start infecting your system as soon as you insert it in the drive.

RULE OF THUMB If you aren't sure a CD or DVD is clean (for example, if it was given to you by a friend who either isn't familiar with the dangers of viruses or isn't much of a friend), hold your keyboard Shift key down while inserting the CD or DVD into the drive, and keep it down until the CD has spun up. Holding the Shift key down disables the autorun feature.[1] Be sure you use a virus scanning program to scan the CD or DVD before accessing any of its files.

- If you run an infected program on a CD or DVD, obviously it will be able to infect your system.

Your Network

There are three common ways for viruses to invade a computer across a network. Here's a quick summary—you'll read more about each one later in this chapter:

---

[1] In Appendix B you'll learn a technique for turning off autorun completely.

- *Network shares:* It's possible for your computer to "share" its disk drive so it can be accessed by other computers on a local network. If you do so, it's possible for another computer to access the files on your hard drive. If that computer is infected by a virus, it can go ahead and infect the files on your computer directly across the network, through the shared drives.[2]

- *E-mail, IM, peer-to-peer (P2P), or web pages:* Many viruses travel as attachments across e-mail or file downloads through an instant messaging service or P2P services such as Kazaa. Others appear as links on a web page. Be sure to scan any downloaded files or attachments for viruses before you run them. It's also possible that flaws in your e-mail program or web browser will automatically run such attachments even if you don't do anything. Installing the latest security updates for your operating system can help prevent this.

- *Direct network connections:* Every time you browse to a web site, your computer asks the web server computer to send it data. Look at it for a moment the other way—a web server computer spends all its time *listening* for requests from other computers. Well, it turns out that your computer may be listening for requests as well, not necessarily web requests, but other kinds of requests. For example, it might be listening for a request to share files. You may not even know all the programs on your computer that are listening for different types of requests, and some of those programs may have bugs that would allow another computer to access yours without your knowledge. This is especially the case if you haven't installed the latest updates for your system.

By now you should be getting a good sense of the physical means that viruses use to invade your system. So allow me to turn the book over to my colleague, who has his own unique perspective on the situation.

Dr. H, the Holistic Social Scientist, Says . . .

I hope you enjoyed Dr. T's discussion, though I dare say that in her focus on technology she really misses the most important aspects of fighting viruses. So let me start by clearing a few things up. Now please don't get me wrong, and know that I really have no intention to cause you any distress, but understand . . .

If your computer gets infected by a virus, it's almost always going to be your fault.

---

[2] *I'm not actually going to teach you how to share drives—it varies depending on the version of Windows you're using and can involve some pretty complex configuration. So you'll have to look in your Windows help for that information. I will however talk about what you need to do to secure shared drives if you choose to do so—that will be in Chapter 7.*

Please, I don't mean to offend. But we're dealing with human nature here, and viruses mostly spread due to carelessness, laziness, curiosity, and ignorance, with a dose of good old-fashioned stupidity and greed thrown in for good measure.

I know that most of you reading this are teenagers, but I expect there are a few parents here as well.[3] But I want to address only the teens for a moment.

First, let me assure you of one thing—don't think for an instant that my comments have anything to do with you being teenagers. I assure you that your parents and other adults have plenty of carelessness, laziness, and ignorance to go around. In fact, between you and me, it's my hope and expectation that by the time you're done with this book you'll know more about virus protection than they do, and will be able to get them out of jams when they get into them.

OK parents, you can pay attention again.

Dr. T divided the ways viruses spread into physical media and network transfer—which makes sense considering her more technological viewpoint. But you need to understand that the way viruses spread really divides into two completely different categories:

- *Viruses that trick your computer into running them:* These are attacks that rely on bugs in your system, errors in system configuration, or other software vulnerabilities. You don't have to actually run an infected program for these infections to occur—simply browsing to a web site, opening an e-mail message, or even connecting to the Internet can be enough for these attacks to succeed. Keeping your system software up to date and using a virus scanner and firewall will be your best defenses against this type of attack.[4]

- *Viruses that trick you into running them:* These are attacks that rely on convincing you to run a program that will infect your computer. While a virus scanner will help here, staying vigilant and using common sense are by far your best defenses for this kind of attack.

In the next few chapters, you'll learn all about the various defenses against viruses. But I must stress this: Your biggest enemy is yourself, your own complacency, and laziness. Many of the people who read this book will still run into problems, not because of a problem with the book but simply because they don't get around to following the recommendations, or follow them for a little while and then forget.

---

[3] *For those of you who are adults and aren't parents, rest assured that by reading this book, you're infinitely smarter than the many adults who would rather remain in vulnerable ignorance than read a book with "Teen" in the title.*

[4] *You'll learn about virus scanners in Chapter 4 and firewalls in Chapter 5.*

Keeping your computer secure requires attention. You have to think about the files you download and run not just now, but all the time. You need to update your virus scanning software and operating system not just now, but frequently. Even daily.[5]

I hate to say it, but your greatest vulnerability is yourself.

Now, I don't want to leave you on such a sad note. I know security is a rather depressing subject—all about people trying to attack your computer and invade your privacy. Before I turn the book back to your nonfictional author, please let me assure you that security is a really easy habit to get into, and once you've set things up it becomes mostly an automatic process. And believe me, the time you spend on it will be nothing compared to the time and hassle of cleaning or repairing an infected system.

How Viruses Spread

I hope you enjoyed our two fictional guest authors. In the rest of the chapter I'll go into more detail on the various ways that viruses spread, incorporating both Dr. T's and Dr. H's approaches.

Physical Media

You've already read about some of the issues relating to physical media: floppies, CDs, and DVDs. You know not to boot from infected media, or allow an infected CD or DVD to automatically start, and not to run programs without checking them first.

But Dr. T's description skipped a step. How do viruses get on the media in the first place?

Here's where floppies and CDs differ. Because a floppy disk is easily writable, just inserting a floppy disk on an infected system is enough for it to become infected in turn. But at least to date, viruses don't write themselves to CDs. So CDs are most often infected unintentionally, when someone copies infected files to it when burning a CD.

Commercial CDs are generally safe—companies check them for viruses before they ship. So the real risk is in media given to you by friends. Before putting them in your machine, you need to ask yourself these questions:

- Do I trust my friend's machine? Was it clean of viruses when the CD was burned?

- Do I trust my friend? Not that any of you would have friends who would intentionally infect a CD they gave you . . .

---

[5] *One of the teen reviewers for this book complained to me recently that his computer was acting strangely. I asked him if he had done a virus scan. He answered that his dad did one for him. "When?" I asked. "About four months ago," he answered.*

By the way, that burned music CD you were just given? It may have programs on it as well (yep, CDs can contain both software and music), so be careful with those, too.

E-Mail and Spam

One of the most common ways for viruses to spread is through e-mail or spam.[6] It works something like this:

1. You open an infected e-mail attachment.

2. The virus looks on your system for other e-mail addresses, preferably those from your own address book.

3. The virus sends out e-mails containing an infected attachment to every e-mail address it can find.

4. The virus does whatever other harmful or annoying act it was designed to do on your system.

And thus the virus spreads.

Some attachments are more dangerous than others. The most dangerous types are executable files. You can tell which these are by their filename extension. Table 3-1 shows some of the common ones.

Table 3-1 Dangerous File Extensions

Extension	Description
.EXE	Executable file.
.COM	An older extension used by executable files.
.BIN	Binary executable files.
.PIF	Program information file. Contains instructions to run a different file.
.BAT	A batch file. Can execute a variety of commands including launching other programs.
.VB, .VBE, .VBS	A Visual Basic Script file. Contains instructions in a language called *VBScript* that can perform a wide variety of system tasks.
.DOC	A Word document file. Word document files can contain programs called *macros*. There are quite a few macro viruses in circulation.

[6] There is some disagreement as to when the term **spam** became used to refer to junk e-mail. Some say it stands for **Simultaneously Posted Advertising Message**, others for the famous Monty Python skit where the word **Spam** is repeated endlessly to everyone's annoyance. Source: Laura Mitrovich's Sept. 2002 article at http://www.marketingprofs.com.

Extension	Description
.INF	An installation file.
.MSI	A Windows installer file—used to install applications.
.LNK	A program file shortcut.
.MDB, .MDE, .MDW	A Microsoft Access database—it can include viruses as well.
.REG	A file that can modify your registry.
.WS, .WSF, .WSH	A Windows Scripting Host command file. Can also perform a variety of system tasks.
.ZIP	Archive file—it can hold infected files of various types.

The spread of e-mail–based viruses depends first and foremost on the first step—an attachment containing the virus somehow has to run on your system. There are two ways that an e-mail attachment can be opened on a system:

1. It can convince you to open the attachment.

2. It can trick the e-mail program into opening and running the attachment. This is most common when running obsolete versions of Microsoft Outlook or Outlook Express. For example, some viruses hide the damaging code in a file with the .jpg extension, indicating a graphic file. But the headers in the e-mail message indicate that it's an executable, so when an obsolete e-mail reader opens the image to display it, instead of displaying the image it executes the application, thus installing the virus.

You'll learn more about protecting yourself from the second type of attack in Chapter 6. For now, let's talk about the ways e-mail will try to trick you into opening an infected attachment.

Masters of Disguise

E-mail is based on a protocol called SMTP—Simple Mail Transfer Protocol. This protocol consists of the rules that an e-mail program uses to send e-mail from one computer to another. SMTP was created during the earliest days of the Internet, a time that most will agree was much more trusting and open than today's Internet.[7]

---

[7] *Today's Internet grew out of the original DARPA-Net—built by the Defense Advanced Research Projects Agency, an agency that does research for the Department of Defense. DARPA-Net was originally limited to government agencies and major universities, with little or no commercial application, so it's easy to see why things have changed.*

With SMTP, an e-mail message can claim to be from whomever it wants.

If you're using a web-based e-mail program, such as Hotmail or MSN, an e-mail you send is always marked as coming from your e-mail address. But if you're using a POP3 account (an account based on a protocol called *Post Office Protocol 3*) through an e-mail program such as Outlook, Outlook Express, Eudora, or Netscape, you can label the e-mail as coming from anyone you wish.

Figure 3-1 shows an example from Outlook Express.

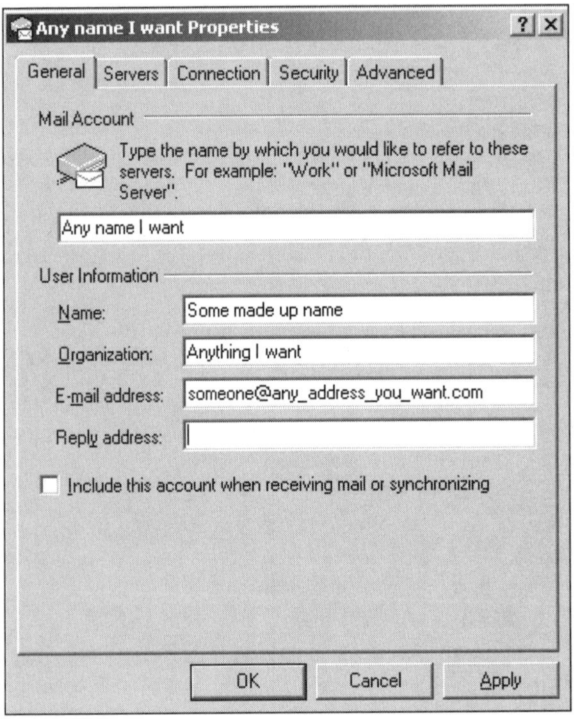

Figure 3-1 A POP3 client relies on the user to specify a correct e-mail address.

Some SMTP programs will do verification on the sending address to make sure it's legitimate, but there is little they can do to verify that you are who you say you are. So if you put in a valid domain name,[8] the e-mail you send with such a client will probably go through.

Well, if you can do it, a virus can as well. So when you get an e-mail that claims to be from a friend of yours, it may not be from your friend's computer. It's very possible that the virus lifted your friend's address on a completely different computer, and mailed you from that computer claiming to be from your friend.

---

[8] *The domain name is the part after the @ sign in an e-mail address. For example, in someone@microsoft.com, microsoft.com is the domain name.*

E-mail spam filters are usually configured to let in mail from people on your own address book, so you can't rely on them for protection.

So, if you get an e-mail from your friend Tom that looks something like this:

```
From: Tom
Subject: Here's a great program that I think you'll like
```

It's possible that your friend Tom really found a program that you'll like. But it's just as likely that a virus is trying to use Tom's name to trick you into opening an attachment.

False Virus Warnings

This particular fraud may also result in your getting warnings from other systems that your computer is infected. Figure 3-2 illustrates how this might work.

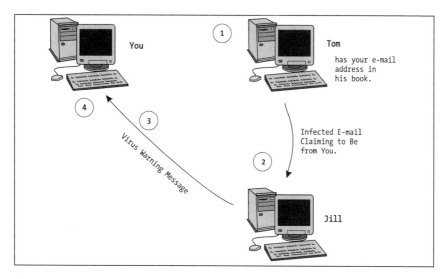

Figure 3-2 False virus warnings

1. Your friend Tom has your address in his e-mail address book.

2. Tom gets infected by a virus that sends out messages claiming to be from you (it's filled in your e-mail address in the "From" address field in the e-mail message). One of those messages goes to his friend Jill.

3. Jill's e-mail server has antivirus protection and detects the virus. The server then sends a message warning the sender that he sent out an e-mail containing a virus. But the server thinks the message came from you.

4. You get a message from Jill's server warning that you sent out a virus. This leaves you very confused, because your machine is clean (you should run a virus scan to make sure), and you never sent anything to Jill.

Masters of Temptation

Viruses choose subjects that are designed to tempt you into opening the message.

- *Polite messages:* Thanking you for something, but you have to open the message to find out what.

- *Friendly messages:* Seeming to come from a friend, telling you that they love you.

- *Tempting messages:* From free computers, to vacations, to software, to offers for just about every obscene act you can imagine. All you need to do is click here . . .

- *Fake confirmation messages:* Seeming to respond to requests you made, confirming new account information or an order or reservation.

- *Warning messages:* We'll cancel your account! We think your information has been compromised! You're doomed if you don't follow these instructions . . .

- *Curious messages:* Containing various phrases designed to provoke your curiosity, like "someone has a crush on you."

Greed. Curiosity. Fear. Temptation.

None of us are completely immune, and virus authors (like spammers) are infinitely creative in the approaches they take.

I wish I could offer a sure guarantee on how to deal with these. A spam filter will help, but none of them are perfect yet. And sooner or later you'll open one of those messages.

In most cases, as long as you don't open the attachment, you'll still be safe. But in some cases your computer can be infected even if you don't open the attachment. You already know that older e-mail clients have bugs that allow them to be tricked into automatically opening an attachment when you view a message. Also, an HTML-based message (which you'll read about shortly) might infect your system by way of an HTML viewer.

Masters of Gullibility

This actually isn't a virus at all—it's an e-mail scam that convinces you to wreck your own system!

Basically you get an e-mail from someone you know telling you about a new virus that antivirus programs can't catch. Your friend tells you to first forward the warning to all your friends, and then to search for and delete a file on your system in order to protect yourself.[9]

---

[9] *My dad got tricked by this once.*

Since this message has come in from a trusted friend, you naturally do as instructed.

Well, guess what, you just deleted an important system file.[10] And you just spread the message to your friends who will perhaps trust you. In other words—you're the virus!

When you get a message warning you about a virus and instructing you on how to deal with it, even if it is from someone you trust completely, check it out first with one of the antivirus software vendors. Chances are good that it's just a scam.

HTML E-Mail

Most e-mail programs now allow you to send e-mail text that includes HTML, not just text. That allows you to include images, fonts and text styles, and so on. E-mail readers display the e-mail in a built-in web browser, and if that browser is vulnerable, the very act of viewing e-mail can run a script, install a plug-in, or redirect you to a page that might infect your system. You'll read more about browser-based vulnerabilities shortly.

Downloaded Files

E-mail attachments are only one way infected software can get on your system. One of the most common ways is completely under your control—the files you choose to download.

People download files from a number of different sources: the Web, FTP sites, Usenet (Internet news) sites, P2P networks such as Kazaa, Grokster, Napster, Morpheus, Gnutella, etc.

Shareware and software downloads from reputable sites (such as CNET.com) and software you purchase for immediate download from reputable companies are generally safe. These sites tend to be very careful about checking out software before they allow it on their site. However, you should still take nothing for granted, and make sure you have your own virus scanning active as a backup.

Sites that are dependent on individual submissions, including newsgroups and P2P sites, are considerably more risky. File descriptions and names are often designed to trick you into installing and running the software. Be especially careful of game hacks and mods, and pirated software. Remember—the virus authors are out to tempt you with the files you want most.

RULE OF THUMB Never download a file that has been posted recently. Always wait until it has been up for at least a couple of weeks. Then be sure you've updated your antivirus software before downloading the file. This reduces the risk of your catching a new virus that isn't yet caught by your antivirus software.

---

[10] *Any file located in your Windows or WinNT directory or any of its subdirectories has a good chance of being an important system file.*

Watch the Source

One factor you may want to consider when downloading files or browsing web sites is where that site is located. Different countries have different laws and levels of enforcement when it comes to dealing with viruses and software piracy.

There are two ways to possibly determine where a web site is located. The first is by the domain extension, the other is by the Whois database. The web site `http://www.iana.com` can help you determine both.

While .com can be from anywhere, different countries have two-letter extensions they can allocate as well. If you go to `http://www.iana.com`, you'll find a link to the IANA ccTLD database. This links the two-letter code for every country. Examples of codes include

.cn	China
.de	Germany
.ph	Philippines
.ru	Russia
.kr	Korea
.jp	Japan

While viruses and spyware come from many different countries (including the US), these countries seem to have more than their fair share of questionable sites. Watch out for Germany especially for spyware, the others for viruses.

The Whois database can also help determine where a web site is registered. From `http://www.iana.com`, choose the link to the IANA Whois service. Other Whois services can be found at `http://www.internic.net/whois.html` and `http://www.networksolutions.com` (click the WHOIS menu at the top for this page).

These can help you track down who owns a domain in some cases, but they are quite useless against domains that host spammers, pirated software, and viruses. That's because while you're supposed to provide accurate registration information, registrars don't actually do any investigating to make sure the records are accurate or useful—all they care about is that the owner of the domain has paid for their registration.

Your Local Network

Many homes nowadays have local networks—where several machines are networked together using wires or a wireless connection. They are often configured to share drives and printers.

You've already read that if you're sharing a drive, any system that connects to that drive sees it as if it is local to that computer. That means if the other computer is infected, it can in turn infect yours.

There are some obvious precautions you can take to prevent this:

- Disable drive sharing. Or at least make sure the drive shares require use of a password (more on this in Chapter 7).

- Don't connect to drives you aren't using, and configure your system so it doesn't restore mapped connections when your machine starts up.[11] That can slow the spread of an infection if it occurs.

- Make sure all the machines on your network are clean. Yes, I know that may mean spending time cleaning your parents' computer, or that of a favorite sibling, but it's far better to do that then have to clean up the mess afterwards.

- In Chapter 5 you'll learn about software firewalls, which can also protect you on your local network.

There are some less obvious precautions as well.

If you have a wireless network, and have just installed it with the default settings, anybody with a wireless card can access your local network. This includes neighbors and people driving by.[12] In fact, some people do that for fun—just drive through neighborhoods looking for open networks. If you're sharing drives without passwords, those people can easily browse your hard drives. Aside from the privacy issues, anyone with an infected laptop can spread a virus onto your systems.[13]

In the next section, you'll learn about direct network attacks through the Internet. All of the attacks described there can occur within a local network as well.

Internet Attacks

Ring . . .ring . . . Hi, I'm Shelly from Super Discount Mortgages, can I interest you in refinancing?

Ring . . . ring . . . Congratulations! You've just won a free trip to Hawaii. Just give us your credit card number and . . .

Ring . . . ring . . . Would you like super-cheap long distance? We can switch you over . . .

---

[11] When you use the Map Network Drive command—which you know how to use if you're sharing drives, and don't care about if you're not—there's a check box labeled Reconnect on Startup in the dialog box that appears. This check box is checked by default, which is really a lousy choice on the part of Microsoft. You should always uncheck it when mapping drives unless you really need to stay connected to the other drive.

[12] **Wardriving** is a term used to describe driving around neighborhoods looking for open networks.

[13] Chapter 7 will cover how to protect your wireless network.

Yes, few things are more annoying than telemarketers. Even if all they want is to talk to your parents, if you're the one who answers you need to first figure out they are telemarketers, decide if this is the one-in-a-million case where you actually need to call your parents, and decide the best way to insult them before you hang up.

How do they get your phone number?

Some of them go by various lists and phone directories. But some of them just use automatic dialers to dial every possible number in an area code.[14]

Computers have an equivalent of phone numbers called *IP addresses* (IP stands for Internet Protocol). You can find the IP address for many web sites using the Ping command. Bring up a command window and type in **ping** followed by the URL of the web site. For example:

```
F:\>ping www.google.com
Pinging www.google.com [216.239.41.99] with 32 bytes of data:
```

This shows that at least one of the computers at http://www.google.com has an IP address of 216.239.41.99. Each of the four numbers ranges from 0 to 255 (though just as with phone numbers, not every number combination is valid).

Your phone number is given to you by the phone company. An IP address is given to you by your Internet provider. With modem dial-up connections and many DSL and cable connections, your IP address changes every time you call in or at regular intervals. This is called a *dynamic IP address*. With some DSL connections and high-speed T1 and T3 connections, your IP address is fixed.

The phone line in your house might be shared with several devices: a regular phone, a fax, a modem, an alarm system, a TiVo, and an answering machine, for example. Each of these devices provides a service to you by using the phone line. Of course, in most cases only one of these devices can use the line at a time—they have to share them.

Just as different devices can answer a phone line, different programs on a computer can answer an incoming request on its IP address. A program that listens for Internet requests is often called a *service*, and a computer that runs these services is often called a *server*.

One big difference between devices on a phone line and services on a computer is that a computer can have lots of services sharing the same IP address—it does this by assigning each one a port number between 1 and 65535. Here's another way of looking at it:

Imagine that each port is a different door onto your computer. Each door can have a service behind it listening for someone to "ring the doorbell." Doors that don't have a service listening are effectively locked. Doors that do have a service open the door when someone rings. As long as the visitor is

---

[14] Telemarketers can still use this technique in the US, but must first check if the number is on the National Do Not Call Registry to make sure the number isn't listed. Visit http://www.donotcall.gov to sign up.

friendly, there is no problem. But if your computer opens the door to someone who is unfriendly . . . well, you get the point.

Some of the services a computer might run include

- *A web server service:* Allows other people to browse web sites you create on your computer

- *An e-mail service:* Lets your computer handle e-mail accounts for multiple users on your machine

- *A database service:* Stores various types of data

- *A printer and file-sharing service:* Used by the computer to share drives and devices

- *A game service:* Where you host games that can be played by others (Counterstrike is a classic example of a game where individuals host their own game servers.)

- And a variety of system configuration and networking services

In fact, your computer is capable of running many different network services. Each one involves having your computer listen for requests on the machine's IP address. Each service listens on one or more different ports.

For example, a computer that hosts a web site it called a *web server*. The web site itself consists of a program called a *web server service*—Microsoft's web server service is called Internet Information Server (IIS). The web service listens on the IP address of the computer at port 80 (port 80 is the standard for web servers).

Most services are designed for businesses—often large corporations. Yet many of them can be and are installed even on home systems. And many of them pose risks to your systems. Here are a few examples:

- If your computer is sharing drives and doesn't provide security using a password, any computer on the Internet can potentially access that drive, delete files, place new files, or read any information on the drive.

- There's a service called *Remote Procedure Call* (RPC) that allows a computer to perform instructions requested from a remote computer. This is very useful in a corporation, where you want centralized control over many computers, or corporate applications that run on multiple computers at once. It's less useful on your home machine, but no less vulnerable to certain kinds of worms that have learned how to use a bug in older versions of the RPC service program to take over machines.

- There are two ways to build your own web site. You might be building it on your ISP's computer, but you might also choose to experiment with building web sites on your own computer. Many tools that allow you to build web sites include having a web server running on your computer. In most cases the web server will be accessible from other computers as well as your own.

IP Telemarketing

Just as telemarketers will dial every possible number to try to sell you something, hackers and viruses will try every possible IP address to find a port that your computer is listening to.[15] Then they will try to exploit any bugs in the service listening on that port to invade your computer. One common bug they'll exploit is called a *buffer overrun error*.

When a computer connects to your computer, it sends a request in the form of data. This data gets loaded into a buffer (a block of memory that holds data) on your computer to be examined and processed as shown in Figure 3-3.

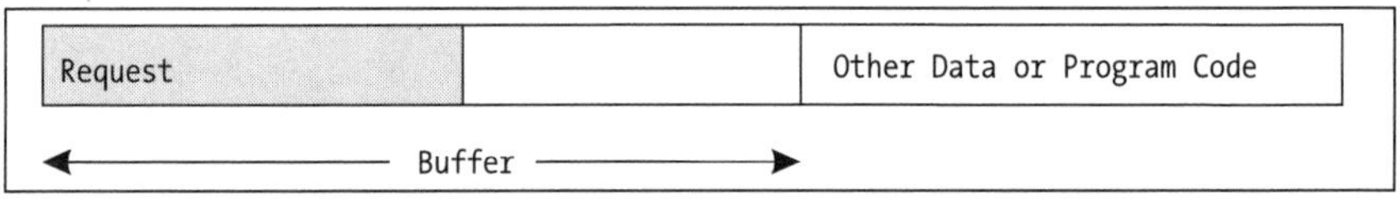

Request		Other Data or Program Code

◄─────────── Buffer ───────────►

Figure 3-3 A properly working service examines the contents of the buffer and performs the requested operation.

Many attacks work by trying to send more data than the computer's buffer can hold. In this case, you might end up with a situation such as that shown in Figure 3-4.

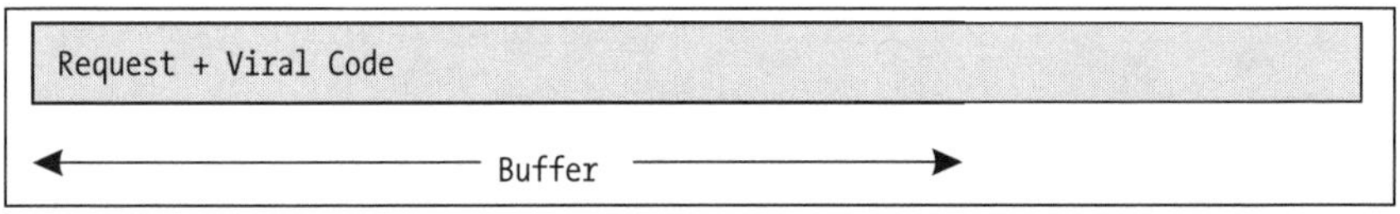

Request + Viral Code

◄─────────── Buffer ───────────►

Figure 3-4 A buggy service doesn't check the size of the request before loading it into a memory buffer.

As you can see, in this example the request has not only filled the buffer, but also overwritten another block of memory—one that perhaps contains other data or program code. If the hacker is very, very clever, they can overwrite data in such a way that the service will execute code that was included in the request. In effect, this attack tricks your computer into running any code they provide.

---

[15] *You can also think of this as people knocking on every door in a neighborhood to see if anyone is home.*

There are three ways to defend yourself from all types of Internet attacks:

- Use a firewall to block outside requests. You'll learn more about this in Chapter 5.

- Keep your operating system up to date. Many security patches address exactly this kind of problem. Chapter 6 covers this topic.

- Turn off services you don't need. You'll learn more about this in Chapter 7.

Internet attacks are among the most dangerous, because they come entirely from outside—not due to some action on your part. However, you can take effective action to block them.

The Web

Chances are that you spend quite a bit of time browsing the World Wide Web. One way viruses can arrive on your system from the Web is pretty obvious—if you click a link that downloads a virus file, and then run or open the file, it's found a new home. The kinds of files that are dangerous are exactly the same as those discussed earlier when we covered e-mail attachments.

But there are other risks to browsing the Web. Before telling you about them, it's important that you know a little bit about how the Web works. You can skip over this part if you're already familiar with HTML and JavaScript.

How the World Wide Web Works

When you browse to a web site, what actually happens is that your computer requests the web server computer to send you a page of information. Remember the part about computers running services that listen for requests? Computers running web servers traditionally listen on port 80.

What's in that page of information returned from a web server?

Most of the time it consists entirely of text in a language called Hypertext Markup Language (HTML). HTML looks something like this:

```
<html>
<body>
<p><font face="Verdana"><b><font size="7">HTML</font></b>
<i><font size="5">makes this look
<font color="#0000FF"><b><u>cool</u></b></font>!</font></i></font></p>
</body>
</html>
```

Your browser reads the HTML and uses it to determine what to display. This HTML will appear in your browser something like the image shown in Figure 3-5.

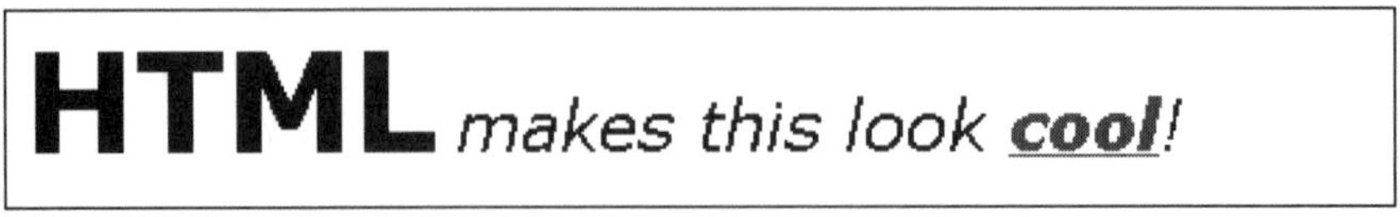

HTML *makes this look cool!*

Figure 3-5 HTML generates nice-looking pages.

HTML can include links to images—instructions to your computer to contact that web site or another to retrieve an image. It can include instructions to display a form—the list boxes, text boxes, and buttons that allow you to send information to a web site. It can also include a program in a language called *JavaScript*—which includes additional instructions on how to display or work with the web page. Menus and pop-up windows are typically implemented using JavaScript. JavaScript programs are designed to be limited in what they can do—typically the worst harm they can do is to bring up endless pop-up windows that are difficult to get rid of.[16] However, if you're using an older browser, it's possible that JavaScript alone can be used to bring in a virus from another site and install it on your computer.

ActiveX Controls and Plug-Ins

HTML can also include requests to run more sophisticated programs called *plug-ins* or *ActiveX controls*.[17] For example, a page that uses Flash actually runs a Flash plug-in to give you pages with animations, graphical effects, and other features that aren't possible with HTML alone.

When you run an HTML page that requires a plug-in, and the plug-in isn't yet installed, you'll be prompted on what needs to be done to display that page. In some cases you'll be directed to a page where you can install the plug-in. For example, to display a QuickTime movie file, you'll likely be directed to Apple's web site where you can download and install the QuickTime plug-in and movie player.

The major plug-ins like QuickTime and Flash are both common and reasonably safe. But many pages use other ActiveX controls, and those raise other issues. You see, an ActiveX control is a program, and like any other program, it can do anything it wants once it's on your system. So it's important that you trust the control and the people who create it.

The default security setting for Microsoft's Internet Explorer causes the browser to look inside the ActiveX control for a piece of data called an *Authenticode signature*—this is a digital signature that tells you who created the control. If the signature is missing, the control isn't loaded. If there, you're prompted whether or not to load and run the control. Figure 3-6 shows an example of such a prompt.

[16] You can get pop-up blockers. These are utilities that modify your browser to control or prevent pop-ups from appearing. One of the most popular is Google's. See http://toolbar.google.com.

[17] A **plug-in** is a piece of software that runs on your computer that adds features to your web browser.

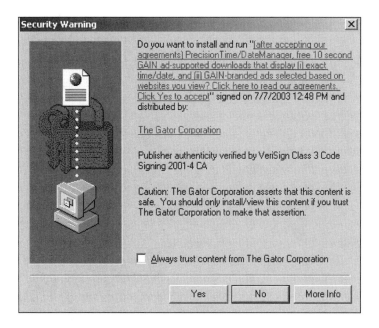

Figure 3-6 A typical ActiveX installation page

You may have already seen this one. This is adware and, coming from a reputable company, does tell you exactly what it does. Your first thought might be to click the Yes button, but before doing so you might want to read exactly what it is you're agreeing to when you allow that control to be installed.

The complete agreement is about 20 pages long.

In a nutshell, when you install this control, you're allowing the control vendor to install software on your machine that is, in effect, a kind of spyware. You grant it permission to watch you as you browse the web, record the sites you visit, and how long you spend there. This information is sent to Gator's servers, where they can send you advertisements based on this information. For example, if you browse a bookstore for a particular book, they could bring up a discount offer from a different bookstore. You're also giving them permission to look on your system to see what software you have installed so they can send you offers based on that information.

You're making some other interesting promises as well: Their current agreement requires you to provide a copy of their privacy agreement to anyone else using your computer to browse the web and obtain consent before they can use it (unless you have the legal right to accept the agreement on their behalf). You also agree not to use any unauthorized method to block display of their ads—I would interpret that to include any utilities or adware removal tools that they don't approve of.

They do promise not to collect any personally identifiable information that would let them track who you are, so while it does qualify as spyware, it probably doesn't qualify as malicious. And who knows, you might appreciate the services they provide. The important thing is that you take the time to understand what is being installed on your system before you install it.

> **RULE OF THUMB** When prompted to install an ActiveX control, answer "No" to the install prompt unless it's part of software that you're trying to install (such as a media plug-in or virus scanner).

> You should never click the check box that says "Always trust content from the ... corporation."

One of the greatest failings of Microsoft's Internet Explorer is that it lacks a check box that allows you to specify that you never want to trust content from a particular corporation. Hopefully they will add this feature.

Another way to avoid ActiveX controls completely is to use a different browser like Netscape, Mozilla, or Opera that doesn't support ActiveX controls. See `http://www.netscape.com`, `http://www.mozilla.org`, and `http://www.opera.com` for information on these browsers.

Are We Paranoid Yet?

At this point you may be ready to just shut off your computer, stick it in a closet, and go watch TV.

Just kidding.

Seriously though, you've just spent the past three chapters learning about the kinds of things viruses can do, the different types of viruses, and how they actually make their way onto your system.

You may be a bit frustrated that I haven't really told you much about how to deal with these problems yet. For that I apologize, but I have good reason.

You see, it's not enough (or even possible) to give you instructions on how to deal with every possible threat that exists today. There are just too many threats, and too many possible computer and network configurations to provide a simple formula. Not only that, but the threats constantly evolve. What you've read so far gives you the foundation that will allow you to figure out how to apply the advice that follows to your particular situation. It gives you knowledge that will help you understand and adapt to future threats as well as those that exist at the time the book is printed.

The next six chapters are all about defense. You're going to learn about the three foundations of protecting your computer: antivirus tools, firewalls, and system updates. You'll learn each one's strengths—and weaknesses. And you'll learn what to do when your computer is the victim.

The Built-In Doctor: Antivirus Programs

Let's get right to the point.

> **Your computer should have an antivirus program installed that includes active scanning and automatic updates.**

That is the single most important thing you need to know. If you don't have an up-to-date antivirus program installed, you should stop reading and get one now.[1] That's the main point of this chapter; all that follows is commentary.

How Antivirus Programs Work

An antivirus program generally does three things. First, it tries to validate itself. That means it tries to make sure that the antivirus program itself isn't infected with a virus. And it scans your computer's memory for viruses that might currently be running. This is important given that the first thing a number of viruses try to do is disable any operating antivirus programs! Antivirus programs aren't always successful at protecting themselves—there's a constant race between the virus authors and the antivirus authors.

> **RULE OF THUMB** If you are infected with a virus, scan your system twice. Even if your antivirus program reports that it has cleaned up any viruses, it's possible that it missed one executing in memory or its own infection, so viruses will still appear on a second scan. Chapter 9 discusses how to deal with more stubborn infections that aren't gone after two scans.

---

[1] OK, you can keep reading, but only because later in this chapter I offer advice on how to choose an antivirus program.

The following is a summary of how to use a typical antivirus program. However, if you actually have an infection, I strongly recommend you read Chapter 9 before starting the cleanup process. It goes into much greater detail on how to deal with viruses while minimizing the chance of scrambling your system software.

File Scanning

Every antivirus program has the ability to scan your system drives for viruses. The way it works is simple in principle. The antivirus program includes a set of virus definitions—patterns of known viruses. The program reads every file in your system and looks for those virus patterns in the file. If it finds one, it considers the file to be a virus and reports it as such.

Some antivirus programs will give you some choices as to what files to scan. Figure 4-1 shows an example of an antivirus control screen, this one from McAfee VirusScan.

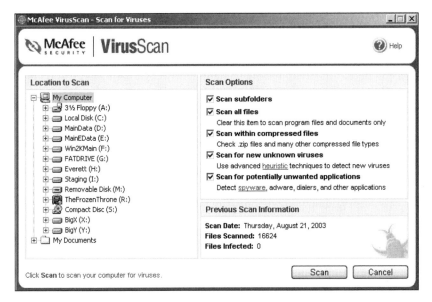

Figure 4-1 The main control screen for McAfee VirusScan

Scanning Options

Let's take a closer look at some of these options.

- *Scan subfolders:* Antivirus programs are capable of scanning your entire system or individual files or directories. Leaving this box checked does no harm when scanning an individual file. The only time you might clear it is if you're checking the files in a directory and know for a fact that all files in the subdirectory are clean. In other words, you should almost always leave this checked.

- *Scan all files:* Antivirus programs give you the option of scanning every file on your system, or only files with extensions that indicate they are programs (these are the same file extensions that you read about in the discussion of e-mail attachments in Chapter 3—for example, .exe, .bat, and .pif). The first time you scan a system, you should scan all files just to be safe. However, for routine scans it's OK to scan programs only in order to save time.

- *Scan within compressed files:* Compressed files are files like ZIP files that contain other files. Many antivirus programs can scan for files within compressed files; however, this also can be very time consuming. As with the "Scan all files" option, you should always scan within compressed files on your first scan of a system. You should use this option for any files you've downloaded or received via e-mail (even if you received them from a trusted friend).

- *Scan for unknown viruses:* It's not uncommon for virus authors to create new viruses by slightly modifying other viruses. Thus a new virus might share many of the characteristics of existing viruses. This option tells the antivirus program to search for these characteristic patterns. In some cases this allows the software to spot brand new viruses. You should always leave this on, even though it will slow the scanning process.

- *Scan potentially unwanted applications:* This option scans for spyware and adware applications. This one is a bit trickier because you're very dependent on the judgment of the company that developed your antivirus software to decide which applications are adware and which aren't. Remember: While you'll never want a virus running on your system, there are cases where you'll have installed adware intentionally. Unlike viruses, the creation and spread of which are generally illegal, adware and some spyware is legal. Also, as you read in Chapter 3, when you install some adware, you're explicitly agreeing not to use other programs such as antivirus programs to remove it or interfere with it.[2] So, whether to leave this box checked or not is entirely up to you.

Virus Cleanup

Some antivirus programs (especially the free ones) stop once they've found and reported viruses. It's then up to you to go to the web site for your antivirus

---

[2] Yes, I know you never actually read the license agreement. But you did agree to it during the installation. And while I personally have no objection to you breaking this agreement and taking the risk that they'll come after you with legions of lawyers, my own bias is to never install those kinds of applications in the first place.

program and find cleaning instructions for that particular virus. Cleaning a virus by hand can be a challenging task, and usually includes both deleting files and deleting registry entries—not something one does casually.

Full-featured antivirus programs will do this for you. The antivirus program will try to identify the particular virus based on the virus pattern found in the file. If it's a true virus (infected file), it will try to remove the virus and restore the file to its original state. If it's a worm, the antivirus program will try to delete the worm. Depending on the program and virus, it may ask you what you want to do with each file, and ask for your confirmation before deleting a file. In most cases you should OK the deletion, the exception being files that may have side effects, as you'll read shortly.

Deleting Infected Files

In some cases it won't be possible for the antivirus program to delete the file or remove the worm. In that case you should either go to the antivirus program's web site for more specific instructions, or delete the file manually. In many cases it will be possible to delete the file after restarting the system. The way it works is this:

Some files can't be deleted while their program is running. So an antivirus program might spot the file as a virus, but be unable to delete it. However, the antivirus program should be able to remove the registry entries or startup settings that started the virus in the first place. So when you restart your machine, the virus or worm won't be running, and thus it should be possible to delete the file. The big exception is when files that are part of the operating system are infected—those can be impossible to delete. Chapter 9 will discuss in more detail how to handle this situation.

Some antivirus programs will offer you the option of "quarantining" a file—putting it in a directory where it's presumably safe. You can do this if you think you'll have a need to look at the file (perhaps it contains data that you want to rescue)—but in most cases quarantining an infected file is just a waste of disk space.

Side Effects of Deleting Infected Files

Sometimes an infected file simply can't be cleaned and must be deleted. Unfortunately, it may be a critical system file, or a file that one of your programs requires to run. That's why many antivirus programs ask you to confirm if you want to delete the file. The only time you might want to say no is if the infected file is a critical system file that your system needs to run—in which case you might allow it to stay as you try other cleanup approaches. However, ultimately you must clean or delete every infected file.

In these cases you may need to reinstall the original program or reinstall your operating system.

All Windows operating systems include a reinstall or repair option (depending on operating system). With Windows 9x and ME you can simply install Windows over the current installation—your current settings should be maintained. This may repair and restore missing files, but isn't guaranteed to do so. With Windows 2000/XP, a repair option is available when you reinstall the operating system. This does a pretty good job of restoring missing files. Remember to perform a system update (described in Chapter 6) after doing a system repair.

In cases of extremely serious infections, you may have no choice but to do a full system restore—either restoring from the CDs provided when you bought your system, or doing a complete hard drive format and operating system installation if yours is a custom system or doesn't have system restore discs.

Chapter 9 will go into more detail of what kinds of problems can occur while cleaning an infected system, and how to minimize the damage and loss that can occur.

Active Scanning

The better antivirus programs include ongoing virus scanning or "active" scanning. With this feature on, the virus scanning program constantly monitors the system and automatically scans every file that is created, modified, or opened. This provides ongoing protection, and largely eliminates the need to routinely scan your entire system.

I strongly recommend that you use an antivirus program that offers this feature.

There are, however, some situations where you'll want to temporarily disable this feature:

- When doing video editing

- When doing image editing of larger images

- When accessing remote drives through a virtual private network (VPN) that aren't on your local area network

Scanning files can be time consuming, especially with larger files. In the case of video editing, the ongoing scanning can severely impact the performance of your video editing software. The same applies to image editing of large pictures.

In the case of remote access to another computer[3] through a relatively slow connection (and even a cable or DSL line is slow compared to a local area network), the antivirus program can double the time it takes to do file transfers because it may be trying to scan files on the remote system.

Your best bet is to leave the antivirus software on unless you notice a performance impact. If you do, turn it off. Just remember to turn it back on when you're finished with the task at hand.

---

[3] Most home users will never do this, but a few of you may have a virtual private network set up to work or school that allows you to access a remote computer as if it were on your local network.

Where Antivirus Programs Fail

Antivirus vendors are quick to promise safety with their programs, but sad to say there are places where even the best antivirus programs fail.

Viral Leapfrog

Each of the major antivirus software vendors maintains a team whose job it is to spot new viruses and update their antivirus software to protect against it. The lifespan of every virus goes something like this:

- Somewhere in the world, someone writes a virus or worm.

- The virus spreads unimpeded, as existing antivirus programs don't defend against it.

- Antivirus software vendors find out about the virus either through infection of their own machines, or samples sent by customers.

- Antivirus software vendors modify their programs, and make updates available that detect the virus and remove infections.

- Customers download the updates, reducing the number of vulnerable machines.

- The number of infections drops, and the spread of the virus slows.

Curiously, this is another place where technology mimics reality, because the spread of a mutated virus like those that cause a cold or flu follows a similar pattern. The virus spreads, doctors recognize it and try to isolate it, immunity spreads among those who survive the infection, and the spread of the virus slows.

But it rarely stops. That's an important point—even in nature it's very hard to completely eradicate a disease. With computer viruses there are almost always some vulnerable machines remaining, allowing the virus to continue to exist in some places.

The Unavoidable Failure of Antivirus Programs

This life cycle also illustrates one place where every antivirus program fails. Between the time a virus is created and the time an antivirus program is updated, there is a window of vulnerability in which a virus can infect your system.

Thus even if you have an updated antivirus program on your system, it's essential that you follow the precautions you've already learned—not to open e-mail attachments you're unsure of—and follow other precautions you'll learn about in the next two chapters: Maintain an effective firewall, and keep your system up to date.

This window of vulnerability also means that you should never download a file from a newsgroup or other file site until it has been available for at least a couple of weeks. That hot new file might be just a bit too hot—and contain a virus that your antivirus program hasn't yet been updated to handle.

The window of vulnerability is a technological reason why antivirus programs can fail. But as Dr. Holistic might say—most of the reasons antivirus programs fail are due to human error and human nature, not technology.

Update? What Update?

Most new computers from major companies ship with antivirus software installed. In some cases they include a subscription for updates for the first six months or a year.

But you won't believe how many times I've had a conversation like this:

Me: So, does your computer have antivirus software installed?

Friend: Yep, it came with it.

Me: Do you know if it's downloading updates?

Friend: Uh, I don't know.

Me: Did you renew the subscription for updates when it expired?

Friend: No, I'll probably get around to it sometime.

Or maybe . . .

Friend: I'm still getting updates to the program, but it wants me to pay for updates to the virus definition file, so I'm not getting those.

Folks, the level of protection these people are getting is virtually useless.

You now know about the life cycle of a virus—you know that a virus spreads fastest when it's new. If even up-to-date antivirus software doesn't give you perfect protection, imagine how bad old virus software is! Failing to update for even one or two months is enough to make you vulnerable to the worst new viruses.

And so it is that once again, most people are vulnerable not due to technological failures, but because of human nature. They forget or don't bother to update the subscription on their antivirus software. They don't check for updates (though nowadays most antivirus software checks for updates automatically as long as the subscription is active).

Other Human Failures

Not bothering to update your antivirus software is just the main human failure that helps viruses spread. There are others.

Trust

Your best friend sends you a really cool new application to try out. Naturally you trust him. But what does that really mean?

- You trust him not to intentionally infect you with a virus.

- You trust him to know enough about computer security to know if the file he's sending is a potential virus.

- You have to trust that his idea of a practical joke doesn't include a virus.

- You trust him to have a clean system.

- You trust him to have the same approach towards spyware and adware as you, or at least warn you if the software has spyware or adware.

That's an awful lot of trust.

Now I'm a firm believer in trusting my friends, coworkers, and associates. But I nevertheless scan everything I'm sent.

And as for files sent by strangers, they get deleted right away. Which brings me to the next issue.

Curiosity

In Chapter 3 you learned about all the tricks that viruses use to convince you to open e-mail attachments. One of the things they appeal to most is your curiosity. This applies to any file you receive, whether by e-mail or one you download yourself. All it takes is for the filename or description to spark your curiosity enough to double-click the file—and you've opened the door to trouble.

By the way, I do want to emphasize that though this book is directed at teens, adults are equally susceptible to trust and curiosity issues. I recently talked to an executive at a computer company, one with years of experience, who sheepishly described how he found an executable file on his system and, just out of curiosity opened it. Nothing happened. Then over the next few days parts of his system stopped working. He couldn't figure out what the trouble was, and didn't suspect a virus because his antivirus software didn't report a problem. Well, a week later his antivirus software was updated and sure enough, it detected a major infection on his computer. His curiosity caused him to open a virus file during the window of vulnerability between the time the virus was created and the antivirus software was updated.

Fraudulent Reports

In Chapter 3, in the section on e-mail, you learned how some e-mail chain letters act as viruses in a way. They convince you to forward warnings to your friends instructing them to manually delete a file that supposedly is a virus that can't be detected by antivirus programs. The file, it turns out, is one your system needs to run properly.

I mention this type of e-mail again to stress one point. This kind of e-mail message is correct in one thing—it isn't stopped by antivirus programs. Only your good sense and a willingness to check up on stories before taking action or spreading them will protect you and your friends from this one.

Anti-Antivirus Software

One of the most dangerous types of viruses actually targets and disables your antivirus software. The danger here is that by disabling the antivirus software not only is the virus given free reign to do whatever it wants, it opens the door to further infection as well.

Most antivirus software provides some indication that it at least thinks it's working—typically an icon in the system tray (by default at the lower-right side of your screen). Other antivirus software brings up a screen at startup indicating that it's protecting your computer. Keep your eyes open for changes in the behavior of your antivirus software. If the icon vanishes from the taskbar, or looks different, or if you stop seeing a notice on startup, you may have been infected by this type of virus.

Otherwise, the techniques for avoiding this type of virus are the same as any other virus. Your best bet is to keep it from being installed on your system in the first place using the techniques you've already learned (and those you'll learn as you read on).[4]

Choosing Antivirus Software

Antivirus software is one of those items for which more isn't necessarily better. In other words, you don't want to have more than one antivirus application running on your system at a given time. Not only is there a chance that they will interfere with each other (or detect another antivirus program as itself being a virus), but having more than one scanning in the background can significantly slow your system down.

In many cases you'll just use the antivirus software that comes with your system. As long as you keep your subscription up to date, and either update frequently or allow it to automatically update itself, you should be perfectly fine with that choice. Chances are, if your computer came with antivirus software, it came with either Norton AntiVirus or McAfee VirusScan.

---

[4] *The virus removal instructions in Chapter 9 offer further suggestions on how to remove this kind of virus.*

Antivirus Choices

Quite a few antivirus programs are available, but chances are good you'll end up using one of three products:

Product Name	Company	Web Site
Norton AntiVirus	Symantec	http://www.norton.com or http://www.symantec.com
McAfee VirusScan (packaged version)	Network Associates	http://www.mcafee.com
McAfee VirusScan web service (also called McAfee VirusScan Online)	Network Associates	http://www.mcafee.com

These products are constantly evolving, and are often bundled with other products or features that aren't directly related to their antivirus features. So if you don't have a virus scanner and are trying to choose between them, see who has the best deal at the moment. Technically speaking, anything I tried to tell you about which one was "better" at a given task right now would without doubt be obsolete by the time you read this. But you won't go wrong with either choice.

Just remember to remove any existing antivirus software (including any that came with your system) before installing new antivirus software.[5]

What About Other Antivirus Programs?

When you do a search for antivirus software (use the keyword antivirus, not anti-virus), you'll see many results. I've focused on the Norton and McAfee products because they are the most popular and widely used. In theory, this means that both companies have the resources to commit to research—to keep their software up to date. They have a larger customer base to potentially report new viruses to them.

But it doesn't mean they are necessarily the "best" antivirus software.

Not only that, but with size comes other types of vulnerability. Authors of anti-antivirus software are more likely to create viruses that disable the products of these two companies than others.

So, if you really feel like putting in research to find another antivirus program, go right ahead. My guess is most of you will stick with one of these products. Also, be sure to visit AlwaysUseProtection.com, where I'll be posting updated information including details on other antivirus programs.

---

[5] *Running two antivirus programs at once will, of course, slow your system down. Worse—the two programs might each decide that the other is a virus, leading them into mortal combat, which can tie up all available computing power.*

Online or Offline

One of the interesting options provided by McAfee is that of a web service–based antivirus tool. The differences between this and a regular packaged product are subtle.

You can't buy the online version in a store—there is no retail packaged product. Instead, you purchase it online and create an account on the McAfee web site. The antivirus program is installed using an ActiveX control. You can reinstall it any time you want just by entering your user name and password on the McAfee site—you don't have to worry about losing a CD.

You can also buy the packaged VirusScan program or Norton's AntiVirus program via the Internet. But in that case, you download an installation package that is installed just as if you were installing it from a CD.

The way you buy and install the product is the only real difference. Once on your system, they are comparable. The big advantages of the online-based antivirus tool is that it's always up to date. If you're restoring a system, you don't have to find the CD, and you don't have to install an older version and then download an update. The version you download will always be the latest. Its big disadvantage is that McAfee's web site currently has incredibly annoying pop-up ads that really go overboard trying to sell you their other products.

The advantage of a packaged product is that it allows you to install antivirus software before you're connected to the Internet. In Chapter 6, you'll learn how to deal with the problem of updating a system after a system restore or when installing a new operating system.

The Freebees

- It's 2:00 a.m., you're at a friend's house, you accidentally opened a downloaded file, and now you're wondering if you may have infected your friend's computer. You need to do a virus scan fast, but you don't have one and the stores are closed.

- You've argued with your parents, but they just won't buy you virus scanning software until you've cleaned your room. A quick look at your room suggests that the world may end before it's clean enough to satisfy them (or even allow someone to see the floor), so you need another option.

- You have the money for virus scanning software, and get to your local computer shop, only to discover that 3D Realms has finally shipped "Duke Nukem Forever". Antivirus software or Duke Nukem? Your computer is well protected for the next few weeks because you're too busy playing to check your e-mail or download any files. But sooner or later, you have to return to the real world.

It's always best to have full-featured antivirus software installed and running on your system. But for those times when you need to do a virus scan quickly, both Norton and McAfee offer free online virus scanning. For McAfee, go to their home page at **http://www.mcafee.com** and look for the link to McAfee FreeScan.

For Norton, go to their home page (**http://www.symantec.com**) and look for something called Symantec Security Check—at the time this book was printed it was in their Downloads section.

Both of these free services use ActiveX controls—the kind I warned you about in Chapter 3. But in this case, when prompted as to whether or not to install the control, you should answer Yes. Figure 4-2 shows an example of an ActiveX control prompt for an online virus scanner—this one for Symantec's free security check.

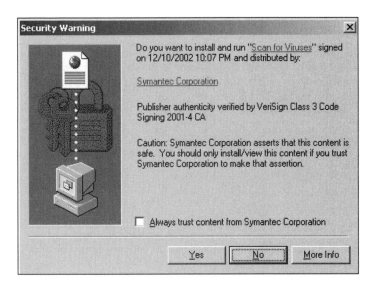

Figure 4-2 ActiveX control prompt for Symantec's free virus scanner

You may (in fact probably will) see more than one of these as the site loads multiple ActiveX controls. Go ahead and click Yes for all of them.

After the ActiveX control is installed, follow the instructions on the screen. Be sure to disable any existing antivirus software before running one of these scanners.

As of the date this book was published, both free scanning programs are very similar. The big difference is that the McAfee one actually requires you to create an account on McAfee.com (using a valid e-mail address) before it allows you to download and install the scanner.

These free scanners do a good job of helping you determine whether your computer has an active infection, but they typically lack many critical features of a full antivirus program.

- They don't clean viruses from your system.

- They may not scan inside compressed files.

- They have little or no flexibility in terms of specifying what files to scan.

- They don't provide ongoing protection.

- They start with your C drive, which is a problem if your operating system is installed on another drive.[6]

If they find a virus, they let you know of the fact and which virus they've found. You then have to remove the virus manually using one of the virus removal tools or instructions you'll find on their web sites.

The free scanners are great tools when you have nothing better available, but I strongly recommend you invest in a full-featured program.

Spam Filters

Spam filters aren't really security products, and I had some doubts as to how much coverage to give them. But they are deserving of at least a brief mention.

A *spam filter* is basically a filtering program that tries to decide which e-mails you want to see and which you don't. Because many of the e-mails you don't want to see contain viruses or messages that try to trick you into divulging personal information, spam filters do provide some additional protection. But because they aren't perfect (or even close), they should be thought of more as a convenience to help you handle e-mail than a real security tool.

If you're using one of the major online services for e-mail—AOL, MSN, Earthlink, etc., or web mail such as Yahoo or Hotmail, you should check their e-mail documentation for configuring spam filtering options. They all have at least some spam filtering built in. If you're using a POP3 account (using Outlook, Outlook Express, or other e-mail client program), you can find a wide variety of spam filtering products.

Some of the most popular are iHateSpam (`http://www.sunbelt-software.com`), McAfee SpamKiller (`http://www.mcafee.com`), and the free open source SpamBayes (`http://spambayes.sourceforge.net`).

You can also find antispam software that does virus checking on e-mail as well; however, your standard antivirus program should do this for you anyway.

---

[6] *It's possible to have more than one copy of Windows, or even other operating systems, installed on your system. This means that advanced users sometimes have their operating system on a drive other than drive C.*

Other Resources

Most of the time, once you install an antivirus program that does ongoing monitoring and automatic updates, you won't need any more information about specific viruses. The software will detect most viruses before they have a chance to run and do you any harm. The antivirus program will clean most viruses reasonably safely.[7]

But if you're interested in learning more about viruses, or learning details about specific viruses, or determining if a virus warning is a fraud, here are some web sites that will help.[8]

- *CERT Coordination Center:* `http://www.cert.org`

- *Symantec Security Response:* `http://securityresponse.symantec.com`

- *McAfee AVERT Virus Information Library:* `http://vil.nai.com/vil/`

- *Virus Bulletin:* `http://www.virusbtn.com/index.xml`

- *About.com:* `http://netsecurity.about.com`

CERT is a federally funded organization that focuses on all aspects of computer security. You'll also find that every antivirus software vendor has information online. The *Virus Bulletin* is an independent magazine (and thus less likely to try to sell you their brand of antivirus software on every page). About.com has a great deal of information and up-to-date news on specific viruses and threats and antivirus software reviews.

Antivirus software is only the first of the three elements you need to secure a system. In the next chapter, you'll learn about one that is equally important: your firewall.

---

[7] *Be sure you read Chapter 9, which tells you what to do if you actually have an active infection on your system.*

[8] *These links are up to date at the time of printing. Visit* `http://www.AlwaysUseProtection.com` *for updated listings.*

Guardians at the Gate: Firewalls

You've just learned about antivirus programs—the first of the three tools you have available to protect your computer. But you also learned that antivirus programs aren't perfect. Many of their imperfections originate with one obvious fact—an antivirus program can only look at files that are already on your computer. Even though they can do a good job of detecting those files and preventing them from running, the file is nevertheless on your system, which poses some risk.

In this chapter, you're going to learn about a tool whose job it is to prevent viruses from reaching your system in the first place. Firewalls are named after a kind of wall that exists in many buildings that is designed to slow the spread of a fire. They tend to be thicker or more fire resistant than other walls, and have fewer openings.

Computer firewalls are designed to provide some separation between your computer and the Internet, or between your local network and the Internet. Think of the Internet as being "on fire"—a constant source of potential attacks on your system. Your firewall is designed to stop that fire from reaching your computer.

> As with antivirus programs, you should
> always have some type of firewall active.

Later in the chapter you'll learn about the different types of firewalls, how to choose a firewall, and most important, how to open ports in a firewall so you can do things like play games online or host web sites while still keeping your system secure.

> **NOTE** This is a long chapter, one of the longest in the book. Don't feel you have to read it all the way though—once you've gotten past the explanations of firewalls, you'll be able to skim through and focus on only those parts of the chapter that apply to your own situation.

How Firewalls Work

In Chapter 3, you learned about Internet attacks (you might want to go back and review that section before continuing). You learned how every computer has an IP address, and that many attacks are based on outside computers trying to contact your machine and trick it into running some sort of program by accessing one of the services you may be running—preferably a service that has a security flaw that they can exploit.

A firewall is a tool that intercepts and blocks incoming requests to your computer. Firewalls can be implemented in hardware or software, and each approach has advantages and disadvantages, as you'll soon see.

Now, the topic of firewalls is actually very complex—there are entire books written on the subject. The good news is that most of that complexity is only needed by large organizations with complex networks. So rather than trying to give you a broad (but simple) overview of firewalls, I'm going to focus on just two scenarios: one based on using a simple home router, and the other based on software. For each one, I'm going to go into a fair amount of depth. That's because you'll need to understand something about how each of these approaches works in order to know how to bypass it for online gaming or instant messaging without at the same time compromising your overall security.

Routers and NAT

If you have a DSL or cable connection, it's possible for you to have more than one computer sharing your Internet connection. To accomplish this, your cable or DSL line most likely connects to a box called a *router* (because it routes signals from one computer and network to another).

In order to share an Internet connection, a router uses a protocol[1] called *Network Address Translation* or NAT for short. To understand NAT, you have to keep in mind that your DSL or cable modem assigns you a single IP address.[2] Anytime you dial up to the Internet, you are assigned an IP address by the dial-up service. That means that as far as the Internet is concerned, you have one computer on the Internet. This raises an interesting question: If each computer has its own IP address, how can more than one computer share an IP address?[3]

---

[1] A **protocol** is a set of rules that computers use to communicate. For example, web sites use HTTP—Hypertext Transfer Protocol.

[2] Some DSL and cable lines, and other technologies such as T1, T3, IDSL, SDSL, etc., allow your Internet service provider to assign you more than one IP address. But this is uncommon for home users.

[3] Sharing IP addresses is a temporary solution to a problem: We're running out of IP addresses. The 4 billion or so possible addresses sound like a lot, but they were allocated in blocks that leave many unused, and with the trend to giving an IP address to every printer, cell phone, and toaster, there aren't enough. The Internet is gradually being reengineered with a new version of IP called IPv6, which will support over a trillion devices.

Every packet of information on the Internet has a source IP address and destination IP address. So, let's say you have two computers on your home network sharing the fictional IP address A.B.C.D[4] as shown in Figure 5-1. If one sends out a request for information to the apress.com server,[5] the server will receive the request (1), and try to send a response back. However, the response packet won't be able to find its way to the correct computer (2). Two computers on a network with the same IP address can't communicate with each other. In fact, in most cases your computer will detect the presence of two computers with the same IP address on a network and will report an error (and disable access to the network).

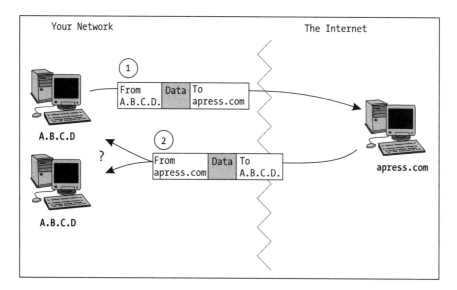

Figure 5-1 Two computers sharing an IP address just doesn't work.

The trick for solving this problem is shown in Figure 5-2. Instead of assigning your IP address to a computer, you assign it to a router. As far as the Internet is concerned, your router is the computer on the Internet with IP address A.B.C.D. Your router then assigns each computer on your home network a private IP address, typically 192.168.1.N,[6] where N is a number

---

[4] Every IP address has four numbers, each from 0 to 255, so assume A.B.C.D represents whatever IP address you have been assigned by your Internet service provider.

[5] Whenever you type in a domain name, such as apress.com, your computer uses a service called Domain Name Service (DNS) to look up the correct IP address for that domain name. So in effect domain names and IP addresses are two ways of saying the same thing: an address on the Internet.

[6] Some routers use 192.168.0.N.

between 2 and 255. The router itself tells your local network that your Internet gateway—the first machine your computer should contact to send data to the Internet—is 192.168.1.1, which is the IP address of the router (as seen on the local network). That's right—the router has two different IP addresses: one on the private network and the other one (assigned by your ISP) on the Internet.

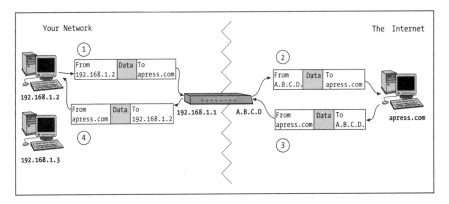

Figure 5-2 Two computers are assigned private IP addresses by a router that uses NAT.

Let's say your first computer, 192.168.1.2, wants to connect to http://www.apress.com. Here's what happens:

- The request from 192.168.1.2 with destination apress.com is first sent to the router at 192.168.1.1 ①.

- The router strips off the "from" IP address, and swaps in your assigned IP address A.B.C.D ②.

- The router stores in memory the fact that a request was made to http://www.apress.com from 192.168.1.2.

- The Apress server receives the request and sends a response. The response data is marked as from http://www.apress.com and going to A.B.C.D ③.

- The router receives the response. It examines the packet and looks in its own memory and discovers that 192.168.1.2 had previously made a request to http://www.apress.com and is expecting a response. So the router strips off the "to" IP address of A.B.C.D and swaps in 192.168.1.2 ④.

- 192.168.1.2 receives the response.

As you can see, the router "tricks" each computer on your network into thinking that it's directly on the Internet. As far as the Internet is concerned, there is only one computer connected—it doesn't know it's just a router.

Internet Connection Sharing on XP

Windows XP includes a feature called *Internet Connection Sharing*, which allows one Internet connection to be shared with other computers on your local network. In effect, this turns the computer into a router.

I'm not going to go into any further detail on this feature for two reasons:

1. I think it's very uncommon in home systems. Dial-up connections are too slow to be worth sharing, and few home computers have the dual network cards needed to configure the system as a true router replacement.

2. External routers are so inexpensive now, and provide such a high level of reliable security, that they are a much better approach overall.

Security Implications of NAT

Now imagine for a moment that your computer at 192.168.1.3 is loaded with obsolete software, and is running several services that are known to be vulnerable to Internet attacks. What happens when an infected computer on the Internet or hacker tries to attack your computer?

- The infected computer sends a request to your IP address at A.B.C.D.

- The router receives the request and looks in memory to see if any of your computers had made a request of the infected computer.

- Seeing none, the router checks to see if it has any instructions with regards to the particular port—if requests to that port have been assigned to one of your computers.

- If not, the router just ignores the request.

In other words—even though one of your computers is very vulnerable to attack, the router blocks dangerous requests before they can get to the system.

This is one of the true "good news" stories with regards to computer security. All the routers that people have installed in order to share Internet connections provide, as a side effect, excellent firewall protection as well!

On the other hand, NAT can pose challenges when it comes to online gaming or hosting services. You'll learn how to handle those challenges later in this chapter.

Firewall Software

If you connect to the Internet through a modem, or your computer is connected directly to a DSL or cable modem, your computer is given an IP address (either during dial-up or other configuration provided by your ISP). With this IP address, your computer is directly on the Internet—in fact, the Internet is really nothing more than a large number of computers that are connected together.

Now, if you are using a dial-up modem, you're pretty much stuck with this. However, if you are using a DSL line or cable modem, you can use a router with NAT even if all you have is that one computer.

> Because a router provides outstanding firewall protection
> and can be purchased for under $40, I recommend you use
> one on your DSL or cable modem line even if you will
> never connect more than one computer.

But if you are using dial-up, or don't want to invest in a router, you can add firewall protection to your computer using software. Even if you have a router, you may want to add firewall software as an extra level of protection.

Firewall software is actually pretty easy to understand.

Think for a moment about the problem a firewall is trying to solve. Your computer may have programs (services) running that are listening to requests from the Internet (your computer is acting as a server). Some of those services may have vulnerabilities that would allow an Internet request to invade your system—even if you don't do anything. A router solves this problem by blocking those requests before they even get to your computer.

A software firewall is a program that intercepts Internet requests before they are forwarded to the service programs on your computer.

Just as computers communicate with each other, programs communicate with each other as well. When a program or service wants to communicate with the network, it doesn't communicate directly to your network card—it goes through the operating system. This means that all Internet communication goes through the operating system first. A software firewall is a piece of software that is designed so that all Internet communication goes through the firewall as well. Sometimes the firewall is part of the operating system, sometimes it hooks itself into the operating system to perform its task.

The firewall software contains a set of rules that you define that allow it to decide whether each network request should go through. These rules can take many factors into account including the following:

- Is it an outgoing request from your computer, or an incoming request from another computer?

- Is the other computer within your local network, or on the Internet?

- What application (e-mail, browser, etc.) is making the request?

- What application is trying to become a server (listen to incoming network requests)?

- What is the port number of the request?[7]

And so on . . .

Software firewalls provide a great deal of flexibility; however, with that flexibility comes a certain amount of complexity, which raises security issues as you will read shortly.

Firewalls and Dial-Up Connections

Once upon a time, it was common knowledge that people who dial up to the Internet with a modem don't need firewall software. There used to be some truth to this. Dial-up connections are less vulnerable than DSL and cable modem connections for a number of reasons:

- With a dial-up connection, you get a different IP address each time. This makes it a bit more difficult to find you (if you're an attacker), but more important, makes your computer less useful. You see, if someone wants to use your computer as a server (say, a porn site, pirate software site, etc.), they prefer your computer to have a fixed IP address.

- Dial-up connections are limited to 56 kbits/sec going into your computer (download speeds) and only 28 kbits/sec coming out of your computer. This also makes it less useful as a server, and means any attack would take longer to accomplish.

- In the past, dial-up connections were expensive—10 cents/minute was not unheard of. So people did not stay logged on for hours at a time. This significantly reduced the chance of a computer being attacked.

While dial-up connections are still slow compared to DSL and cable modem lines, most of these arguments no longer apply.

- With most services offering unlimited access plans, and the spread of online gaming, instant messaging, and increased use of the web, it's not unusual for your computer to be logged on for hours at a time. That's plenty of time to find and attack a system even through a modem.

- There are many more computers on the Internet, and significantly more viruses and Trojans out there. A vulnerable computer connected to the Internet may be attacked and infected in a matter of minutes.

---

[7] *Ports were described in Chapter 3.*

- While dynamic IP addresses may make a computer less useful as a server, they don't prevent it from being used by a Trojan—some of which can contact a hacker's computer to let them know the current IP address. Also, the lack of a fixed IP is an advantage for hackers who are planning Denial of Service attacks, because they are harder for a victim to block.[8]

It's therefore essential that you use firewall software if you are connecting to the Internet through a modem.

Where Firewalls Fail

Firewalls, like antivirus programs, have weaknesses. And like antivirus programs, those weaknesses most often have to do with how you use them.

The Window of Vulnerability

Picture this scenario.

- You just bought a new computer. The operating system doesn't include a firewall. You have a DSL line that you plan to connect to, or you're connecting through a modem, and you know that you need to install a firewall. So you decide to buy one online.

- You boot up your computer, connect to the Internet, find an online store, and buy and download the firewall software.

- You install the firewall software.

What's wrong with this picture?

The problem with this scenario is that between the time you connected your computer to the Internet for the first time, and the time you installed the firewall, your computer was unprotected. Sure, it may only have been 10 or 15 minutes, but that can be enough for an attack to succeed.[9]

 RULE OF THUMB If you are using a software firewall, buy a retail package or be sure one is installed on the computer BEFORE you connect to the Internet for the first time.

---

[8] Sites block Denial of Service attacks by filtering out attacking IP addresses. If a computer keeps changing IP addresses, its attack is much harder to block.

[9] Remember, there are large numbers of machines just randomly targeting IP addresses, searching for a vulnerable computer. Some of them belong to hackers, but most are those infected by viruses and worms that are trying to spread themselves.

If you are using a router with NAT, you don't have to worry about this problem.

Your Local Network

The big difference between a router and a software firewall is where the protection occurs.

Figure 5-3 shows a typical configuration with a router-based firewall. An attack from the Internet (symbolized by a thick arrow on the right) is blocked. However, a router doesn't protect you from attacks from other computers on your local network.

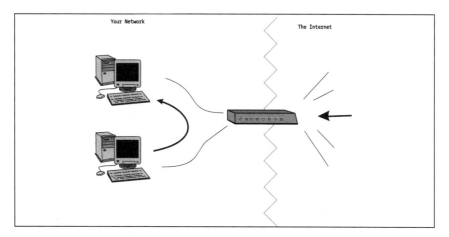

Figure 5-3 A router doesn't protect you from local attacks.

A software firewall (symbolized by the brick wall) protects you at the computer, thus providing you with protection against attacks from local infected systems as shown in Figure 5-4.

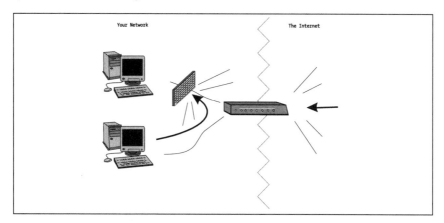

Figure 5-4 A software firewall protects your computer from local attacks.

You might want to conclude from this that you should always have a software firewall, but that isn't necessarily the case. If all of your local machines have active antivirus software and you are behind a router, the chances of you suffering from internal attacks in your home network are very slim. Businesses are much more likely to benefit from having the extra protection, as they may have dozens, hundreds, or thousands of computers on their local networks.

Human Nature and Firewalls

I sometimes host LAN parties,[10] so here's a scenario I've seen many times:

- A friend brings over his computer in order to play games or do some file exchanges.

- He starts running a game server, but nobody else can see the game . . . or he shares a drive so that you can exchange files, but you can't connect to his machine.

- After trying a whole bunch of different things, somebody suddenly figures out, "Hey, did you turn off your software firewall?"

- After yelling at each other for a few minutes for being idiots, he turns off his firewall and the game or file sharing commences.

Do you see the problem here?
Or here's a related scenario that I've also seen many times:

- You've been on your instant messaging service with a friend, and suddenly she wants to send you a cool picture or file.

- She tries to send a file, or open a direct connection to your computer, but after an endless delay (with her asking every few seconds "Did you click Accept? Did you click Accept?"), you get a message saying the connection could not be established—you may be behind a firewall.

- "Oops!" she says. She turns off the firewall and presto—the connection succeeds and you get the file.

Do you see the problem now?
The key phrase is "turns off the firewall."
Now, as you will see in the next section, it's quite possible to open holes in your firewall so you can do things like host games, share files, and start IM direct connections without compromising your overall security.

---

[10] For those who aren't aware of the term—a **LAN party** is when a group of friends get together, each bringing over their computer, and play network games late into the night and often well into the next day.

But when you're in a hurry, because your friend needs to log off IM, or because your friends are all yelling at you to start the game, and you need to bypass the firewall security, you aren't going to take the time to search through the online help and figure out how to do it. You're going to disable the firewall.

That's human nature.

When I've been in these situations, I have NEVER seen anyone, teen or adult, do it the correct way. They just disable the firewall "only for now" to get on with the task at hand.

In the case of a LAN party that I host, the risk of turning off the firewall is fairly small. My entire network is behind a router, and I keep my computers up to date and configured properly (as you'll read about in the next chapter). I also ask my friends to do a virus scan before they arrive, and if they haven't, I install antivirus software and do it for them.

But turning off that software firewall completely is risky if any of the machines brought over for the party are infected. And it's never safe for allowing a direct connection (including P2P file sharing).

This is probably the greatest flaw in firewall software—and it's not a technical flaw at all. It's purely human nature.

That's why I always recommend people with DSL or cable modem connections to use a router even if you only have one computer. As with software firewalls, you can open ports to allow direct connections, host games sites, and so on, but unlike software firewalls, there is no trivial way to just turn off all protection.[11]

Sometimes It's Just Too Late

Router-based firewalls do a great job blocking incoming requests. But they generally do nothing to block outgoing requests. This means that once a computer is infected with a Trojan, there is nothing to prevent the Trojan from opening connections to a cracker's system. Once that connection is open, the cracker can have full access to your system.

Many software-based firewalls can be configured to work in both directions—where only certain applications are permitted to access the Internet. For example, they'll allow only your web browser or e-mail client to initiate an Internet connection. They can prompt you when a program is trying to access the Internet or act as a server. This allows you to effectively block viruses and Trojans because they won't be on the list of approved applications.

This is one argument in favor of installing a software firewall on your system in addition to using a router—it does provide an extra level of protection, in the event that a virus or Trojan does get on your system.

---

[11] *Many routers do allow you to assign one connection as a DMZ or* **demilitarized zone**—*a computer that is effectively directly on the Internet—where all requests are forwarded to that computer by default. However, this has little application to any home use. You are much better off directing individual ports as described in the next section because using a DMZ is like using no firewall at all.*

Choosing a Firewall

The best strategies for using a firewall should now be pretty clear to you.

If you are using a dial-up connection with a modem, you should always have a software firewall. You should never turn it off. If you need to bypass it for some reason, take the time to learn how to use the program to allow you to bypass it for the one service you need, rather than turning it off completely (you'll learn how to do this later in this chapter).

If you are using a DSL connection or cable modem, spend the $40 to buy a router that supports NAT (it will say that it allows sharing of your Internet connection by multiple computers). If you wish to be extra safe, or if you're concerned about the security of other computers on your local network, you may want to use a software firewall as well. The section "Choosing Firewall Software" that appears later in this chapter has more information to help you decide if you wish to do so.

Choosing a Router

Routers come in many different sizes and price ranges, from the $40 home unit to large corporate systems costing tens of thousands of dollars.

For home use, the key feature you're looking for is Internet Connection Sharing (which is the marketing term router manufacturers use for NAT— Network Address Translation). Most routers will also claim to have firewalls built in. Unfortunately, while not dishonest, it can be hard to determine what this actually means. As you've already learned, NAT itself acts as a firewall, so marketers can legitimately claim that any NAT router is a firewall. Some routers include keyword filters—blocking access to sites that have certain keywords in their URL[12] and call that a firewall feature. Other routers include the same kind of IP filter rule settings as software firewalls. This sounds like it will provide even better protection, until you remember that NAT itself is already providing excellent protection. What the IP filter rules really provide is more flexibility. For example, NAT allows you to direct incoming web requests to a particular computer, but IP filters would also allow you to restrict incoming web requests to those coming from specified computers. This kind of flexibility is rarely needed for home use.

One reason that routers are so inexpensive is that there is a lot of competition. The good news is that they are all very comparable—you're unlikely to go wrong choosing any of the major brands. The bad news is that at those kinds of

---

[12] This is presumably intended for parents to filter out obscene sites. Given that the worst pornography sites do their best to keep obscene terms out of their names, the level of protection provided by keyword filters is questionable.

prices the companies generally can't afford high-quality technical support. Because router models change frequently, it's not possible for me to review and recommend specific routers here—by the time you read this the information will be obsolete. So here's how you go about choosing a router:

Visit your local retailer or an online store and write down a list of routers that look like good candidates. Be sure you first decide if you are getting a wired or wireless router (wireless are more expensive, and typically slower, but you don't have to run cables between the computers).

- Visit the web site for the manufacturer of each router.

- See if you can download the manual for the router from the manufacturer's web site. If they don't have the manual available, consider a different router.

- See if the manual is clear and includes the features you need.[13] Chances are it has far more capability than you need. Don't worry if you don't understand all the features—some are designed for network experts. However, be sure you understand how to use the features that you care about—especially how to assign server ports to particular computers.

- Look at the support section on the web site. Look for a good FAQ section—that's going to be your best source of information if you run into trouble.

- Check the downloads section for the router. Does it look like the company provides updated firmware[14] for their routers?

- Check out customer comments online at Amazon.com, Epinions.com (or other online retailers), and comments and reviews at CNET.com.

Because routers at this level all have similar features, and similar prices, choosing based on the quality of support available on the web site is a very reasonable approach.

Router Manufacturers

There are many router manufacturers to choose from. I'm going to list a few in Table 5-1, but let me stress that even a cheap off-brand router will probably do the job.

---

[13] *In this book I've only discussed security-related features. Your Internet service provider should be able to help you determine what other features you may need in a router for use with their particular service.*

[14] **Firmware** *is the internal software that a router uses to perform its job. That's right—a router is also a computer, but specialized for handling network traffic.*

Table 5-1 Major Router Manufacturers[15]

Manufacturer	URL	Comments
3Com	http://www.3com.com	A bit more focused on small business than home users.
D-Link	http://www.dlink.com	Also a fine choice.
Hawking	http://www.hawkingtech.com	If you have two DSL lines, they have a router that can let you use both at once for reliability and improved bandwidth.
Linksys	http://www.linksys.com	Recently purchased by Cisco, the leader in high-end routers (that is, expensive business routers). It's not clear yet how this will impact their product line or support.
Netgear	http://www.netgear.com	Several people I know have had good luck with their equipment.
Siemens	http://www.speedstream.com	Huge multinational corporation—be sure to go to their Speedstream web site or you can spend hours trying to find the site that covers their home products.

Choosing Firewall Software

There are probably just as many (or more) choices for firewall software as there are antivirus programs. But as with antivirus programs, you'll probably end up using one of the more popular choices. The good news is that you may already have one—firewall software is often packaged with antivirus software (for example, at the time this book was printed, McAfee included their personal firewall product with their retail antivirus software). Both Symantec and McAfee sell security bundles that include both antivirus and firewall protection.

---

[15] Another manufacterer is Belkin (http://www.belkin.com), which was recently involved in a "scandal" where some of their routers, as installed out of the box, would every eight hours or so randomly redirect a web request to a site in which they tried to sell parental control software. While they have apologized (sort of) and are offering a fix to those routers, the fact that they'd even consider doing such a thing in the first place is enough to kick them off this list. I mean, it's sort of fundamental to the idea of a router that it always at least tries to give you the page you ask for, don't you think?

On Software Bundles

All the major antivirus and firewall vendors sell software bundles beyond the core product. So, for example, you can buy Norton AntiVirus software, or you can buy Norton Internet Security, which includes a firewall, privacy control, antispam software, parental control, and so on. Obviously, they make more money on the entire bundle.

In working on this book, I faced two possible approaches: I could evaluate and talk about the various bundles available, or I could focus on individual products and features.

I chose the latter approach for several reasons:

First, bundles and features change—so today's product recommendations won't necessarily apply tomorrow.

Second, most teens I know want to purchase the least amount of software possible. Many bundled features simply make it easier to do something that you can actually do quite easily on your own (like clearing your browser history).

Finally, and most importantly—I have a strong bias towards installing the least amount of software protection needed to provide good security. That's because Windows is complex, and invasive software (which includes most of these security products) inevitably changes the behavior of your system. It can lead to performance slowdowns. It can cause other applications to fail in unexpected ways. It can lead to problems with Windows itself. Your operating system and the applications you have installed form a very complex system—and every system is different. Thus there is no way for a software vendor to test their software against every possible scenario. Plus, Murphy's Law[16] says that any nontrivial computer program has bugs (any computer program with more than 10 lines of code is nontrivial). So every time you install a security or privacy tool, you increase the chances of some unpleasant side effect occurring.[17]

This is, in fact, the main argument for avoiding a software firewall if you are using a router. The firewall software itself has the potential to interfere with the operation of other applications.

If you buy a bundled package, take the time to read about the various products and tools that are included and only install those that you want and understand. Some of these products can be somewhat invasive—meaning they modify the way your system works in various ways, and they can interfere with each other. For example, if you install a software firewall you got with a Norton bundle, you definitely don't want to install another firewall!

---

[16] The First Murphy's Law is, "Anything that can go wrong, will go wrong." There are hundreds of others.

[17] I develop software using a Microsoft product called **Visual Studio .NET**. After a recent antivirus software update, I started getting warnings every time I ran the program. McAfee had installed a new feature called **Script Stopper** that was designed to prevent dangerous scripts from running, and it decided that Visual Studio was running a dangerous script. Script Stopper did bring up a prompt that allowed me to either stop the script, or let it continue. However, Visual Studio .NET would crash even after I told Script Stopper to allow the script to run. Fortunately, it's possible to disable Script Stopper, but it shows you how two working programs can interfere with each other to cause problems.

There is value in having software that performs additional security checks for you—it can serve as a backup in case you miss something. It can make things easier. It can automate tasks that you would otherwise have to do yourself. In doing so it improves your level of security, but remember: There is no such thing as "perfect" security. There are only various degrees of security. My focus is to bring you to a level that is good enough to protect you from almost every threat, while at the same time minimizing both the cost and hassle of doing so.

Firewall Software Manufacturers

Speaking of which, the most popular standalone firewall software is probably ZoneAlarm. ZoneAlarm comes in a standard Firewall-only edition that is currently free. (Visit `http://www.zonealarm.com`.) They also sell higher-end packages that include a number of other privacy and security features. However, some of these features duplicate capability already built into many antivirus products, and some of the features just make it easy to do things like managing cookies that I'll be showing you how to do yourself later.

I've already mentioned McAfee and Symantec, which both have personal firewall products.

I'm not going to go into detail on installing any of these firewalls—the instructions that come with each one should be fine to get you started. However, there is one firewall you may already have that may need nothing more than some quick configuration to enable.

The Windows XP Firewall

If you're using Windows XP or later, your operating system includes a built-in firewall, so you may not need to buy a third-party product at all. However, you may need to turn it on.[18] Here's how:

From your Start menu, choose the Control Panel. Then choose Network Connections. Choose the Internet connection you use. Figure 5-5 shows a typical screen for a system connected to a DSL line or cable modem. You may also have a list of dial-up connections that you choose from if you use a modem to connect to the Internet.

On Windows XP, you configure your firewall for each connection separately—so if you use more than one Internet connection, be sure to set the firewall for each of them.

To enable the firewall, right-click the Internet connection and choose the Properties menu. You'll see a dialog box—click the Advanced tab and you'll see a dialog box similar to the one shown in Figure 5-6.

If you're using a dial-up connection, you'll see additional settings that allow Internet connection sharing or other features, but you're only concerned with the firewall.

---

[18] Microsoft left the firewall off by default in Windows XP until recently.

Figure 5-5 The Windows XP Network connections screen

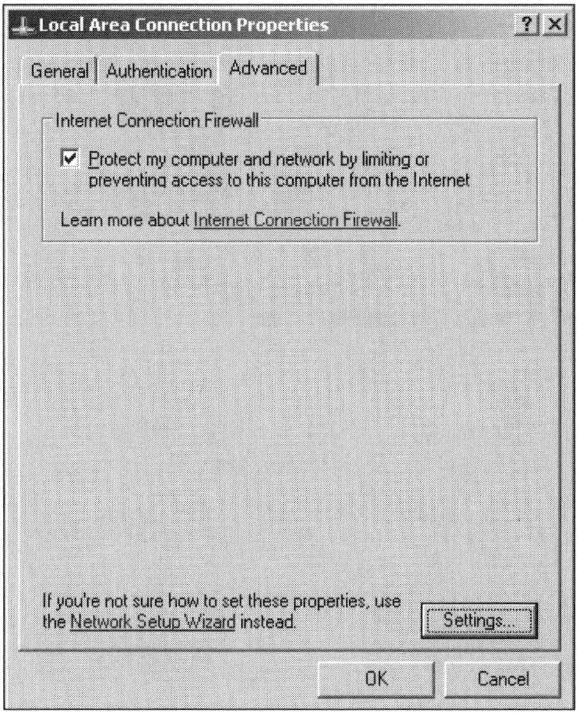

Figure 5-6 Dialog box to enable the XP Internet Connection Firewall

When the Internet Connection Firewall checkbox is checked, the XP software firewall is enabled. You'll learn about additional firewall settings in the next section.

Remember—like all software firewalls, it can interfere with communication within your local area network (affecting things like drive sharing). The XP firewall is designed to protect computers connected directly to the Internet, not those on an in-house network. It's a very good choice for those using dial-up Internet connections.

Firewalls, Online Gaming, and Other Services

You've already learned that while firewalls are able to block outgoing connections (Internet requests made by your computer to others), in most cases your firewall won't be set up to do that. Routers using NAT don't block outgoing connections by default (some advanced routers allow you to create outgoing filters, but they are disabled by default, and if you turn any of them on you presumably know how to turn them back off). The XP firewall doesn't block outgoing connections. Other firewall software does allow blocking of outgoing connections but makes it fairly easy to disable this feature.[19]

On the other hand, most firewalls, including all routers that use NAT, by default block all incoming connections—requests made by other computers to your computer.

Curiously enough, this is just fine for most adult users. All they do is browse the web, check e-mail, share drives and printers, and occasionally connect to work using a virtual private network (VPN).[20] All of these tasks only require outgoing connections.

But some of the most common ways teens use computers require your computer to act as a server as well. For example:

- Hosting a game server like Counterstrike

- Using a game service (like Battlenet) that works better (fewer drops, less lag) when your computer can receive incoming connections

- Performing instant messaging file transfers and direct connections

- Using Kazaa and other P2P services

- Experimenting with web sites

All of these require you to allow access from the Internet to a specific port on your computer.

---

[19] *Experts may scream at this point that I haven't even mentioned proxy servers. To which I answer, home users don't have proxy servers. If you're looking to apply knowledge gained in this book to a business/corporate setting, you should go out and learn about proxy servers, too.*

[20] *A network protocol that allows a remote computer to securely become part of a corporate network*

Common Server Ports

The first step to opening a hole in your firewall is to figure out what port the service needs. Your best bet for finding this information is to check on the web for the particular service where you can usually find an FAQ section containing advanced networking information.

There are two different kinds of Internet connection: TCP and UDP. The difference between them isn't really important—basically the TCP protocol is a more reliable kind of connection, but is not quite as fast because the sending computer receives confirmation that the data was sent. The UDP protocol doesn't require confirmation, but the sender is never certain the data was actually received. When configuring your firewall you need to know the protocol (TCP or UDP) as well as the port number

Table 5-2 lists some of the most common ports. Note that only incoming ports are listed—if your firewall is blocking outgoing ports, you'll have to research the web sites and help files for each service to determine the outgoing ports.

Table 5-2 Common Ports

Service	Port	Description
Age of Empires II	See DirectPlay	
America's Army	1716–1718 UDP, 8777 UDP, 27900 UDP, 20045 TCP	Some of these only apply when running a server. See http://www.americasarmy.com for more information.
AOL Instant Messenger	5190 TCP	Default port for file transfers and direct connect. You can override this in the Preferences menu.
Baldurs Gate	47624 TCP, 2300–2399 TCP and UDP	
BattleField 1942	14567 UDP	Need only for servers. Open the ports specified under Gamespy, plus 23000 to 23009 UDP if you want your server to be listed with Gamespy.
Battlenet	6112 UDP and TCP	Most Battlenet games.
Battlenet	4000 TCP	Diablo II.
Battlenet	6113–6119 TCP	Warcraft III custom games (must configure the game to use a custom port).

Continues

Table 5-2 Common Ports (*Continued*)

Service	Port	Description
BattleZone II	17770–17771 UDP	Only needed for running your own server.
Counterstrike and Halflife	27015 UDP	Only needed for running your own server.
DirectPlay	2300–2400 UDP and TCP 6073UDP, 47624TCP	Many Microsoft games use this technology. 6073 and 47624 are only needed for hosting games.
Everquest	1024–6000 UDP, 7000 TCP	Warning—this opens a very wide port range.
Gamespy	3783, 6667, 6500, 6515, 12300, 27900 UDP, 28900, 29900, 29901 TCP	See http://www.gamesspy arcade.com for more details. You won't need all of these to play games— most are only needed if you're running a server.
MSN Messenger	6891–6901 TCP	6891–6900 are used for file transfers, 6901 for voice.
MSN Game Zone	6667, 28800–29000 TCP	
NeverWinter Nights	5121 UDP	You can specify other ports from 5121 to 5129 by configuring the nwnplayer.ini file. See http://nwn.bioware.com for more information.
Kazaa and Morpheus	1214 TCP	Improves file sharing and file availability, and allows you to be a supernode.[21]
Rainbow Six	2346 TCP	
Ultima	5001–5010, 7775–7777, 8888, 9999, 8800–8900, 7875 TCP	7875 is not required for the game but by UO Monitor.
Unreal Tournament	7777–7783, 27900, 8080	Modify the server.ini file [UWeb.WebServer] section. Change ListenPort to 8080, ServerName to your IP address (obtain via IPConfig as described later in this chapter).

---

[21] *Of course, acting as a supernode can get you sued if you are sharing copyrighted material.*

The technical support or online help for your particular game or application will have updated information on the ports required by that application. Some router and firewall manufacturers include configuration settings for popular services on their web sites.

Configuring NAT

Every router has its own configuration, so it's not possible to provide one formula or set of instructions that will work on every router. But the principles involved are similar.

A NAT-based router isn't actually blocking a port—it's just discarding it because it doesn't know to which computer it belongs. So your job is to instruct the router to forward requests to that port to your computer. This involves three steps:

1. Determine your IP address.

2. If possible, tell the router to always assign the current IP address to your computer. Remember, a NAT router assigns computers IP addresses from a local range (typically starting at 192.168.1.2). Some routers allow you to reserve an IP address, some don't, but most do tend to remember which computer got which address and reassign the same one. If you find your software has stopped working, you can check your IP address and see if it has changed, and then update the router accordingly.

3. Instruct the router to forward requests to a certain port to your computer's IP address.

Determining Your IP Address

Open a command window.[22]

Type in the command **ipconfig** and press the Enter key.

You'll see a result similar to what's shown in Figure 5-7.

As you can see, my computer was assigned port 192.168.0.2 by this router.

---

[22] *From the Start menu, look for Command Prompt. It may be under Programs ➤ Accessories, or All Programs ➤ Accessories. You can also use the Run command from the Start menu and type in* **cmd***.*

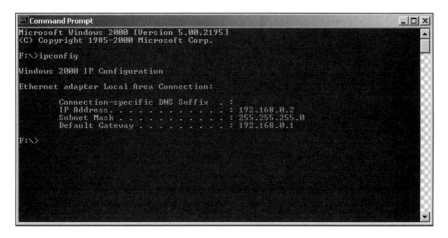

Figure 5-7 Using the IPConfig command

Configuring Your Router Using a Browser

Most modern routers can be configured using a web browser. Look at the
default gateway address given to you by the IPConfig program. Then enter
that IP address in the browser address bar. For example, in this case I would
use **http://192.168.0.1**.

You will be prompted for an account name and password.

You probably won't know what it is.

But that's OK, because 99 percent of the time people don't bother to
change the password. So look in the router manual for the default login name
and password. If you don't have the router manual, you can probably download it from the manufacturer's web site. If you or your parents have changed
the password and forgotten it, you'll need to check the manufacturer's web site
for information on resetting the router to its factory defaults, then reconfigur-
ing it for your network.[23]

For this example, I'll use an older but popular[24] Netgear router, the
RT314.

After searching the menus for a while, I found a menu called Ports, or Port
Forwarding, as shown in Figure 5-8. Some routers will call this Server Ports.

In this example, you can see that I've directed the Battlenet ports to my
computer. Generally speaking, routers make it easy to redirect entire blocks of
ports to a single computer, which is essential for some games.

---

[23] *I recently bought a router and couldn't log on until after I had reset it to the factory defaults as
described in the manual. It turns out it had been returned by a dissatisfied customer who had
changed the password. The store just restocked it without verifying that it worked. Those of you who
live in Silicon Valley can probably guess which store it was.*

[24] *I could use a newer router for the example, but since they're all different anyway, and the newer
ones are if anything easier to configure, this is a reasonable choice.*

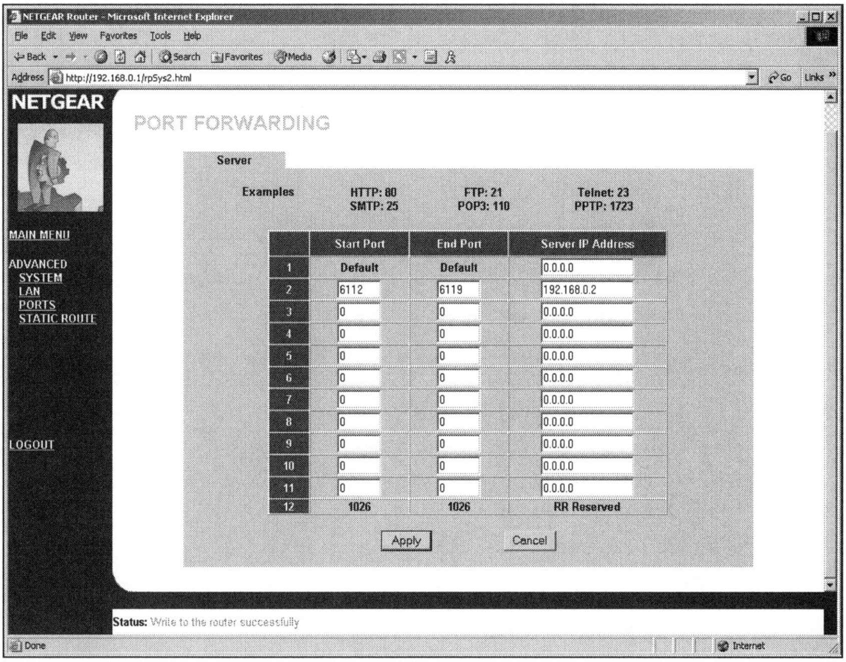

Figure 5-8 Example of a router configuration screen in a browser

When using NAT, depending on the game, you may be able to play it online from only one computer at a time. Check the documentation for your particular game for details.[25]

This particular router did not allow you to assign specific IP addresses to a computer.

Figure 5-9 shows the configuration window from another router, this one a Hawking router, in which an IP address is reserved for a particular computer based on its MAC address. The MAC address identifies a unique network card. You can find out the MAC address for your machine using the IPConfig command, but this time type in **ipconfig /all** and look for an entry called Physical Address.

---

[25] FYI: Warcraft III can be configured to run on different computers on your network simultaneously. There's a game setting that lets you specify the incoming port number (change it from 6112). Next you configure your router to send each port to the correct machine.

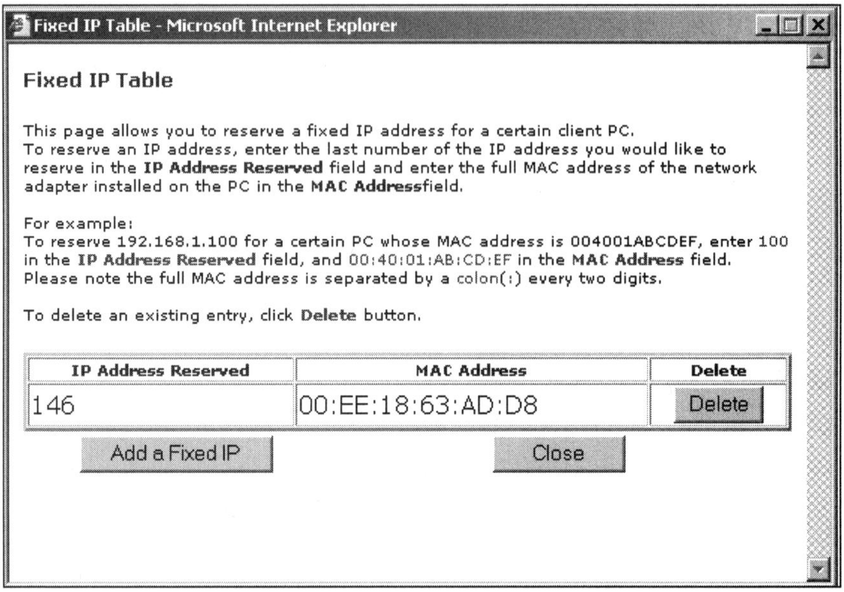

Figure 5-9 An example of reserving IP addresses for a specific machine

Configuring a Router Through Telnet

Most routers also allow an older style of configuration through an application called *Telnet*. This is an old-style terminal program. Even newer routers still support Telnet because it allows a router to be configured through a serial port.

To configure a router with Telnet, bring up a command window (as described earlier), type in **telnet 192.168.0.1**,[26] and then press Enter (obviously using the default gateway address for your router). You'll be prompted for a user name and password (or perhaps only a password). You'll then be brought to a configuration screen such as the one shown in Figure 5-10.

Can you guess which menu selection you would use to set the port forwarding?

That's right—number 15: the one dealing with server setup.

You'll obviously need to refer to your own router's documentation for details on configuring your particular router. But these examples should at least point you in the right direction to help you find and understand your own router's features.

---

[26] *On some routers this will be 192.168.1.1—try it both ways to see which one works.*

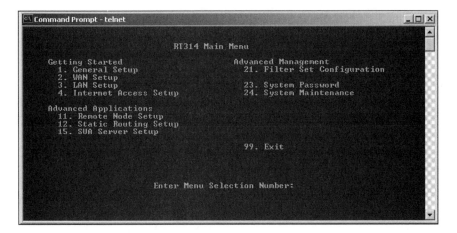

Figure 5-10 A Telnet configuration screen

Configuring Software Firewalls

Unlike routers, software firewalls have no problem figuring out which computer is supposed to receive an Internet request—they are running on the computer that is receiving the request. So the question with software firewalls is whether or not the computer should see that request.

To illustrate this, we'll look at two software firewall examples: the Internet Connection Firewall built into Windows XP, and ZoneAlarm.

Configuring an Internet Connection Firewall on XP

The firewall on Windows XP is an example of a very simple yet effective firewall. Why simple? For one thing, it only works in one direction—monitoring incoming requests from the Internet. It doesn't care what applications are running on your computer, and in fact doesn't prevent applications from trying to listen for incoming requests (and thus acting as servers). It just blocks incoming messages that it doesn't recognize.

Earlier in this chapter you learned how to turn on the Internet Connection Firewall. In Figure 5-6 you saw a button labeled Settings—this is what you'll use to open ports in the firewall, allowing requests to come through. When you click the Settings button, you'll see the dialog box in Figure 5-11. This figure shows how you would allow your computer to act as a web server.

> **NOTE** You shouldn't turn this on unless you are actually running your own web server on the computer, and its software is completely up to date. Web servers are special targets for attackers and if incorrectly configured can pose a huge security risk!

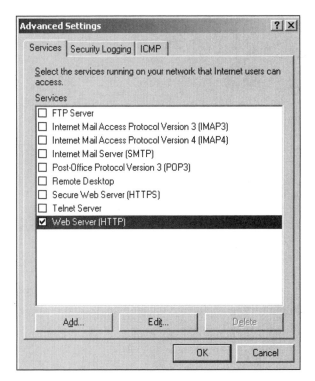

Figure 5-11 Opening a port in a firewall

The Add button is used to open additional ports in the firewall. Figure 5-12 shows how you would add an entry for Battlenet to use port 6112 TCP.

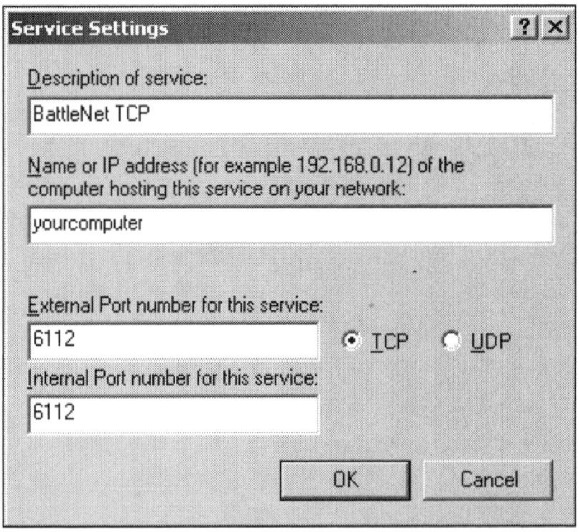

Figure 5-12 One of the entries for running Battlenet

To find the name of your computer, go back to the previous dialog box (shown in Figure 5-11), highlight any of the entries (don't check it), and click the Edit button. Copy whatever name you see in that entry and use it in your new entry.

For Battlenet, you'll create a second entry for port 6112, this time selecting UDP.

If you're trying to run a game that needs to listen to requests on many incoming ports, this is not the right firewall for you. You'll want to move up to a more advanced firewall.

Configuring ZoneAlarm

As mentioned earlier, ZoneAlarm is one of the most popular firewall products, and their basic firewall is free for personal use (at least at the time this book was printed).

ZoneAlarm, like other advanced firewalls, does a lot more than block incoming requests. It also

- Detects when an application is trying to connect to the Internet, and lets you decide if that application should be allowed to do so.

- Detects when an application is trying to act as a server—to listen to incoming Internet requests—and lets you decide if that should be allowed.

- Remembers what different applications are allowed to do, effectively learning as it goes based on the software actually installed on your machine.

- Allows you to distinguish between data sent to and from the Internet, and data sent to and from systems on your local network (or other trusted systems).

When trying to connect to Battlenet from Warcraft III, you'll notice that your application freezes. If you press Alt-Tab to get to the main screen, you'll find a prompt such as that shown in Figure 5-13.

You would typically click Yes, and check the box telling ZoneAlarm to remember Warcraft III for next time.

The same thing will happen when you try to create a game on Battlenet, except that your entire computer may seem to freeze. That's because Warcraft III is a full-screen application, and it's sometimes difficult for Windows to switch between graphic modes. So you may never actually see the warning in Figure 5-14 that comes up when Warcraft III tries to act as a server.[27]

---

[27] So how did I get to it? Pressed Ctrl-Alt-Del to bring up the Windows Security dialog box (this was on Windows 2000), clicked Cancel to see the screen with the alert, and pressed Alt-Tab to get back to Warcraft.

Figure 5-13 ZoneAlarm alert for Battlenet

Figure 5-14 ZoneAlarm alert for Warcraft III trying to act as a server. Note that it's listening on port 6112.

A better approach is to configure Warcraft III using the advanced program configuration option. Figure 5-15 shows the Program configuration screen in ZoneAlarm where you can add specific applications and set whether it's just accessing the Internet, or also acting as a server.

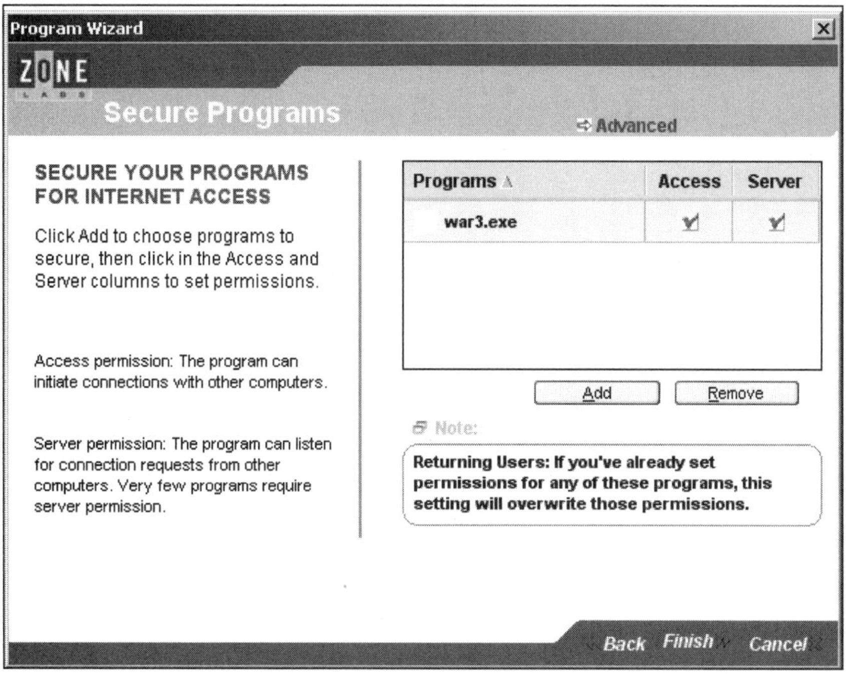

Figure 5-15 ZoneAlarm advanced program configuration screen

Once an application is configured in this way, you should no longer see those alerts, and ZoneAlarm should no longer interfere with the program.

This is obviously just the briefest introduction to ZoneAlarm, and your version may differ (especially if you have the more advanced Plus or Pro edition). But the principle applies to other software firewall products as well, and this introduction should at least give you a good start.

Remember, your game or firewall manufacturer will have online help and FAQ information that can help you configure your firewall for specific games.

Things to Remember

This has been a long chapter—the longest in the book, actually. But it's one of the most important subjects, and probably the most complex. The good news is, you actually now know quite a lot about how the Internet actually works, and should know enough to more easily understand the specific instructions of your own firewall, and the applications you run (at least as far as Internet connectivity is concerned).

For those who are feeling a bit lost, here's a quick summary of the key recommendations:

For those of you using a dial-up Internet connection:

- Install a software firewall. Learn how to use it.

- If you have XP, you can use the built-in firewall.

For those of you using a DSL, cable modem, or other high-speed connection:

- Use a router that supports NAT (Internet Connection Sharing).

- If you download a lot of software, or would like an extra level of protection, consider using a software firewall as well. **If you are not using a router, you MUST use a software firewall.**

If you use a software firewall, learn how to perform any tasks you need without disabling the firewall completely—your firewall documentation will help you with this. Now it's time to look at ways to help your computer resist attack, even in cases where your antivirus software or firewall aren't enough to do the job.

Locking Up, Part 1: Software Updates

You've learned about antivirus tools and firewalls, the first two of the three pillars of computer security. In this chapter, you're going to learn about software updates, which are in their own way just as important as what you've learned up until now.

It might have struck you as odd that in both of the previous chapters I talked about not only the value of antivirus tools and firewalls, but also the ways in which each of them can fail. This is important, because most security vulnerabilities come from a failure of some sort—whether a failure in technology (such as bugs in Windows), or a failure in human judgment (such as being tricked into opening a virus).

Look at it this way:

It's quite unlikely that you would intentionally install and run a virus on your system, right?

So anytime your system is infected, something has gone wrong. Something has failed.

No human is perfect. The assaults and trickery of e-mail, temptingly named downloads, and our own curiosity to just see what that strange program will do, means that even security experts will sometimes find themselves frantically cleaning their system—despite the best protection of antivirus tools and firewalls. When it happens, we tend to be rather upset at ourselves—after all, who likes to make mistakes?

But if we beat ourselves up when we make a mistake, it's nothing next to the fury we feel when a problem occurs that isn't our fault.

I mean, there are certain things that should be safe—always.

- It should be safe to plug your computer into the Internet—it shouldn't be possible for some outsider to somehow connect into a system unless you do something to make that possible.

- It should be safe to browse the Web. I'm not talking about software downloads, I'm talking about just browsing web sites. There should be no way that just clicking a page link could damage your system.

- It should be safe to view e-mail. I'm not talking about opening attachments—I mean simply viewing the content of the text part of the e-mail message.

These things should be safe. They should be safe always.

But they aren't.

And the fault of this lies squarely with Microsoft.[1] For a very long time, they did not take security seriously—we know this because recently they have claimed to have changed their priorities so that safety is now their top priority.

Now, to be fair, they have finally woken up to the problem and have become a lot more responsive to security threats, and getting out updates, and notifying people about them. But it's a tough problem for a number of reasons.

- An operating system is incredibly complex, and even if Microsoft had made security their top priority from the beginning, there would still be some security flaws in their software. Not as many, perhaps, but they would exist.

- Microsoft is a victim of their own success. If you were a malicious virus author, what system would you focus your efforts on targeting. Mac? Linux? Of course not—you'd target Windows, because most everyone uses it.

- By the same token, there are lots of white hats[2] out there trying to find security flaws so that Microsoft will fix them. This puts Microsoft in a dilemma—if they ignore the flaw, sooner or later some virus will be created to take advantage of it. If they announce the flaw and create an update, someone will quickly create a virus to try to take advantage of it before people download and install the update.

So the good news is that Microsoft has seen the light—they are now much more aggressive than they have been in the past at not only making their software more secure from the start, but also providing updates to fix problems that exist.

Unfortunately, that leaves tens of millions of computers out there that need to be updated in order to be secure. That's your job. Until you update your computer, it will be vulnerable to attacks even if you don't make any "mistakes."

---

[1] And I'm probably going to get endless grief from my friends at Microsoft for saying so. Sigh ...
[2] The good kind of hacker

Updating New Computers

You just brought home that new computer, with the very latest version of Windows and included antivirus protection. You're safe right?

Wrong!

In fact, your computer may be at its most vulnerable, because your confidence that it's safe might make you careless.

You see, when I said that Microsoft is finally taking security seriously, I mean they really are taking it seriously. And they're finding security flaws. Lots of them. Weekly. Go to `http://www.microsoft.com/security` and take a look at the list of security bulletins with updates. For example, I wrote this chapter originally in September 2003, and at that time I saw bulletins for 9/10/2003, 9/3/2003 (five updates), 8/20/2003 (three updates), 8/13/2003 . . . you see what I mean?

The software on your new computer isn't as new as you think. The computer may have been sitting on a shelf for a while. And, when the computer's manufacturer installs the operating system on a computer, they only install the most recent full version of the operating system. They do NOT install all of the updates that are available as of the date of manufacturing.[3] So your computer may have software that is six months or a year old on the day you buy it.

And yes, the antivirus software on that computer may be that old as well—which makes it, as you now know, pretty close to useless.

So, even new machines need to be updated.

Using Windows Update

The good news is that Microsoft makes it remarkably easy to update your system. But before you begin, I must offer a few cautions.

Before You Start

Microsoft allows you to update your computer through the Internet. But think about it:

You're about to connect to the Internet in order to install software updates to close vulnerabilities to attacks from the Internet.

Do you see the problem here? The last thing you want is for your computer to be attacked while you're updating your system!

So, before you connect your computer to the Internet (even if it's a new system), be sure you're using a router with NAT or have first installed a software firewall as described in the last chapter.

Then go directly to Windows Update—do not browse the Web, do not check e-mail, do not pass Go, do not collect $200.

---

[3] For example, I just bought a new IBM ThinkPad laptop with Windows XP Professional—great machine. But I had to spend an evening installing software updates to bring it up to date.

Risks of Updating Your System

I'm about to tell you about a web site that will automatically update your system. It does the best it can to update your system correctly and safely. But it can't know, nor can Microsoft possibly test, every possible combination of software on your system. I mean, by the time you add up the different versions of operating systems, the possible existence of different service packs[4] or updates, the number and variety of other possible applications on your system (in all their possible versions), plus the possible existence of viruses and the many possible configuration settings—well, the truth is that each system is pretty close to unique.

So there is a chance—a small one, but a definite chance—that installing a software update will screw up your system. This can range from minor errors like Internet Explorer failing to work[5] to major errors like the system failing to boot.[6]

So, before updating your system, take a few minutes and prepare. The minimum you should do depends on your operating system.

Regardless of operating system, you should back up any critical data[7] as described in Chapter 8.

Windows 95/98/ME

- Be sure you have a Windows startup disk. Create a startup disk by bringing up the Control Panel, choosing Add/Remove Programs, selecting the Startup Disk tab, and clicking the Create Disk button— then follow the directions.

The startup disk will allow you to at least boot your system to a command prompt if the worst occurs. Once you've created a startup disk, store it somewhere safe. You don't need to create one before each update.

Windows 2000

- Be sure you know where your original Windows 2000 CD is, or, if your system didn't come with one, make sure you're familiar with the system restore procedure for your computer.

---

[4] A **service pack** is a major update that consists of many smaller updates. I'll talk more about them shortly.

[5] As happened to me recently when trying to install an Internet Explorer update on an older system

[6] As happened just last week to a coworker when installing a Windows XP update

[7] Backing up, as you'll read in Chapter 8, is always a good idea. However, it isn't absolutely critical to do so before an update. That's because update failures, if they occur, may cause your system to fail to boot. However, an update failure shouldn't cause you to lose your files.

- Create an emergency rescue disk. Do this by going to the Start menu, choosing Program ➤ Accessories ➤ System Tools ➤ Backup, and then clicking the Emergency Repair Disk button. You'll need two blank floppy disks before starting. If you're on a machine that doesn't have a floppy drive, you should still do this—just be sure you check the box labeled "Also backup registry to the repair directory". The floppy backup will fail, but you'll have a backup of the registry on your hard drive.

You don't need to create an emergency rescue disk before each update. You should create one if you've installed any major applications or changed your hardware since you created your previous rescue disk.[8]

Windows XP

- Be sure to back up any critical data—just in case.

- Be sure you know where your original Windows XP CD is, or, if your system did not come with one, make sure you're familiar with the system restore procedure for your computer.

- Windows XP has a more advanced System Restore capability than previous Microsoft operating systems. Most Windows updates automatically create a system restore point—which you can restore from to go back to the prior state of the system (one that presumably worked) in case of difficulty. You can manually define a system restore point by going to the Start menu, choosing Program ➤ Accessories ➤ System Tools ➤ System Restore and following the directions to create a new system restore point. You might also want to do this before installing other applications just to be safe.

All Operating Systems

Did I mention making a backup of any critical data? You know, of course, the importance of keeping good backups just in case of problems with viruses or updates, not to mention the inevitable disk crashes.[9] I apologize,

---

[8] *That's because application and hardware configuration settings are kept in the registry. If your emergency rescue disk isn't up to date, you may have to reinstall any applications or reconfigure hardware installed after your rescue disk was created.*

[9] *Disk drives should be considered the one truly disposable part of your computer. It's a mechanical device and it will fail sooner or later—usually at the most inconvenient possible time. This I know from harsh personal experience. How long should a good hard drive last? From what I've seen, any drive older than five years is living on borrowed time and could die at any moment. By the way, a disk can actually "crash"—the magnetic head that floats over the magnetic disk can crash into it, gouging deep scars into the coating and scattering metal particles containing what's left of your data throughout the now useless drive. These particles in turn cause the other heads to crash in a chain reaction of high-speed self-destruction.*

but it is important, so I'm afraid you'll have to put up with me repeating it periodically.

When the update is complete, if you have trouble with a particular application that was updated, you can in most cases uninstall that update. This can be done through the Control Panel ➤ Add/Remove Programs command. Of course, uninstalling a security update is something you should avoid if at all possible, as doing so reopens your computer to the kind of attack the update was designed to stop.

If serious problems occur during or after the update process, read Chapter 9, where I discuss ways to try to rescue systems that have been demolished by viruses.[10]

Running Windows Update

Now it's time to do the update. Type **http://windowsupdate.microsoft.com** in the address bar of your browser. You'll be brought to a site that will automatically update your system. You may see one or more ActiveX control dialog boxes such as that shown in Figure 6-1.

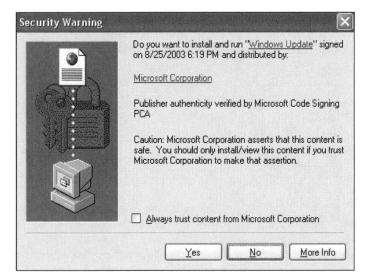

Figure 6-1 Windows Update ActiveX prompt

Click Yes to these prompts.

Shortly thereafter you'll see a welcome page. Click the button labeled Scan for updates. There will be a delay while the control scans your system, and then you'll see a result page similar to that shown in Figure 6-2.

---

[10] *I know it sounds odd, but yes—the errors caused by a failed update can be exactly the same as those caused by a virus.*

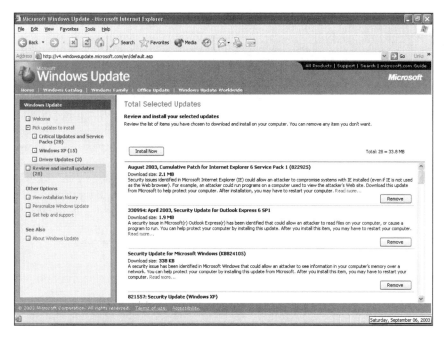

Figure 6-2 Typical Windows Update results

Now you're ready to decide what updates to install.

Choosing Full or Partial Updates

Windows Update divides updates into three different categories. *Critical updates* are updates that Microsoft believes are essential because they contain security fixes. There are two types of critical updates: service packs and smaller updates.

A *service pack* is a major operating system update. It includes not only security updates, but general bug fixes as well. Service packs also tend to be quite large—often tens of megabytes. Also, service packs typically must be installed alone—in other words, Windows Update won't be able to install them along with other updates.

The ideal sequence for updating is as follows:

1. Run Windows Update.

2. Click Install Now. If a service pack is in the list, Windows Update will tell you that your update list includes an update that must be installed by itself, and will allow you to continue with just that update.

3. Complete the service pack installation—your system will typically need to be restarted.

4. Go back to step 1 and run Windows Update again. Repeat this sequence until all critical patches are installed.

Now here's the bad news. Even on a new computer with a DSL connection, you're going to spend a few hours updating your software. If you're on a dial-up modem connection, the amount of time can be impractical.

If you do have a dial-up connection, consider just letting your computer download the updates overnight. Otherwise, just install the security updates—they are a lot smaller and will close off most vulnerabilities even if you don't install the full service pack. I do recommend installing the latest service packs if at all possible though—not only do they fix other bugs on your system, but also they tend to be better tested. You'll find after installing a service pack that there are fewer security updates in the list next time you go to the Windows Update web site. That's because a service pack already includes many security updates.

The update list shows how large each file is, and anything under a few megabytes is reasonable for a modem download. However, don't trust the download sizes of service packs—the size there is that of the service pack installation file, which in turn will try to download the rest of the service pack files.

The Update Process

Once you click the Install button, you'll typically see a license agreement such as the one shown in Figure 6-3.

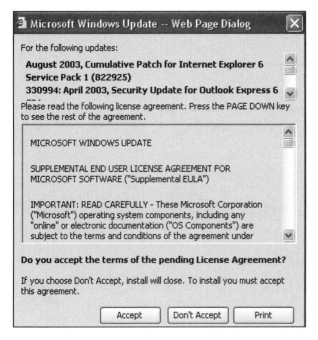

Figure 6-3 Typical Windows Update license agreement

As always, you should read the license agreement. As usual, you probably won't. After all, it isn't much of a choice—either accept the license, or accept the fact that your system will be vulnerable to attack.[11]

Figure 6-4 shows the dialog box displayed during the installation. You'll see each update installed in turn.

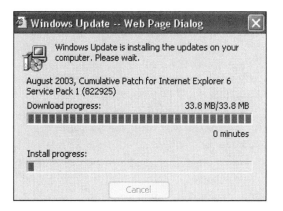

Figure 6-4 Windows Update installing a 33.8-megabyte service pack

Recommended Updates and Driver Updates

The Windows Update site will also offer a set of recommended updates and possibly driver updates. These are updates that typically fix bugs in your system but don't represent security vulnerabilities. It's up to you as to whether or not you want to install these. Certainly, if you're having trouble with a particular application, you should see if updates are available. For example, if a newer game isn't working, an updated video driver may be available that solves the problem.[12] Read the explanation for each update and decide for each one if it relates to anything you do on your computer and if you want to install it.

Office Update

If you use Microsoft Office, you can go to the web site **http://office. microsoft.com/officeupdate**,[13] which performs a similar update process

---

[11] This assumes, of course, that it's even possible to understand the license agreement. Like most such agreements, this one has been crafted by legions of skilled lawyers, resulting in text that is perfectly clear—to other legions of skilled lawyers.

[12] Also check the web site of your computer manufacturer and the video card manufacturer. There may be updates available that are more recent than the one on Microsoft's site. That's because Microsoft will generally only offer the latest driver that is fully certified and tested by Microsoft, whereas the video card manufacturer may offer later drivers that haven't gone through the test process, or even beta drivers that aren't yet even fully tested.

[13] Alternatively, go to http://office.microsoft.com and click the Downloads link.

for Microsoft Office applications. Because Office documents (such as Word, Excel, and PowerPoint files) can contain programs, they can contain viruses. These are caught by most antivirus programs, but the Office applications themselves have security updates available. Just click the Check for Updates button to see if any are available for your system.

Automatic Windows Update

New Windows operating systems include a built-in automatic update feature. You can access it from the Control Panel (choose System) by selecting the Automatic Update tab. Some systems have an automatic update icon in the taskbar as well.

The automatic update software goes to the Microsoft web site and performs the update tasks automatically based on your settings as shown in Figure 6-5.

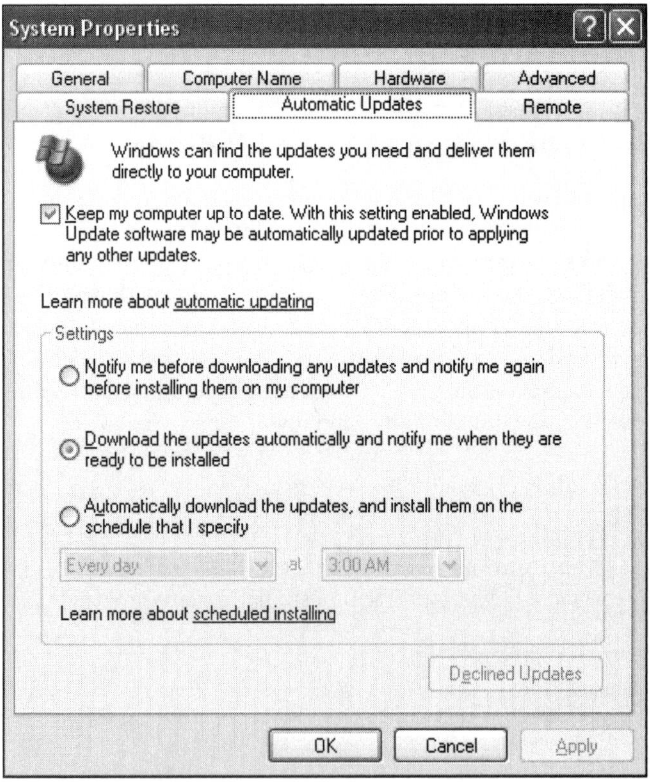

Figure 6-5 Automatic update settings

If you have automatic Windows Update installed, I would recommend the following settings:

If you're on a dial-up connection, either disable the automatic update feature or choose the first option. This will prevent Windows Update from using your limited available bandwidth for updates while you're trying to do other things.[14]

If you have a high-speed connection, the second option is a good one. Windows will download the update in the background, and then notify you before it installs that update—giving you a chance to back up your data before the installation proceeds.

The third option only makes sense for computers that are on all the time—it allows you to schedule a time for downloads. I don't like this option because it also installs the update without prompting you further, and thus doesn't give you a chance to back up your files before it does the update.

Fake Update Notices

If you received an e-mail from SecurityUpdate@microsoft.com that looked like Figure 6-6, what would you do?

I hope your answer is that you would not install it. This e-mail message is a fraud.[15]

RULE OF THUMB Microsoft will NEVER e-mail a software patch to you. In fact, you shouldn't trust anyone who tries to e-mail a software update—reputable companies provide software updates through their web site, not e-mail.

This particular message arrived on my machine carrying the W32/Swen@MM virus. This particular worm doesn't do much harm on its own, but it does turn your machine into a mass mailer to spread the worm. It also turns off most antivirus and firewall software (thus making you vulnerable to other attacks), and blocks other programs (like the registry editor) that could be used to clean the virus.

---

[14] *Bandwidth was discussed in Chapter 2, where you learned how a virus or spyware using the Internet could slow down browsing and file downloads, and cause extreme lag or disconnects with online games. Downloading a software update can do the same.*

[15] *One of my reviewers pointed out a curious fact: Many fake update messages are written by people whose spelling or grammar is questionable (to put it kindly). In this case, "an malicious user" is a tip-off. But don't get into the habit of judging fakes by their writing—it's not a reliable indicator.*

Microsoft

All Products | Support | Search | Microsoft.com Guide

Microsoft Home

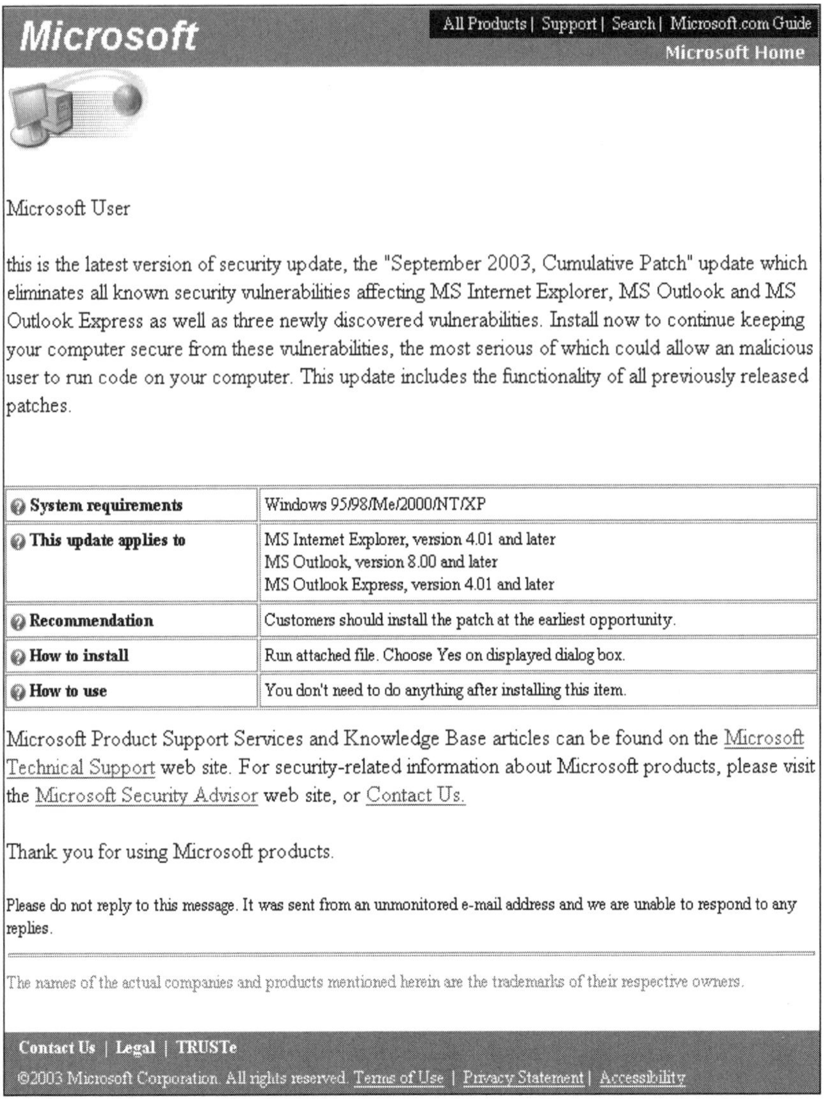

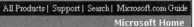

Microsoft User

this is the latest version of security update, the "September 2003, Cumulative Patch" update which eliminates all known security vulnerabilities affecting MS Internet Explorer, MS Outlook and MS Outlook Express as well as three newly discovered vulnerabilities. Install now to continue keeping your computer secure from these vulnerabilities, the most serious of which could allow an malicious user to run code on your computer. This update includes the functionality of all previously released patches.

System requirements	Windows 95/98/Me/2000/NT/XP
This update applies to	MS Internet Explorer, version 4.01 and later MS Outlook, version 8.00 and later MS Outlook Express, version 4.01 and later
Recommendation	Customers should install the patch at the earliest opportunity.
How to install	Run attached file. Choose Yes on displayed dialog box.
How to use	You don't need to do anything after installing this item.

Microsoft Product Support Services and Knowledge Base articles can be found on the Microsoft Technical Support web site. For security-related information about Microsoft products, please visit the Microsoft Security Advisor web site, or Contact Us.

Thank you for using Microsoft products.

Please do not reply to this message. It was sent from an unmonitored e-mail address and we are unable to respond to any replies.

The names of the actual companies and products mentioned herein are the trademarks of their respective owners.

Contact Us | Legal | TRUSTe

©2003 Microsoft Corporation. All rights reserved. Terms of Use | Privacy Statement | Accessibility

Figure 6-6 Fake e-mail example

Into the Home Stretch

Keeping your Windows system up to date is one of the best things you can do to reduce the vulnerability of your system to attacks. In this chapter, you learned how to update your system using Windows Update, and how to minimize the chances of problems on those rare occasions when Windows Update fails.

Once you have a virus scanner and firewall on an updated system, you've closed off most of your computer's vulnerabilities. But there are a few left that need some hands-on attention—that's the subject of the next chapter.

Locking Up, Part 2: System and Application Configuration

Updating your system is a critical part of making it secure. But it turns out that there are also a variety of ways you can change your computer's configuration to make it more secure, and equally important, to help you to avoid making mistakes or fix problems when they occur.

In this chapter, the focus will be purely on security. In Part II of the book I'll revisit application configuration with an eye to protecting your privacy.

E-Mail Settings

If you are using an e-mail client program such as Outlook, Outlook Express, Eudora, Netscape Messenger, etc. (as compared to a web-based e-mail program), you can do a number of things to improve security.

The examples shown here will be for Outlook Express, but most e-mail clients have similar settings.

Turn off Automatic Downloading of Messages

Outlook Express settings can be found by running the program, and then choosing the Tools menu and selecting Options. Choose the Read tab, as shown in Figure 7-1.

You should uncheck the box labeled "Automatically download message when viewing in the preview pane".

Outlook Express shows a list of available messages to view. Many of those will typically be spam. With this option off, clicking a message header will not automatically download the message. Instead, you'll be able to delete the message without downloading it.

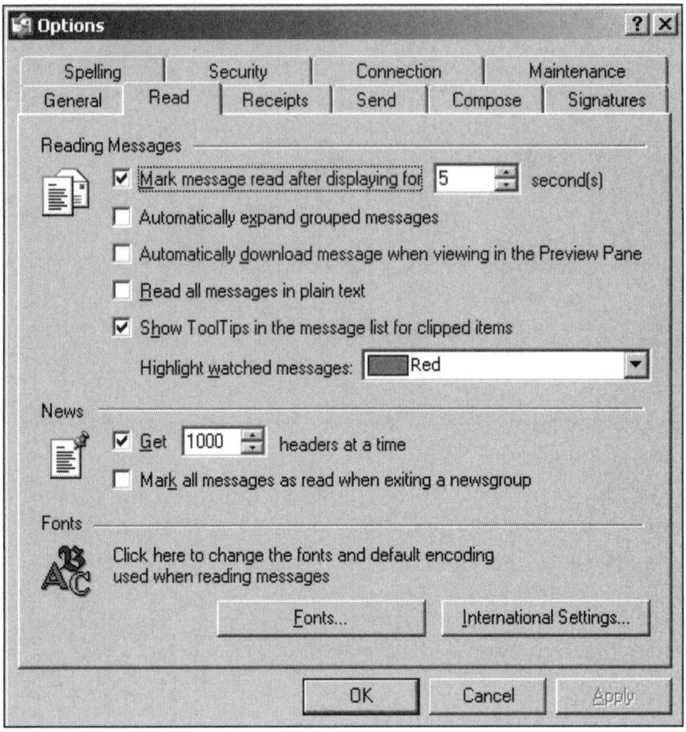

Figure 7-1 Options for Outlook Express

This not only prevents a potential virus from being downloaded to your system, it eliminates the risk of flaws in which just viewing a message can exploit a bug in the e-mail program to infect your system.[1]

You can also check the box labeled "Read all messages in plain text". This provides added security, but you lose the ability to display HTML-based graphics in the message.

Turn off JavaScript and ActiveX Controls

Figure 7-2 shows the Security settings for Outlook Express.

An e-mail message can contain plain text (which is safe) or HTML (which is potentially dangerous). HTML makes an e-mail message work just like a web page, meaning it can normally run JavaScript or load ActiveX controls—just like any other web page. Just viewing such a message can be dangerous—especially if your software is not up to date.

---

[1] A risk that is already reduced because you've updated your system software, right?

To prevent this, be sure your e-mail program is set to use the Restricted Sites Zone. This prevents messages from using ActiveX controls or running JavaScript. On other e-mail clients, be sure you disable JavaScript in your e-mail program.

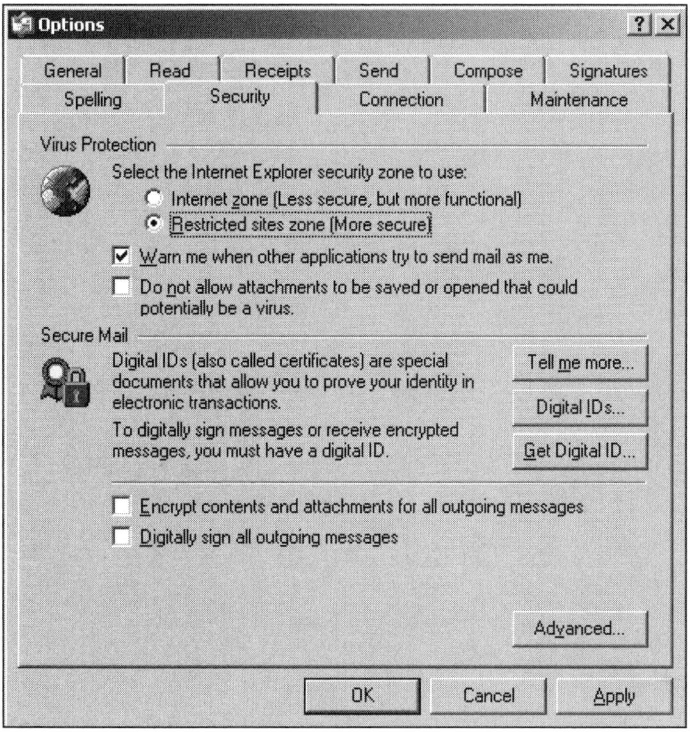

Figure 7-2 The Outlook Express Security tab

The "Warn me when other applications try to send mail as me" check box causes a warning to come up if another program tries to use Outlook Express to mail messages—something viruses often try to do.[2]

The "Do not allow attachments to be saved or opened . . ." check box is a tough choice. If you check it, you won't be able to save or open many types of attachments—some of which you will actually want. If you have a good antivirus program, and are very careful with what you do with attachments, it's safe to leave this option unchecked.

---

[2] *Other viruses include their own e-mail programs, allowing them to send e-mail without using Outlook Express.*

Turn on Display File Extensions

The default settings for the Windows Explorer (that's the program that lets you examine your hard drives and system—not the Internet browser) hide information that can be important to you.

From your Explorer window, choose the Tools menu, and then select Folder Options. Click the View tab and you'll see a dialog box similar to that shown in Figure 7-3.

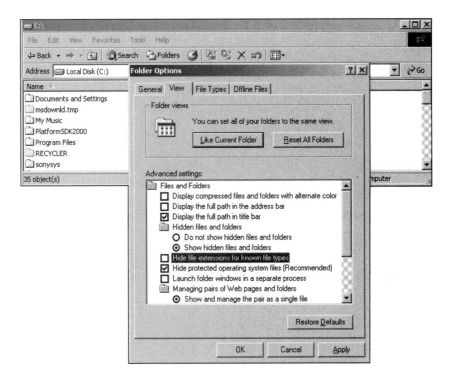

Figure 7-3 Setting folder options

Uncheck the option "Hide file extensions for known file types". In Chapter 3, you learned that the file extension can help you determine if a file is potentially risky. For example, a file with the extension .exe is an executable and carries the highest risk (meaning you should never run it unless you're sure it's safe). But it's hard to know the file type if the file extensions are hidden. (Windows does use different icons for different file types—but who actually remembers what those icons mean?)

When searching for a virus, you might also want to select the "Show hidden files and folders" option for hidden files and folders. This allows you to find worms that are trying to hide themselves.[3]

Sharing Drives

Those of you who have only one computer at home, or those who have more than one but don't connect them together, can skip this section. But if you do have multiple computers at home, there's a good chance they are on a local network. One of the advantages of a local network is you can share certain equipment—for example, instead of having a printer on each computer, you can have all your computers share one printer.

It is also possible on a local network to share drives.

I'm not going to go into specifics of how to share drives here. It varies on each operating system, and there are enough issues that can come up on each operating system to fill a chapter on its own.

From a security perspective, you should do two things with regards to sharing drives:

- If you don't have a local network, never share drives. After all, you don't want to share your drives with strangers on the Internet, right? Don't panic though—your firewall will block the attempts of outsiders to connect to your drives even if they are shared.

- If you do want to share drives, always use a password on the share. For Windows 98/ME, this means assigning a specific password to the drive. For Windows 2000/XP, it means making sure that all accounts on your computer have a password.[4]

I'll talk more about passwords in Part II of this book, where I discuss privacy issues and how passwords make it harder for others to look at the contents of your drive. The important thing to realize here is that some viruses don't just infect the system on which they land—they explore the local network to try to find other systems they can connect to—especially looking for shared drives. If your share is protected by a password, it becomes much more difficult for a virus to connect to your system.

---

[3] *Normally, files are set to "hidden" because they are critical operating system files, or otherwise files that should never be modified by the user.*

[4] *You can actually fine-tune security of shared drives on Windows 2000 and XP to allow access only to specific accounts. Read the built-in help on drive sharing to find out how.*

Turn off Services

You already read about *services*—programs that run in the background listening to the Internet.[5] There are certain services on Windows 2000/XP that you should either turn off or make sure they are turned off. These are services used by business systems that are almost never used on home systems. The concept of services does exist on Windows 95/98/ME, but it works differently, and the services that come by default with those operating systems pose little risk. So if you're using 95/98/ME, you can skip this section.

Bring up your Control Panel and first click Administrative Tools. Then click Services. You'll see a list of running services as shown in Figure 7-4.

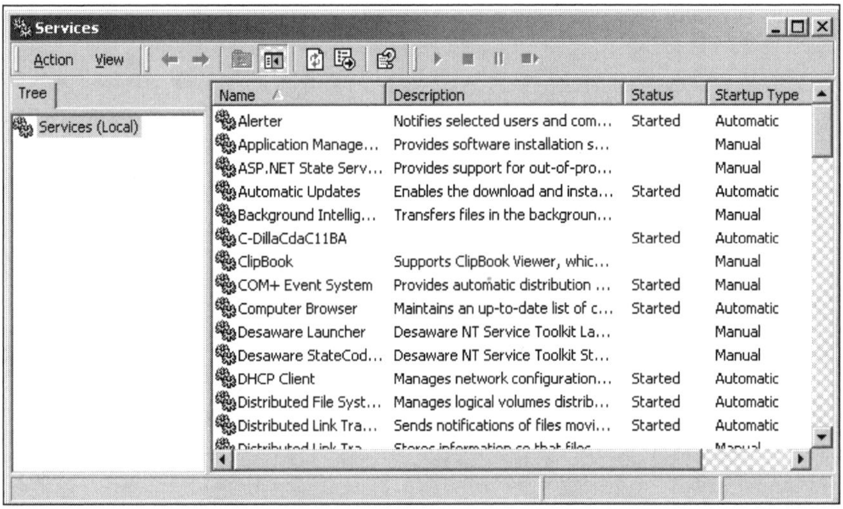

Figure 7-4 The Services window

You can see the name of each service, along with a short description. When you double-click a service, you'll see the Properties dialog box for that service as shown in Figure 7-5.

You can stop a running service by clicking the Stop button. But of more interest is the Startup type combo box, which has three options: Automatic, Manual, and Disabled. In this example, you see the Windows Messenger service, which up until the very latest versions of Windows XP by default had a startup type of Automatic, meaning it is started automatically when Windows starts. This service is used by system administrators on large networks to send instant messages to people on the network. It is more often used by IM spam-

---

[5] This was covered in both Chapter 3, which discussed Internet attacks, and Chapter 5, where you learned how firewalls can block outside access to services running on your computer.

mers to try to send messages (usually obscene) to random machines on the Internet that aren't firewalled (though I believe earlier versions of this service also made a system vulnerable to certain attacks). By setting it to Manual, those messages are blocked—the service is turned off.

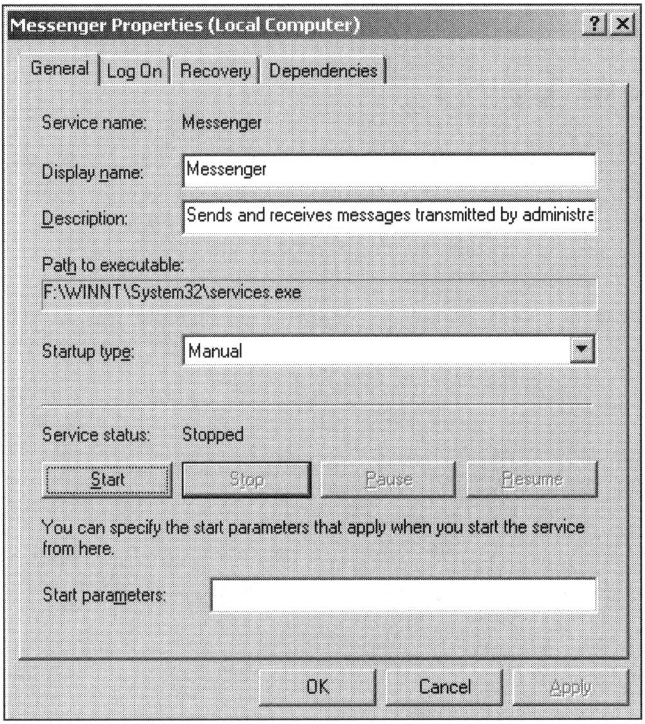

Figure 7-5 Configuring a service

Here is a list of services that you should set to Manual or Disabled unless you are certain you need them.[6]

- *Windows Messenger:* Leaving this on allows incoming spam messages.
- *Telnet:* Leaving this on allows outsiders to log in as a user on your system.
- *World Wide Web Publishing Service:* Leave this on if you are hosting a web site or using your system to develop web sites. Turn it off otherwise.

---

[6] *Not every machine will have all of these services installed.*

- *FTP Publishing Service:* Leave this on only if you are hosting an FTP site.

- *TFTP Service:* Leaving this on allows outsiders to transfer files to and from your system.

Change Your Login

Windows 2000 and XP distinguish between two types of users: administrators and ordinary users. Normally, most people just use the default account they created when setting up the system. This is an administrator account.

One effective way to protect your system is to create additional user accounts.

On Windows 2000, bring up the Control Panel, choose Administrative Tools ➤ Computer Management, and then select the Users entry under Local Users and Groups as shown in Figure 7-6.

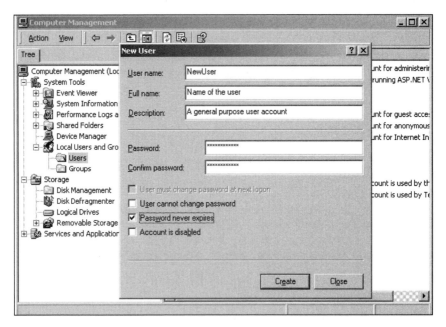

Figure 7-6 Adding a user

You should uncheck the "User must change password at next logon" check box, and check the "Password never expires" check box—these options are designed to allow tighter security for business networks, but provide little benefit on a home system.

The new user you created will have its own application and desktop settings (so you'll want to go back and check the other configuration settings described in this chapter). This user will not be an administrator, so you'll need to log on to the administrator account to do a variety of tasks (including updating your system, installing most antivirus and firewall software, and installing many applications).

On Windows XP, bring up the control panel and choose User Accounts. You'll see a wizard that has a number of self-explanatory options. In terms of account type, XP Home refers to a user account as a Limited account. Just follow the instructions on the wizard. XP Professional can be configured using the wizard, or using the same approach as Windows 2000.

Remember to create a password for all of your accounts to provide the best protection.

The reason to run under a user account, even though it can be inconvenient at times, is that any viruses or worms you accidentally run while under this account will also be running under that account—so they may not have enough permission to do all the things they want to do, and thus will cause less damage than they would under an administrator account.[7]

Are User Accounts Worth the Trouble?

The big dilemma with user accounts is simple: The restrictions they put in place that prevent viruses from doing harm at the same time often prevent you from doing things you want to do. If you choose this approach, you will at times find yourself switching between your user and administrator account as you struggle to get software installed or configured correctly.

So here's the answer:

Yes, you *should* use user accounts, and remain logged in under a user account unless you absolutely have to switch over to an administrator account to perform a certain task.

But . . .

Most of you *won't* use user accounts. I know this because almost everyone I know—including those who know better—use administrator accounts almost exclusively. I personally use administrator accounts almost exclusively.[8]

So, unfortunately, this is a case where what you should do, and what you probably will do, are very different.[9] I've pointed out this option because you should know about it. But if you don't follow this advice, you'll be in good company.

---

[7] One of my reviewers was wondering if using user accounts will slow down your system. No, your software will run just as quickly in a user account as in an administrator account.

[8] One of my reviewers roundly thrashed me for recommending something that I myself don't do. OK, so I'm not perfect. But the fact that I don't follow my own advice doesn't make it bad advice. And if it will make you feel better, there is one place where I DO use user accounts—anytime I have a guest over using one of my machines, I always log them in under a user account.

[9] There are many of these situations in life: eating enough fruits and vegetables, getting enough exercise . . . you know what I mean.

Wireless Networks

I had some friends over a few months back, and one of them brought his laptop. He was sitting in the living room browsing the Internet and at some point he looked up and said "Hey, it's great of you to provide wireless Internet access to visitors, but you really should add some security—anyone driving by can access your network."

At which point I responded "Huh? What are you talking about?—I don't have wireless Internet."

It turns out that he was accessing my next-door neighbor's network.

Wireless Internet is becoming more and more popular—though the routers and network cards are a bit more expensive than the wired kind, the convenience of not having to run wires everywhere is a huge advantage (and potentially a huge cost savings). But wireless networks pose their own security issues that you need to be aware of.

Wireless Risks

The degree and type of risk you face with a wireless network depends on the intent of the person trying to use it. If the person driving by with their laptop just wants to use your network to access the Internet, little harm will occur.[10] You might see a bit of a delay on downloads as they start using your available bandwidth, but chances are you won't even notice it happening.

But here's the key thing to remember about a wireless network: That stranger who uses your wireless network is not just on the Internet—they are on your local network. What does this mean?

- They are inside your firewall—so your router-based firewall provides you no protection.[11]

- If any of your drives or system resources are shared without a password, your uninvited guest will have an easy time accessing them. Once connected to your hard drive, they might cause damage (erasing or modifying files, or planting Trojans) or might simply steal any personal information you may have on your computer.

- Remember the part about configuring routers—how I mentioned that you can look up your router's password in its manual because hardly anyone ever changes their router password? Well, on a wired network this poses little risk, because routers generally don't allow people to log

---

[10] There are people who drive around neighborhoods with a laptop looking for these open networks—a "sport" called **wardriving.**

[11] Any software-based firewall installed on your computer will continue to provide protection from these visitors, as it protects you from other computers on your local network. This was covered in Chapter 5.

in from the Internet—they only accept login attempts from your local network. But on a wireless network, your uninvited guest is on your local network and can thus configure your router as well.

Protecting Your Wireless Network

Some of the techniques you've already learned will help protect your wireless network. I just mentioned securing any shared drives. A software firewall on your system provides good protection (just as it protects your computer from other computers on your local network with wired networks).

But the single most important thing you should do on a wireless network is to secure it. This means you need to do the following:

1. Change your router password.

2. Change your SSID[12]—this is the name of your network.

3. Turn on encryption. I'll tell you more about this in the next section.

You'll need to check the documentation for your router and for your network cards to learn how to do these. Each one is different. However, Windows XP does have a standard way to configure wireless devices that I'll show you now.

Always Use Encryption

Encryption is a way of scrambling information so as to keep it private. I'm not going to spend a lot of time explaining it now—it's another one of those subjects on which entire books are written. What you need to know about encryption right now is simple: The only way to read encrypted text is to have another piece of data called a *key*. A key is typically 40 bits or 128 bits. As long as two computers have the same key, they can both exchange encrypted information, and it is extremely unlikely that anyone else will be able to understand that encrypted data if they were to somehow intercept it.

To turn on encryption on your wireless network, you have to enter the same key into the wireless router and each computer using the network. Before transmitting data, the router and computers encrypt it—so any stranger driving by who intercepts the signal won't be able to figure out what it actually contains—they just see the scrambled data.

You'll read more about encryption in Part II of the book, because it is a great tool for protecting your privacy.

---

[12] *This stands for **Service Set Identifier** in case you're curious, but you don't need to remember it.*

Figure 7-7 shows the dialog box for encryption setting in Windows XP. Your network card may come with its own utility software to set this information as well.

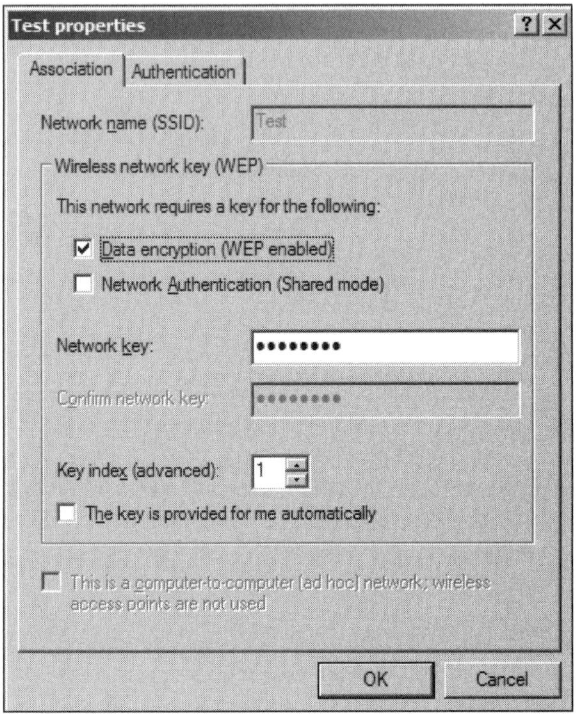

Test properties ? X

Association | Authentication |

Network name (SSID): | Test |

Wireless network key (WEP)

This network requires a key for the following:

☑ Data encryption (WEP enabled)

☐ Network Authentication (Shared mode)

Network key: | •••••••• |

Confirm network key: | •••••••• |

Key index (advanced): | 1 |

☐ The key is provided for me automatically

☐ This is a computer-to-computer (ad hoc) network; wireless access points are not used

OK   Cancel

Figure 7-7 Typical wireless network configuration dialog box

RULE OF THUMB You should always use 128-bit encryption. Modern computers can crack 40-bit encryption fairly easily.[13]

Change Passwords Periodically

It turns out there is a flaw in the current design of wireless networks with regards to the way they encrypt data. This makes it possible for an outsider listening in on your network to determine the key just by listening to the encrypted signals being sent in your network. It does take time though, and depends on how heavily your network is used.

[13] Rumor has it that the supercomputers owned by the National Security Agency (NSA) can read 40-bit encrypted data as easily as unencrypted data.

This problem is a greater risk to businesses than individuals, because it actually requires some time and effort to break into the network—and a lot of network traffic to pull it off. A casual drive-by user looking for an access point is unlikely to take the trouble.

However, it's a good practice to change your wireless network password periodically. And if you have reason to believe that someone actually wants to break into your network, you should change them weekly.

Is Life Possible Without Microsoft?

Some people love Microsoft. Some people hate them. Some people wonder what the fuss is all about.

Regardless of how you feel about Microsoft, there is one clear fact:

Microsoft Windows rules the desktop—meaning that it's on the vast majority of computers run as home and school systems.[14]

That means that anyone who writes a virus, Trojan, spyware, or any other type of malicious program will first target Microsoft software. The result is a race—with hackers (both good and bad) trying to find security flaws in Microsoft software and Microsoft racing to release security updates to block them. Then you racing to update your system and antivirus software before a virus is released that exploits that security flaw.

It's a game—and a rather risky, time-consuming, and unpleasant one.

But it's not the only game in town.

You can quit. Since most viruses target Microsoft software, you can gain quite a measure of safety by not using Microsoft software.

For e-mail, consider using web-based mail or e-mail clients other than Outlook or Outlook Express.

For browsing the web, look at Netscape, Mozilla, or Opera.

You can even avoid Windows entirely and go to Linux. It has the advantage of being free and having huge numbers of free applications available, but the disadvantage of still not being quite as friendly or easy to use as Windows (plus if you're used to Windows, it will be very unfamiliar, so you'll have a lot to learn in order to use it). And many of your favorite applications (especially games) won't run under Linux (though there are Windows emulators that can handle some of them). If you're curious about what Linux looks like, but don't want to go through the hassle of installing it on your system, you can download a bootable CD from `http://www.knoppix.com` that allows you to boot directly from the CD and run Linux from the CD without interfering with your current system.

Of course, if large numbers of people switched to non-Microsoft software, the virus writers would start focusing more on those products as well. But when and if this will occur is a question that only time will answer.

---

[14] *Business workstations as well, but most teens aren't using business workstations. In fact, the typical home system is often more powerful than a mere business workstation.*

Safe at Last! (More or Less)

From antivirus programs, to firewalls, to system updates, to system configuration—you now have all the tools you need to protect your computer from the vast majority of threats. If you follow the recommendations you've read here, chances are good you will never see a virus or suffer an attack.

But there is always that "window of vulnerability"—that slight chance that something will get through. And of course, there is always the chance of other system failures such as hard drive crashes. And for those possibilities, an ounce of preparation can save you hours of hassle and grief—if you have extraordinary discipline and willpower. But that's the subject of the next chapter.

Backups: The Most Important Thing You'll Probably Never Do

Originally this chapter was going to be about what to do when you're hit with a virus (which is now Chapter 9). But as I was writing that chapter, I realized that I had missed one very important issue—even though it's not really one that comes to mind when you think about computer security. Everything you've read up until now really focuses on preventing trouble in the first place—because believe me, preventing an attack is infinitely easier than cleaning up after one occurs. And while having good backups won't protect your system from an attack, it can prevent a disaster from becoming truly devastating.

Why Back Up Your Data?

You already know that some viruses and Trojans like to target data on your hard drive, modifying it or deleting it (depending on the type of virus).

In Chapter 6, I mentioned that disk drives sometimes crash. Well, actually I said that sooner or later almost every disk drive will inevitably crash. This means that at any time, without notice, you might lose everything you have stored on that drive—even if you don't get infected with a virus or Trojan that deletes files. In fact, there are all sorts of things that can cause you to lose data—I've even seen power surges do it.[1]

Most businesses have routine backup systems in place—large companies have people whose sole job is to perform backups and prepare for possible

---

[1] A **power surge** is a sudden increase in voltage that can damage your equipment. These can be caused by lightning, or sudden increases or decreases in demand in your home or neighborhood. One of the best things you can do to protect your drive and system is to connect it to an uninterruptible power supply (UPS)—basically a surge protector connected to a battery that will even keep your computer running for a few minutes during a power outage, enough to shut down your system safely. Surge protectors provide some protection, but a UPS provides really excellent protection. APC makes some pretty good ones—visit http://www.apc.com for details.

disasters. Consider the example of the New York Board of Trade. They have a trading floor for commodities—you may have seen it in the movie *Trading Places*. On September 11, 2001, their trading floor in the World Trade Center was destroyed. They not only had good backups though, they had an entire backup trading floor that could have been up and running that evening (though in fact they waited for the rest of the financial markets to reopen on September 17th).

On the other hand, some businesses that should have great backups don't, as demonstrated in this story sent to me by one of my reviewers.[2]

> Back in March of 2003, everything was going great. Linkin Park was just about to release another album, and my fan site was doing quite alright.[3] Then about one week before the album was released (3/25/03), I noticed my site was no longer loading. After checking that it was not a problem with my computer, I sent an e-mail to the administrator of the hosting service I was using at the time. I didn't get a response for about 24 hours, and I was wondering why this was taking so long. The next day I received an e-mail that said Server #2 (which is the server I was on) had suffered a major hard drive failure; all data had been lost. My first thought was relief—because I had a backup of all the files. But then it hit me that I had never been able to get a backup of the MySQL database with all the user and membership information and forum messages—all that information was lost. Keeping backups is such a simple thing, and in the end will make you the happiest person on the planet.

Most home users and many small businesses do not have backup systems in place. To be honest, most people are terrible when it comes to backups—which is why large corporations create formal procedures and rules to make sure backups happen.

So chances are pretty good your situation is something like this:

- You haven't backed up your system recently, if ever.

- You don't know where many of the original CDs are for the programs you've installed on your system.

- You don't know where the manuals for your computer are, or where the original CDs are that came with your system.

So here it is, the moment you've been waiting for. The obligatory speech:

You should always keep up-to-date backups of anything on your computer that you don't want to lose.

---

[2] *Submitted by D. B.*
[3] *The current URL is* http://www.lp-musix.net.

OK, I realize this probably won't do any good. I'm enough of a realist to know that despite knowledge of the risks and best intentions, most people don't back up their computer. So while I'll tell you about preventive backups here, in the next chapter I'll also talk about how to at least try to back up your data after a disaster has already occurred.

But there is some good news.

Most (but not all) teens don't have too much critical data to lose. Music and video files can be replaced. As for past homework assignments—you may be glad to see them go. You probably don't have things like tax or financial records that would take a huge amount of time to re-create.

But you should at least think about it, because there might be some data that you may really want to keep around, like . . .

- Digital pictures you've taken and downloaded to your computer and already deleted from your camera

- Any videos you've edited

- Any other content you've created—like game mods or other software, or drawings, or other projects

So do yourself a favor and make a backup of anything you don't want to lose. And take a few minutes and make sure you know where your original application and system CDs are stored.

Oh, and here's one more bit of advice.

Talk to your parents about backups. Because they may have some really important data on their disk drives and they're probably not backing up their data either. Do them a favor and show them how its done—they'll be a lot less depressed if disaster strikes.

What About Applications?

Your hard drive basically holds two types of information. There are your applications—this includes the operating system and any applications you have installed. And there is the data—any information that you have created, edited, or collected that you work with.

One of the backup choices you have is whether you want to back up your applications or just your data. Backing up your data can be as easy in many cases as copying the contents of your My Documents folder to a CD-R (remember to back up everyone's My Documents folder if your system has multiple users).

It is also possible to back up an entire hard drive including all of the applications. This, of course, takes a lot more space—in most cases several CDs or a DVD. But it has the advantage that you can restore your system to a previous state without spending hours reinstalling all of your software.

Keep in mind, just copying the folder containing an application is not enough if you need to restore it later. Windows applications often need to be configured properly (including settings in the system registry). If the registry information isn't correct, the application won't run.

If you use backup software to back up your entire system, it should back up the registry as well.

It's up to you which approach you take (or whether you take both). If you don't back up your entire disk, be sure you have your original program CDs (and any installation or activation codes) and know where to find them.

Backup Techniques

Backing up consists of placing your critical data somewhere other than your hard drive. Common choices include

- *CD-R or CD-RW:* A good choice for most. CD-R drives are inexpensive and come on most newer systems. Plus the discs are very inexpensive. It may seem that they are too small (700MB or so) for backing up today's large hard drives, but most people don't have that much irreplaceable data—the big exception being any videos that you've edited.

- *DVD-RW or DVD+RW:* A good choice for those who really do need to back up large amounts of data. The drives and media cost more than CD-Rs but are rapidly coming down in price.

- *Another machine on your network:* If you routinely copy your data to another machine on your local network, you've reduced the risk of loss in case your hard drive crashes.

- *An external hard drive:* These plug into a USB or IEEE 1394 (FireWire) port. Maxtor (`http://www.maxtor.com`) has a series called OneTouch that makes it easy to back up a drive. Just plug in the drive, insert a CD into your CD drive, press a button, and go.

- *An Internet backup service:* Services such as `http://www.backup.com` allow you to store data on a secure server in a remote location. It can be expensive though—especially for larger amounts of data.

Offsite or Onsite

Backing up your software to a CD, DVD, or another system on your network protects you from hard drive crashes and viruses, but it won't protect your information from a major disaster like a fire. Businesses address this problem by keeping a set of backups offsite. They might put a backup CD set or DVDs in a safe deposit box in a bank, or at another business location, or they might use one of the Internet-based backup services.

This is probably overkill for most home users—if that level of misfortune strikes, you'll probably have a lot more on your mind than the contents of your computer drive. But here again, your parents might really need that information—so you should mention it to them if you end up helping them with a backup plan.

Backup Software

There are many backup programs available, so I won't go into them here. If you have a CD or DVD writer, it almost certainly came with some type of backup software. Take a few minutes to learn to use it.

Windows 2000 and XP come with a built-in backup program that is effective, but probably not as easy to use as the one that came with your CD or DVD writer. You can access it from the Start menu by selecting Accessories ➤ System Tools ➤ Backup command.[4]

The way you are supposed to use backup programs is to first do a full backup of your drives, then perform an incremental daily backup. What does this mean? Every file on your system has a bit of information called the *Archive bit*. When you back up a file using a backup program, this bit is cleared. Any time the file is modified, this bit is set. That way a backup program can tell if a file has been changed since the last backup. In an incremental backup, only those files that have changed since the last backup are stored—which can save quite a bit of time on the backup.

In practice, most people aren't going to do this. Ultimately it's your decision how often you want to back up your files and which files. Even if you copy the contents of your My Documents folder to a CD once every week or two, you'll be doing better than the vast majority of computer owners.

A Simple Backup Strategy

So far I've tried to convince you that backing up is important, and I've offered you a number of choices as to how to back up your software. I didn't really go into detail because there are so many different backup choices and software available that it's difficult to describe a solution that will be good for everyone. I encourage you to look at the backup software you have available (that comes with Windows or with your CD burner) and see if it's something you are comfortable with.[5]

---

[4] Windows XP Professional also includes a feature called **Automatic System Recovery**, which combines a backup of your system configuration and an entire partition. Refer to your Windows XP help for more information on this feature.

[5] My own backup strategy, for those who are curious, is this: I keep a second system with a large hard drive on my local network. Once every couple of weeks I copy all of my data files from my main computer to that system. Critical information (such as software I develop) is copied daily to a computer at another location. Other important information is burned onto CDs. I have numerous stories of cases where backups have saved me from major grief or financial loss.

But one of my reviewers pointed out that this isn't good enough; he felt if I left readers to figure it out for themselves, they would end up doing nothing. I'm not sure this is true, or rather I fear most people will do nothing regardless. Nevertheless, for those of you who are looking for a really simple answer to the backup problem that will save most of your important information most of the time, here is one that can help, assuming you have a CD burner:

1. Figure out where you are storing the files you care about. Many will be in your Document and Settings/*yourname*/My Documents folder. Some might be in music or photo folders. Make a list of these folders.

2. Using your CD burning program, burn the contents of those folders onto a CD or CD-RW.

3. Anytime you create something you really care about, copy it to a CD. This might be a web site, or video you've edited,[6] or photos.

4. Back up anything that is new or has changed at least once a month. More often is better, but only you can decide how critical your data is, and how much it would hurt to lose it.

I could write a whole book on backing up (maybe someday I will). I'll add more information to the AlwaysUseProtection.com web site as I have the chance. The truth is, if you continue to use computers (which is inevitable in this day and age), the day will come where you will have a hard drive failure or other computer disaster and need your backups. So take some time and learn to use your backup software. You'll be glad that you did.[7]

I'll talk more about backups in the next chapter, but there the story won't be how to back up your system to prevent disaster, but rather how to try to retrieve your data from a system that is already in deep trouble.

---

[6] If you have a file that doesn't fit on a CD, which is often the case with video, you'll have to use a backup program that can split files across multiple CDs. Or you can buy a DVD burner.

[7] For those looking for extra reliability, it is possible to add a RAID to a computer. RAID means redundant array of independent drives—it's a way of using more than one drive to store your data in a way that if one fails, the information can be recovered from the other (in effect, the data is written to multiple drives at once). Our e-mail server at work recently died a horrible death (the drive started making loud noises and the system crashed). Fortunately, we had a RAID installed. We pulled out the bad drive, and installed a new empty drive. The system started right up with no loss of data, and proceeded to back up data to the new drive.

What to Do When You've Been Hit

Reading about security can be rather depressing. You may feel, based on what you've read in this book so far, that your poor computer is under constant attack by evil forces that are out to get you.

This is probably because your poor computer is under constant attack by evil forces that are out to get you.

But there is some good news.

If you follow all of the precautions, or even most of the precautions, you've read about so far—keeping an up-to-date antivirus program running at all times, using a firewall, and keeping your system up to date—chances are actually good that you'll never be infected by a virus or have your system penetrated by an attack from the Internet. I've been a professional software developer for a long time, and the only virus that (to my knowledge) has ever been on one of my personal systems is one that I captured intentionally for a talk I was doing on security.[1]

I've also been exceptionally lucky and paranoid about what goes on my system. Yet I also know that tomorrow can be the day that I make a mistake, or the day an attack succeeds due to some system vulnerability I have no control over.

Many of you reading this book will make a mistake, or get unlucky. And many of your computers will get infected before you have a chance to put the precautions you've read about into place. Many of your computers are infected right now.

And the best precautions don't do much good when you already have an active infection.

This chapter is all about what to do to clean up your computer as safely as possible.

---

[1] It was the Melissa virus, one of the first really nasty viruses that lived in Microsoft Word documents. I defanged it (removed its ability to spread and replaced the harmful code with messages saying "If I were real I'd be doing something bad to your system"), then used what was left in a presentation illustrating the amount of damage such a virus can actually do.

Introduction to Readers Who Are Starting Here

For those of you who've already read the previous chapters, what you've learned will help you understand the instructions that follow on how to clean your system. So you can skip the next couple of paragraphs.

I'd like to welcome those of you who have flipped directly to this chapter. I know you're out there. Maybe your computer is already infected with a virus and you're desperately looking for an easy solution to your problem. If so, I'll help you as best I can—but you won't necessarily understand everything you find here. I'll try to point out which chapters covered key concepts so you can backtrack if you get confused.

But for those of you who think this is all you need to know—that you don't need to read the first eight chapters, please reconsider. When it comes to dealing with viruses and Internet attacks, prevention is infinitely better than trying to clean up the mess afterwards.

Some Advice Before You Start

Before you begin cleanup, I'd like to offer some observations and suggestions to get you off on the right track.

There Is No Easy Solution

I wish I could offer you a guaranteed way to clean your system—one that will always work and will rescue all your data. But I can't.

> **IMPORTANT WARNING** Anytime you're dealing with viruses or system repairs, you risk loss of data. The information provided here is a set of guidelines that have a good chance of working on most typical home systems. However, because of the huge number of different viruses and possible system configurations, I can't guarantee that the suggestions here will work for your situation. In fact, they may very well make things worse.
>
> So consider yourself warned—whatever happens from here is at your own risk and your own responsibility. If you have information on your system that you can't afford to lose, you should call in expert help from someone who can base their advice and actions on your specific situations.[2]

---

[2] Finding an expert can be a challenge also. A friend of mine recently brought her computer to a major computer chain to have a virus removed. They said it would be back in two days, but it took three weeks, cost her $160, and she ended up losing all the data and programs on her system anyway.

Check for Book Updates

Believe it or not, I rewrote this chapter four times to get to this point, and I'm still not entirely happy with it. What I'd like is to be able to help every reader clean their system—but I know that's impossible, because every system is so different. I can't even include everything I know about cleaning a system, because the result would be a much longer and exceedingly boring book, containing large sections that would only be needed by a few readers. Plus, today's best recommendations may not match tomorrow's.

For that reason, I run the web site AlwaysUseProtection.com, which is dedicated to providing ongoing information and advice. It also includes updates to the book. I encourage you to visit and check for updates to this chapter before you continue.

Take a Deep Breath

I'm going to let you in on a secret. Even the most experienced computer engineer faces an infected system with at least a mild degree of panic. Many times cleanup and system repair is easy and straightforward, but even the experts know that no matter how experienced you are, you may be facing a situation that you just can't fix, and you may be about to lose valuable data beyond any hope of recovery.

So before you start, take a deep breath, and remember these words of advice.

Don't Panic

The Hitchhiker's Guide to the Galaxy[3] was right on this score. If you have a hardware problem like a disk crash, there's not much you'll be able to do about it—other than pay a lot of money to a disk recovery service that might be able to rescue some of your information. Otherwise, you may have a lot of restoration to do, but if you follow the advice here, you should be able to minimize actual loss of data. Just try to stay calm and . . .

Be Patient

Cleaning and restoring a system is a very slow process. Don't rush into things. I know you'll be tempted to just run your virus scanner and delete every infected file—but that can lead to worse problems, so it's best to prepare for them in advance. Read these instructions twice—read the instructions on your antivirus program—and then, when you've thought things through the best you can, don't be afraid to try things.

---

[3] *Great book by Douglas Adams about a galactic encyclopedia that had "Don't panic" stamped on its cover*

Be Persistent

Cleaning and restoring a system can be frustrating. But don't give up. Try not to skip any of the recommendations I offer—they are there to help you and are based on harsh experience.[4] Read them carefully—I've kept them short and every sentence counts. And don't be afraid to ask for help—you can probably find a friend who can answer your questions and get you over the rough spots.

Don't Read This Chapter

Unlike most of the other chapters in this book, this chapter isn't meant to be read from start to finish. It's more like one of those "choose your own adventure" books you may have read as a kid. You'll begin by evaluating the current state of your system, and then read and perform only the tasks that are needed for your situation. If you're lucky, you'll never need to read most of this chapter!

Ready to start? Here we go.

The Three Steps to Cleaning Your System

Regardless of the current state of your system—whether you're doing a routine virus scan or trying to rescue a system that won't even boot—the job divides into three parts:

1. Decide what information on your disk you don't want to lose, and try to rescue it.

2. Prepare for the virus scan, and then do it.

3. Clean up the mess that's left afterwards.

Sounds easy, doesn't it?

If only it were so.

The actual job of cleaning your system may involve a variety of tasks. Later in this chapter, you'll see a section named "The Task List," which goes into detail on how to do the following tasks. (Don't do them now! Think of this as a preview.)

▶ **Prepare for a Scan or Update:** What to do before you scan your system or do a system update.

▶ **Update Your Restore Tools and Information:** Preparing information that can help you rescue your system in case of disaster.

▶ **Disconnect from the Net:** When you need to get off the Net, fast.

---

[4] *My own as well as others*

▶ **Rescue What Data You Can:** This is your last chance to rescue data before you risk losing it all.

▶ **Do a Full Virus Scan:** Here's where you do the scan itself.

▶ **Boot into Safe Mode or the Command Prompt:** A way you may be able to use your system even when Windows won't start.

▶ **Boot from CD:** Another way you may be able to use your system when Windows won't start, and a first step to restoring a system.

▶ **Try to Repair Windows:** Sometimes you can actually repair your operating system.

▶ **Finish Up a Repair or Installation:** Things to do after a system repair or installation.

▶ **Install a Second Operating System:** A technique that can be used on some systems to rescue data.

▶ **Reinstall Your Operating System:** A technique that can sometimes repair an operating system.

▶ **Restore and Start Over:** What you do when all is lost and it's time to start fresh.

Those are the tasks. You'll find that some are quite easy, and some complex. And there are a lot of them, which is why this chapter is long. But don't worry—chances are you'll never have to perform all of these tasks, and you don't need to read about a task until you actually need it.

How Is Your System?

Your first challenge is to figure out which tasks you need to do. What follows is a list of possible problems. Once you've found the one that best describes your situation, follow the instructions and perform the tasks described for that situation.

So to begin, I'd like you to answer the question: How is your system?

🐾 *I'm not seeing any problems (I think…).* It just felt like time to do a routine scan.

🐾 *My antivirus program, while running in the background, just found a virus or Trojan!*

🐾 *My computer has been acting strangely.* This can include anything from slower performance, to applications that no longer run, to sudden system crashes.

🐾 *I've been hacked!* You have evidence that someone is on your system right now!

☠ *Windows is broken!* This can include everything from built-in applications not working to Windows not even starting. This may be the result of a failed system update as well as a virus.

☠ *My antivirus software won't run.* This can include being unable to install or upgrade antivirus software, or being unable to run the antivirus software.

☠ *I turned my computer on, sparks flew out of the power supply, the disk drive is making a loud squealing noise, and I smell smoke.*

Next, we're going to look at each one of these in detail. For each one, you'll get a list of tasks to do.

☠ I'm Not Seeing Any Problems (I Think . . .)

Good for you. The antivirus program that you have running at all times provides good protection, but everyone should do a full virus scan periodically anyway.[5]

The tasks you should perform are as follows (look at the section "The Task List" for detailed instructions for tasks where noted):

- **Prepare for a Scan or Update** (see "The Task List").

- Close all other applications.

- Have your antivirus software scan all of the drives on your system. Have it check all files and within compressed files[6] (this can take a while).

If the full virus scan doesn't detect a virus, you're done. Your system is almost certainly clean.

Otherwise, your antivirus program will display a list of files, and for each one ask you if it should clean the file, delete the file (if it can't be cleaned), or just ignore the file.

What you do here depends on the type of file.

If the antivirus program asks you to delete a system file, you should say NO.

What's going on here?

If you delete system files, your system may stop working. So rather than allow the antivirus program to delete those files, you should close the antivirus program, and perform the instructions in the section called "My Computer Has Been Acting Strangely."

---

[5] How often is up to you. I'd suggest once a week if you want to be extra safe, but at least once a month.

[6] The first time you do a virus scan, after installing antivirus software, you should scan within compressed files. However, you can skip that option on routine scans if you see no other signs of infection.

> **NOTE** A *system file* is a file with the extension .exe, .dll, .ocx, .sys, or .drv that is located in your root directory, or your Windows or WinNT directories (or any of their subdirectories—especially those named System or System32). For example, \windows\system\gdi32.dll would be a system file. It is, however, safe to delete any files with the extension .tmp, or located in a subdirectory containing the word *Temp* or *Temporary*. Any file that can't be deleted when you try to delete it is probably also a system file.

☠ My Antivirus Program, While Running in the Background, Just Found a Virus or Trojan!

First of all, congratulations—because you have an up-to-date antivirus program doing active scanning on your computer, you've probably just saved yourself from a serious infection.

If you're lucky, the warning will appear the very first time the file is being created. In those cases, the antivirus program will almost always be able to clean or delete the file before it's even saved on your system. When this happens, you should check to see if the file is a system file (see the note in the previous section for information on system files).

If it's not a system file, go ahead and clean or delete it as prompted by your antivirus program (it may go ahead and do so automatically).

If you don't see any more virus warnings within the next few minutes, you should be OK. I do recommend you do a routine virus scan as soon as you have time. That's it—you're done.

If you're unlucky, the warning will be your first indication of a major infection. This will happen if your antivirus program has just been updated and suddenly has the information needed to detect a virus already on your system (a virus that was installed during the window of vulnerability described in Chapter 4). You'll know this is the case if the infected file was a system file, or if you suddenly get a series of virus warnings.

If you do have a major infection, your next step is to perform the instructions in the section called "My Computer Has Been Acting Strangely."

☠ My Computer Has Been Acting Strangely

If you've reached this section, either you suspect you may have a virus or your antivirus software has detected a virus (and you've been directed here from one of the other sections of this book).

Your first thought will be to go ahead and just do a full virus scan. But if your system is really infected, the cleanup process could cause problems. Therefore, the tasks you should perform are as follows (look at the section "The Task List" for detailed instructions for tasks where noted):

- **Rescue What Data You Can** (see "The Task List").
- **Prepare for a Scan or Update** (see "The Task List").
- **Do a Full Virus Scan** (see "The Task List").

This time, when you do the full virus scan, allow the scanner to repair or delete system files if it finds they are infected. They do need to be cleaned, and you've already taken steps to prepare to restore your system if necessary.

By the time you're done with this task, your system will either be clean, or you'll be going back to the earlier question, "How is your system?", with your computer in the same or worse condition than it was when you started.[7]

If your system is clean and seems to be operating normally, you should perform this task:

- **Update Your Restore Tools and Information** (see "The Task List").

☠ I've Been Hacked! Someone Is on My System Right Now!

The first sign you may have a Trojan will probably be a warning from your antivirus program. That's because more than viruses and worms, Trojans try to hide their presence. After all, the whole point of a Trojan is for someone to be able to either hijack your computer for their own purposes, or steal your information.

However, Trojans can also be used for threats, extortion, and blackmail, so you can actually find yourself conversing in windows similar to instant message windows with the person who has access to your system.

The tasks you should perform are as follows (look at the section "The Task List" for detailed instructions for tasks where noted):

- **Disconnect from the Net** (see "The Task List").

- **Rescue What Data You Can** (see "The Task List").

- **Prepare for a Scan or Update** (see "The Task List").

- **Do a Full Virus Scan** (see "The Task List").

By the time you're done with this task, your system will either be clean, or you'll be going back to the earlier question, "How is your system?", with your computer in the same or worse condition than it was when you started.

If there are still indications of a Trojan after a full scan has reported a clean system, you might want to try a different antivirus program.

If your system is clean and seems to be operating normally, you should perform this task:

- **Update Your Restore Tools and Information** (see "The Task List").

---

[7] It's the old "we cured the disease but the patient died" story. Those infected files you deleted may have been critical system files your system needs to run.

☠ Windows Is Broken!

If you've reached this section, whether just a few of your applications don't work, or your computer doesn't even start, you're going to have to do some repair work as well.

How you proceed depends on how broken[8] Windows is.

If Your Monitor Is Blank . . .

Make sure your computer and monitor are plugged in and turned on, and all cables are properly connected.[9] If your monitor remains blank, you may have a hardware problem—which is unfortunately beyond the scope of this book. You'll need to contact your computer manufacturer, appropriate repair service, or deal with it in whatever manner you prefer.

Your First Step As Always . . .

If you haven't done so already, do this task:

- **Rescue What Data You Can** (see "The Task List").

If It's Just One or Two Applications That Aren't Part of Windows That Don't Work . . .

Sometimes after a virus scan you'll find that one or more applications are broken. This often happens when one of the files they need was deleted because it was infected.

In many cases, you can repair an application by reinstalling it. Go to the Control Panel, and select Add/Remove Programs. Some programs will have an option to add or remove features and maybe even do an automatic repair. In other cases, you can try uninstalling and then reinstalling the program.

If Windows Is Still Broken . . .

If you did the **Rescue What Data You Can** task, you may have already performed a number of system repair tasks that allowed you to do the backup. But if you're still having trouble—either Windows applications don't run or Windows won't start—try doing these tasks:

- **Try to Repair Windows** (see "The Task List").

If that works, continue to these tasks:

- **Prepare for a Scan or Update** (see "The Task List").
- **Do a Full Virus Scan** (see "The Task List").

---

[8] "Windows is broken" is an attempt to say, in a somewhat lighthearted manner, that something in Windows doesn't work. I'm using the term to refer purely to software failures. If you've dropped your laptop or your monitor has exploded, it's your computer that's broken, not Windows.

[9] As a holder of a degree in electronic engineering, as well as computer science, I can assure you that the most important lesson I learned in college is that 95 percent of all hardware problems consist of systems that are not plugged in, not turned on, or accidentally disconnected from each other.

If You Can't Repair Windows ...

If you've tried everything in the **Try to Repair Windows** task and nothing works, you may have no choice but to just start over with a clean system.

Remember that even at this point, an expert can probably still rescue data from your hard drive. So don't take this step unless you really can afford to lose everything on your hard drive—because if you continue, that definitely will happen. To start over, do this task:

- **Restore and Start Over** (see "The Task List").

☠ My Antivirus Software Won't Run!

As you learned in Chapter 4, some viruses specifically target antivirus programs and try to prevent them from running. Unfortunately, those programs also usually disable other programs you could use to clean your system manually (like the registry editor program).

Here are some things you can try that will hopefully allow you to install, update, and run your antivirus software:

- **Rescue What Data You Can** (see "The Task List"). This is a routine first step to any risky operation on your system.

- **Boot into Safe Mode or the Command Prompt** (see "The Task List"). Boot into Safe mode and try the operation.

- Visit your antivirus software web site. Antivirus software vendors have support FAQ sections on their web sites that might be able to help.

- Try uninstalling and reinstalling your antivirus software. This works best when the problem is a virus that is infecting your antivirus software files. It's less effective on viruses that specifically target antivirus software.

- Remove unfamiliar programs from your Startup program group. These are programs that start every time you start Windows, and some viruses place themselves in this group. To remove them, right-click your Start menu and select Open (the first time), and then Open All Users (the second time). Click Programs and then click Startup. You should recognize every program listed as one you installed. If any are unfamiliar, delete them or drag them into a temporary directory (from which you can restore them later if you want).

- Examine programs in your registry. The registry has an additional place where viruses install themselves to run on startup. This is an advanced technique covered in Appendix B that can allow you to manually prevent some viruses from starting.

- **Install a Second Operating System** (see "The Task List"). This will almost always work, in that the second operating system will be clean and able to detect and delete the infected files on the other operating system's partition.

- **Reinstall Your Operating System** (see "The Task List"). This may disable the virus enough to allow your antivirus program to run.

If none of these work, you may end up with little choice but to start clean with the **Restore and Start Over** task in "The Task List."

☠ I Turned My Computer on, Sparks Flew out of the Power Supply, the Disk Drive Is Making a Loud Squealing Noise, and I Smell Smoke

This is what we in the computer business call "a hardware problem." And while it may sound funny, it can happen.[10] I'm sorry though, if you're the unfortunate victim of this type of problem, this book can't help you.

The Task List

The following tasks are referred to by the scenarios described in the "How Is Your System?" section. **They are NOT intended to be done in the order shown here.** Do them as recommended by the scenarios.

> ⚡ **IMPORTANT WARNING**[11] Any time you're dealing with viruses or system repairs, you risk loss of data. The information provided here is a set of guidelines that have a good chance of working on most typical home systems. However, because of the huge number of different viruses and possible system configurations, I can't guarantee that the suggestions here will work for your situation. In fact, they may very well make things worse.
>
> So consider yourself warned—whatever happens from here is at your own risk and your own responsibility. If you have information on your system that you can't afford to lose, you should call in expert help from someone who can base their advice and actions on your specific situations.

If you have important data on your disk that you can't afford to lose, consider finding an expert to help you recover your data before trying to clean your system.

---

[10] I have experienced each of these symptoms, though I must confess I haven't had them all happen at once.

[11] Yes, this is a repeat of the previous warning. Consider it a friendly reminder.

Prepare for a Scan or Update

Before you start a virus scan or a system update (especially one that involves installing a full service pack), there are a number of things you should do if possible.[12]

- Back up any critical data (see Chapter 8 and the **Rescue What Data You Can** task in "The Task List").

- Be sure your antivirus program is up to date (see Chapter 4).

- Be sure you have a firewall in place and active (see Chapter 5).

- Find your original operating system CD, and installation CDs for your applications (along with installation keys).[13]

Update Your Restore Tools and Information

Each version of Windows allows you to prepare for disaster. The problem is, it's important that these tasks be done when a system is in a clean and known good condition. By the time you're infected, it's too late. For example, if you set a system restore point in XP on an infected system and then clean the system, going back to the restore point can actually make things worse!

- *For Windows 95/98/ME:* Be sure you have a Windows startup disk. Create a startup disk by bringing up the Control Panel, choosing Add/Remove Programs, selecting the Startup Disk tab, and clicking the Create Disk button—then follow the directions.

- *For Windows 2000:* Be sure you have a recent emergency rescue disk. Create a rescue disk by going to the Start menu, choosing Program ➤ Accessories ➤ System Tools ➤ Backup, and then clicking the Emergency Repair Disk button. If you're on a machine that doesn't have a floppy drive, you should still do this, just be sure you check the box labeled "Also back up registry to the repair directory". The floppy backup will fail, but you'll have a backup of the registry on your hard drive.

- *For Windows XP:* Define a system restore point by going to the Start menu, choosing Program ➤ Accessories ➤ System Tools ➤ System Restore, and following the directions to create a new system restore point. Windows XP Professional also includes a feature called

---

[12] Depending on the state of your system, one or more of these may not be possible. Do the best you can.

[13] I realize that this one is hard and may not be possible for everyone. Do your best. The good news is that after you've done it once, you shouldn't have to do it again—just remember where everything is.

Automatic System Recovery, which can restore your system from a set point. Refer to your online documentation for this feature—it won't be covered in this book.

Disconnect from the Net

Viruses and worms connect to the Internet or your local network to spread themselves. Trojans work to let outsiders into your computer. But neither of them can reach the Internet if your computer is physically disconnected from the Internet.

- If you're on a dial-up connection using a modem, unplug the phone line from the modem. If a phone line plugs directly into your computer, the part of your computer it's plugged into is the modem.

- If you're connected to a router, or to a DSL or cable modem, unplug the network cable.

You may need to reconnect in order to download antivirus software or firewall software. If instructed to do so, reconnect to the Net long enough to perform the download, then unplug it again until your system is clean.[14]

Rescue What Data You Can

Chapter 8 discussed backing up data, but its focus was on routine backup—the kind that can save your data if you get into trouble.

If you're reading this task, it's because you're already in trouble and have data on your hard drive that you want to back up if at all possible. The techniques themselves are covered in Chapter 8. This task focuses on the strategy you should take.

If Your System Can Boot to the Windows Desktop . . .

First you need to identify the files that you want to back up. In most cases, your data will be in the My Documents folder, but some applications may store information in different directories. You yourself may have organized your system to store data in other places.

If you don't have too much data, you might be able to copy it to a floppy disk.

---

[14] *If you don't already have a firewall, definitely try to install one before you reconnect to the Internet. However, don't be surprised if it isn't much help. Some Trojans call "out" to the Internet, meaning your router provides no protection once your system is infected. Others can disable software firewalls.*

If your CD burning program works, you should be able to store your data onto a CD.

In either case, mark the floppy or CD to indicate that it may have infected files.

Later, if you do have to restore from the floppy or CD, be sure to copy the files to a temporary directory[15] and perform a virus scan on that directory before you place the files where they belong. Then, if any viruses were found, throw out or erase the floppy or CD.[16]

Network Backup

If your computer is on a local network, and you can share drives so they can be seen by another system, you can copy the files temporarily to that system if it has enough disk space.

This approach means reconnecting your network cable if it has been disconnected, so you should unplug your router from the Internet before proceeding.

First make sure the other system is clean, updated, and has an active antivirus program.[17] Be sure the other system isn't sharing any of its drives, and has passwords assigned to its user accounts (this is to prevent your system from attacking the other system). Share the drive on your system. From the clean system, copy the files across the network from your system to a directory on the other system. You should always share from the infected system and do the copy operation on the clean system because if you do it the other way around, your infected system may proceed to infect the clean system. Be sure to label the directory so you know it may contain infected files—give it a name like "Possibly Infected Files". And don't run any of the programs in that directory!

During the copy process, the clean system may detect and clean viruses on incoming files. But you should do a scan of those files anyway once they are copied.

If Your System Can't Boot to the Windows Desktop ...

Try to boot to Safe mode (see the task **Boot into Safe Mode or the Command Prompt** in "The Task List").

If it succeeds, try to use one of the backup techniques described in the previous section.

If this fails, you can boot to the command prompt (See the task **Boot into Safe Mode or the Command Prompt** in "The Task List") and use the

---

[15] *A temporary directory, or folder, is one you create on your drive for temporary use. It can have any name. Your system may also have a directory somewhere named Temp that the system uses for temporary files, but you shouldn't use that directory for this purpose.*

[16] *You can scan files on the CD for viruses, but it won't do much good because the virus scanning program won't be able to clean the files—they are all read-only.*

[17] *If all the computers on your network are infected, which is possible, you may still want to go ahead and do this backup, just to reduce the chances of the data being lost.*

console commands to copy files to a different partition, second hard drive, floppy disk, and possibly a network share. A small portable USB drive can be a handy backup destination as well.

Consider Calling for Expert Help

There are a number of other things that a Windows expert can do to rescue your data that depends on your particular system. I simply don't have space here to cover them (one could write an entire book on rescuing Windows systems—maybe someday I will).

So if you have valuable data, this would be a good time to call for help if you haven't already.

If All Else Fails . . .

If your system can't boot, or you're unable to make a backup using the techniques described, all isn't lost. You can try both of the following tasks which, if successful, will allow you to back up your existing files in most cases:

- **Try to Repair Windows** (see "The Task List").
- **Install a Second Operating System** (see "The Task List").

Do a Full Virus Scan

Hopefully this is just a routine virus scan, or you're doing a scan to confirm that your system is clean after your virus scanner caught one using active scanning. If not, best of luck—and I hope you've followed the recommendations for backing up your system and preparing for the worst.

Doing a full virus scan involves the following steps:

1. Update your antivirus software. Even automatically updating software provides an option to request an immediate check for updates. If you were instructed earlier to disconnect your computer from the Internet, you may need to temporarily reconnect in order to perform the update. It's worth the risk because scanning with obsolete antivirus software is next to useless.

2. Close all other applications.

3. Have your antivirus software scan all of the drives on your system. Have it check all files and within compressed files (this can take a while). If your antivirus software won't work, go back to the "How Is Your System?" section and follow the instructions listed under "My Antivirus Software Won't Run!"

4. If no viruses were found, you're done. Congratulations, you almost certainly have a clean system! Update your system restore information by going to the **Update Your Restore Tools and Information** task in "The Task List" to prepare you for next time.

5. Follow the recommendation of the antivirus program to clean or delete each infected file that was found. Make a note if any of the infected files were within a compressed file. Make a note if the antivirus program was unable to delete an infected file (write down the name of the file and the virus that was detected).

6. Finish all of the files.

7. If the antivirus program was unable to delete an infected file, reboot your system. Then go back to step 2 and continue from there. The only difference is, if no infected files were found in a compressed file, you can safely skip future scans of compressed files. That will save time (see Chapter 4 for details of types of scans).

8. If your third scan still shows viruses, go to the web site of your antivirus program and see if they have any further information or specialized cleanup tools for the virus that was identified. (You did write down the name of the file and virus earlier, right?)

9. If your fourth scan still shows an infection (which is highly unlikely), you have an extremely active infection that has probably also infected your antivirus program. Try uninstalling and then reinstalling your antivirus program (remember to download any updates if you've reinstalled the antivirus program from a CD). You might also consider trying a different antivirus program at this point—perhaps a free scan or trial period of a different program that might work better against the virus you have.[18]

10. If your fifth scan still shows an infection, try booting your system in Safe mode and scanning in that mode (See the task **Boot into Safe Mode or the Command Prompt** in "The Task List").

11. If you're unable to clean the system after a couple more attempts, call your antivirus program manufacturer for help.[19]

Boot into Safe Mode or the Command Prompt

Each version of Windows has a special startup mode called *Safe mode*. Safe mode is a special mode in which many Windows features and components are

---

[18] *Normally you wouldn't have more than one virus scanner installed on your system at once, but at this point things are getting a bit desperate. Just remember to uninstall the one you won't be using when you're done.*

[19] *This is a last resort, because antivirus support generally involves either costly phone calls or endless waits.*

disabled. This allows your system to boot in cases where one of those features and components are causing you trouble.

When you boot into Safe mode, you'll get a menu of boot options you can try. Don't be afraid to try different options in your effort to get your system to boot—it shouldn't do any harm. Two of the options include regular Safe mode and Safe mode with network access. Only choose network access if you really need to access your network (say, to do a network backup).

The console is a DOS-style command window that lets you enter commands that can help you rescue your system. It's sometimes called the *Recovery Console*.

If you would like to learn more about using the Recovery Console, go to `http://www.microsoft.com` and type **Recovery Console** into the search window. You can also try searching for "Recovery Console" on Google.

Some of the commands you'll learn about are

- *ChkDsk:* Attempts to repair your file system (Windows 2000/XP)

- *Copy:* Copies a file from one location to another

- *Dir:* Lets you view a list of files in a directory

- *FixBoot and FixMBR:* Can fix your boot sector and master boot record

- *ScanDisk:* Attempts to repair your file system (Windows 95/98/ME)

Also check AlwaysUseProtection.com for updates.[20]

Alternate Boot on Windows 95/98/ME

If you get an invalid boot or missing system error when booting, you need to repair your operating system as described in the **Try to Repair Windows** task in "The Task List."

After restarting your system, hold the Ctrl key down. You should see a Safe mode prompt. If not, try pressing the F8 key while Windows 98 or ME is starting. If you press it in time, you'll get the Safe mode menu.

Choose the Safe mode option to boot into Safe mode.

Choose "Command prompt only" to enter the console (DOS window), or if that fails, choose "Safe mode command prompt only".

Alternate Boot on Windows 2000 and Windows XP

There are two ways to boot into Windows 2000 and Windows XP: You can boot from disk or from your operating system CD.

---

[20] *Those of you familiar with DOS or command-line programming will find the Recovery Console familiar and easy to use. The rest of you will have more difficulty. Unfortunately, this is another of those subjects that deserves an entire book to itself, and space doesn't permit me to include more here. I'll be adding further information to the web site as I have the chance.*

Alternate Boot from Disk

If you can't boot from disk, you'll have to boot from CD.

When the Windows 2000 or Windows XP initial startup screen appears, you'll see this line at the bottom of the screen:

```
For Advanced Troubleshooting and Advanced Starutp Options for Windows
Press F8.
```

Press F8 and you'll see a number of options including Safe mode, Safe Mode with Networking, and Safe Mode with Command Prompt. Choose the one you need.

Alternate Boot from CD

Place your operating system disc in the CD drive and boot from CD (see the **Boot from CD** task in "The Task List").

You'll be able to choose between repairing an existing version of the operating system or setting up the operating system. Choose the repairing option to get to the Recovery Console (which provides a command prompt) and other advanced recovery options.

Boot from CD

If you have Windows 95/98/ME, you can boot from a set of startup floppy disks that you create using the techniques described in the **Update Your Restore Tools and Information** task in "The Task List." You'll boot from a Windows 95/98/ME CD to reinstall Windows (see the **Reinstall Your Operating System** task in "The Task List").

If you have a Windows operating system CD, you can boot from the CD on most systems. You may have to configure your BIOS[21] to enable this feature—check your computer configuration documentation for details on how to do this. Only original Microsoft operating system CDs are likely to boot (the CD will be by Microsoft, and have the name of your operating system on it). If you have an MSDN CD (a different way they distribute operating systems) or a system restore CD, you won't be able to boot from CD to enter Safe mode or the command prompt, or to install a second operating system.[22]

Try to Repair Windows

There are two approaches to repairing an operating system: One is to find an expert, the other to do it yourself.

---

[21] When you turn on your system, you'll usually see a brief display along the lines of "Press F1 to enter system setup." System setup is where you configure your BIOS.

[22] Some of these CDs do have a way to create a set of boot floppies, but that is a subject beyond the scope of this book.

If you're trying to restore an operating system in order to back up critical information, you should definitely find an expert. There are things an expert can do to try to repair a system that I can't possibly cover here.[23]

I'll describe here two approaches to repairing a system that will work much of the time, but there are no guarantees.

If Your Computer Boots to the Windows Startup Screen, but Fails to Start Completely ...

When this occurs, it means that your system is booting up, but there is a problem with the Windows installation itself. You may have a configuration error, or a missing or corrupt file. Typical symptoms include the system completely freezing (be sure you wait a long time before you decide the system is frozen), or a blue screen full of cryptic text that looks like it's right out of *The Matrix*. This latter screen is called the *blue screen of death*.[24]

The first thing to try if you're in this situation is to boot into Safe mode. See the **Boot into Safe Mode or the Command Prompt** task in "The Task List."

If you can boot into Safe mode, go ahead and try to back up any files you care about and do a virus scan before you continue with the repair process.

Try an Automatic Restore

If you're using Windows 2000 or XP, it's possible you can restore your system to a previous known good configuration. Choose the Last Known Good Configuration option on the Boot menu. If it boots successfully, shut down and try a normal boot. If it works, you're done—return to the scenario that you were working on.

Try a Chkdsk or ScanDisk

The ScanDisk command (Windows 95/98/ME) or Chkdsk command (Windows 2000/XP) can repair some file system problems that can cause a boot to fail. To run these programs, boot to the command prompt (see the **Boot into Safe Mode or the Command Prompt** task in "The Task List").

Then use the ScanDisk command (for Windows 95/98/ME), or the Chkdsk /F command (Windows 2000/XP).

Try the Recovery Process (Windows 2000/XP)

Even though you can boot to the startup window, Windows 2000 and XP provide additional recovery options when booting from CD.

Try the sequence of operations that appears in the section titled "If Your Computer Fails to Boot Before You See the Startup Screen."

---

[23] *There are probably things an expert can do that I don't know how to do—and I have a lot of experience at this kind of thing.*

[24] *That isn't Microsoft's official name for this phenomenon, but every Windows expert I know of understands the term and uses it.*

Last Resorts

Your next step will probably be to try reinstalling your operating system as described in the **Reinstall Your Operating System** task in "The Task List."

If this fails, you should either call in an expert, or go on to your last resort, the **Restore and Start Over** task in "The Task List."

If Your Computer Fails to Boot Before You See the Startup Screen ...

If you see a message that your disk is unbootable, or an error occurs with NTLDR,[25] you obviously have serious troubles. You may have a corrupt or infected boot sector, a scrambled partition table, or a wiped disk.[26]

The first thing you should do, however, is make sure there are no CDs or floppy disks in your computer. You wouldn't want to start repairing your hard drive because your computer is failing a floppy or CD boot!

Windows 95/98/ME

Hopefully you have a set of startup disks you created earlier (see the **Update Your Restore Tools and Information** task in "The Task List"). Boot from these disks—this will bring you to the command prompt.

Try running the ScanDisk program. This can repair many problems.

> ⚡ **CAUTION** Don't perform the following step if you have more than one operating system on your computer!

If your system still won't boot, try using this command: **Sys C:**.

This will repair the boot record of your hard drive. But if you have both Windows 95/98/ME and Windows 2000/XP on your system, it will make it impossible to boot to Windows 2000/XP.

If neither of these tasks work, your next step will probably be to try reinstalling your operating system as described in the **Reinstall Your Operating System** task in "The Task List."

If that fails, you should either call in an expert, or go on to your last resort: the **Restore and Start Over** task in "The Task List."

Windows 2000/XP

If you have an actual operating system CD, boot from the CD as described in the **Boot into Safe Mode or the Command Prompt** task in "The Task List." If you have multiple operating systems on your computer, use the CD

---

[25] NTLDR is one of the files used for a Windows 2000 or XP startup. A corrupt, missing, or incorrect NTLDR file will cause an error message to display that says that your NTLDR is bad.

[26] You may not know what all of these things mean, but you don't really need to at this point. After all, they all sound suitably intimidating and depressing.

for the version of the operating system you're repairing. However, be aware that a Windows 2000 repair may prevent XP from booting, so you'll have to repair it afterwards as well.

Emergency Repair Process (Windows 2000 Only) When booting, choose the option to repair an existing installation of Windows.

You'll be given two choices: to repair using the Recovery Console, or to repair using the emergency repair process. Choose the emergency repair process.

You can choose automatic or manual repair.

If you have a recent emergency repair floppy disk, the automatic (fast) repair is your best bet. Otherwise, choose manual and don't restore the registry.

If the automated repair process updates your registry from older information (either on disk or from an older emergency repair floppy disk), you could lose recent application settings. In that case, you may need to reinstall those applications.

Emergency Repair Process (Windows XP Only) When booting, choose the option to set up Windows XP.

After agreeing to the license agreement, you'll be shown a list of all existing XP installations and given the option to repair an installation or install a new copy of Windows. Choose to repair the installation.

Recovery Console The Recovery Console is similar to the Command Prompt. It features a number of commands an expert can use to do a variety of repairs. The ones you're most likely to use are the following commands:

- *ChkDsk:* Can repair some file system problems

- *FixBoot:* Reinstalls your main system boot record

- *FixMBR:* Repairs the master boot record for the boot partition

After the Repair
Once you've completed a successful repair, do the **Finish Up a Repair or Installation** task.

Finish Up a Repair or Installation

Part of the repair process may include copying files from your operating system CD to your computer. Unfortunately, these files don't contain the latest bug fixes. Therefore, it's important to do a system update after a repair.

To learn how to update your system, read Chapter 6.

This leads to an interesting question: What if you had to repair your system after a system update? Won't the update cause the problem to occur again? Won't this bring you to a loop—where you install an update, then repair, then install the update, then repair, and so on for all eternity?

Well, hopefully the repair process fixed or removed whatever strange problem caused the first update to fail. But yes, I suppose this kind of loop is possible. If it happens, all I can suggest is backing up your system and doing a complete system installation as described in the **Restore and Start Over** task in "The Task List." Chances are your update failed because of some other application you had on your system, and a completely clean installation will solve that problem. However, I make no promises.

Finally, when your system is fully installed, updated, and repaired, be sure to do the **Update Your Restore Tools and Information** task in "The Task List."

Install a Second Operating System

If you have more than one partition[27] on your system, or a second disk drive, there is another approach you can take to rescue your data—one that will work even if your operating system won't boot.

If your computer is running Windows 2000 or XP,[28] and came with a Windows operating system disk, you can actually install a second operating system on your system on the other partition or drive if it has enough space. This second operating system will be completely independent of the other—it won't share any applications, registry settings, and so on, which means that it will be clean when you install it. And it will remain clean as long as you don't execute any infected files.

Don't worry yet about updating or configuring this second operating system—if things go well, you'll be able to delete it.

To install a second operating system, do the following tasks.[29]

- **Disconnect from the Net** (see "The Task List").

- **Boot from CD** (see "The Task List").

- The installation program will at some point ask you if you want to repair an existing copy of the operating system, or set up your operating system now. You'll choose the setup option.

---

[27] You can divide a disk drive into multiple partitions—each of which has its own drive letter. For example, you can have drive C, D, and E on one physical hard drive. You can use the program PartitionMagic (see http://www.powerquest.com) to divide an existing partition into multiple partitions, but do use caution and make backups before you try to do so.

[28] You can install Windows 2000 or XP as a second operating system even if your first operating system is Windows 95/98 or ME.

[29] Unfortunately, here again is an example of a situation where not only is each version of Windows different, but there are all sorts of potential situations that can come up that I can't cover here. So the instructions here are simple, and will work on many systems, but not all.

- After agreeing to a long license agreement, the installation program will search for existing copies of Windows, and ask you if you wish to upgrade an existing system or install a new copy of the operating system. Choose the new copy and when prompted, choose a partition that doesn't yet have an operating system.[30] **When asked whether to format the partition or leave it as is, you should leave the partition as is**.

From here you should be able to follow the prompts to fully install the new operating system. After installing the new operating system, when you reboot your machine you'll be given a choice as to which operating system to boot. Your latest installed operating system will be the default.[31]

Warning! If you need to install any software from the Internet, or are connected to the Internet, be sure to install a firewall first! Remember—this new operating system isn't updated and will be vulnerable to external attack.

After you install the operating system, you can install antivirus software to scan all of your available drives, or install your CD burning software in order to make backups.

> ⚡ **CAUTION** Don't run any of the programs that were not installed with the new operating system—the last thing you want to do is infect your newly installed system. Remember to use your antivirus software to clean all of your drives before you start using this system.

If you wish to continue to use this second operating system, be sure to update your system as described in Chapter 6.

If you decide to delete this operating system, boot to your main operating system, browse to the partition on which you installed the new operating system, and delete the contents of the following directories: \Windows or \WinNT, Program Files, and Documents and Settings. Then delete the pagefile.sys file on that partition's root directory.

Operating System vs. System Restores

Computer vendors use three approaches to allow you to restore your system in case of this kind of trouble.

---

[30] In most cases, you only have one operating system on the first partition of the first drive. Therefore you can install Windows on any other partition.

[31] You can change the default operating system by going to the Control Panel ➤ System menu, then selecting the Advanced tab and clicking the Startup and Recovery button.

- Some manufacturers provide all of the individual applications and an original Windows operating system CD. This is most common for custom computers from smaller manufacturers. It's also common for people who build their own machines. In this case, you have the actual Windows CD and can install the second operating system from that CD.

- Some manufacturers provide a separate system recovery CD. Unfortunately, the system recovery process they use typically restores the system to exactly the state it was when you bought it, deleting all of your data files in the process. So these CDs are generally not useful for the second operating system approach.

- Some manufacturers place the system recovery data on a hidden partition on your hard drive. While useful for rescuing your system from software problems, this approach is useless for disk crashes— because a disk crash will destroy the hidden partition as well. Restoring from a hidden partition will typically also delete any of your data.

So what do you do if all you have is a vendor's system restore CD set or partition that will destroy your data? Ultimately you have two choices:

- Don't use the second operating system approach.

- Obtain another operating system CD that you can use to install the second operating system.

One important point: If your system has Windows 95/98/ME or Windows 2000, the second operating system you install can be Windows 2000 or Windows XP.

However, if your system currently has Windows XP, you must install Windows XP as your second operating system.[32]

Errors during installation of a second operating system may indicate a hardware problem.

Reinstall Your Operating System

One nice thing about all versions of Windows is that normally if you reinstall your operating system over an existing copy, it will preserve your previous settings (including all personal information, desktop settings, and installed applications) while at the same time fixing many types of problems.

---

[32] Installing Windows 2000 after Windows XP will cause your XP system to fail to boot. In that case, you'll need to repair your XP system in order to use it.

Windows 95/98/ME

Warning—attempting to reinstall Windows 95/98/ME on a system that includes other operating systems will cause those systems to fail to boot. You'll need to repair those systems as well (at least updating the boot using the FixBoot and FixMBR utilities from the Recovery Console).

Boot from CD as described in the **Booting from CD** task (see "The Task List").

Follow the installation instructions to reinstall your Windows operating system.

Windows 2000/XP

If you have an actual operating system CD, boot from the CD as described in the **Boot into Safe Mode or the Command Prompt** task in "The Task List." If you have multiple operating systems on your system, use the CD for the version of the operating system you're installing. However, be aware that a Windows 2000 repair may prevent XP from booting, so you'll have to repair it afterwards as well.

When booting, choose the option to set up Windows.

After agreeing to the license agreement, you'll be shown a list of all existing Windows installations. If given the option to repair an installation or install a new copy of Windows, choose to repair—this will actually reinstall all of the system files.

Remember to do a system update as described in the **Finish Up a Repair or Installation** task after a successful operating system reinstallation.

Restore and Start Over

This will generally be your last resort—when your system is such a mess that you're ready to give up and completely reinstall your operating system.

The good news is that you'll end up with a clean system. The bad news is you'll lose all of the files on your system partition, along with all applications and application settings.

System Restore

Many newer systems don't come with actual Windows operating system disks. Instead they come with system restore CDs or with a hidden partition on the computer's hard drive that contains system restore information.

If this is the case with your system, refer to the documentation that came with your computer to learn how to restore your system to the state it was in when you bought it.

Windows 95/98/ME

Warning—attempting to reinstall Windows 95/98/ME on a system that includes other operating systems will cause those systems to fail to boot. You'll need to repair those systems as well (at least updating the boot using the FixBoot and FixMBR utilities from the Recovery Console).

If you have startup disks, boot to those disks and reformat your C drive using the Format command.

Boot from CD as described in the **Boot from CD** task in "The Task List."

Follow the installation instructions to reinstall your Windows operating system.

Windows 2000/XP

If you have an actual operating system CD, boot from the CD as described in the **Boot from CD** task in "The Task List." If you have multiple operating systems on your system, use the CD for the version of the operating system you're installing. However, be aware that a Windows 2000 repair may prevent XP from booting, so you'll have to repair it afterwards as well.

When booting, choose the option to set up Windows.

After agreeing to the license agreement, you'll be shown a list of all existing Windows installations and partitions.[33] If given the option to repair an installation or install a new copy of Windows, choose to install a new copy.

Remember to do a system update as described in the **Finish Up a Repair or Installation** task after a successful operating system reinstallation.

Are We Safe Yet?

This concludes the first part of the book. Believe it or not, you now know more about protecting a computer than most people—even many who work in the computer industry. You're in a good position to help friends and family protect their machines.

So I'll leave you with one last thought.

The number of computers infected by viruses is huge. The number of computers that lack firewalls and aren't up to date is also huge. And just as software technology continues to advance, the sophistication of viruses and attacks increases constantly.

---

[33] To really clean things up, you can delete and then re-create and reformat the partition on which you're installing Windows. Deleting, creating, and formatting partitions can be done from this screen.

So, think basic economics:

- Few people understand computer security = low supply.

- Many people need improved computer security and help with viruses = high demand.

- Low supply with high demand = high prices and good opportunity!

There are lots of people out there who, rather than reading this book and doing the work themselves, will gladly pay you to do the things you learned how to do in this book. And if a major chain can charge $160 and take three weeks to clean a system while losing all the customer's data, imagine the opportunities available to you. From cleaning systems, to installing firewalls, to performing security audits (making sure the system is set up and configured correctly, and is up to date), you now have knowledge and skills that people will pay for, whether as an employee at a computer store, or running your own small business.[34] And it's a whole lot more fun and profitable than flipping burgers.[35]

Wait, Don't Leave Yet!

Yes, you now know how to protect your computer. In the next part of the book, you'll find out how to help your computer to protect you and your privacy. It may help you keep some of that money you make as a computer security expert (or any other way). It might save you a great deal of embarrassment (should you be part of the 99 percent of the population who has something to be embarrassed about). It might even prevent someone else from taking a walk in your shoes . . .

---

[34] *If you do start your own business, be sure to warn your clients that there are no guarantees— come up with some sort of warning or disclaimer such as the one I used earlier in the chapter.*

[35] *Not that there is anything wrong with flipping burgers. After all, cooking burgers properly also involves killing viruses and worms of a different kind.*

PROTECTING YOUR PRIVACY

Imagine a world where there were no identification cards—where individuals and businesses would simply believe you were who you said you were. Why, you could walk into a bank, claim to be Bill Gates, and walk out with a billion dollars in cash—except in such a world, nobody would dream of doing such a thing.

Imagine a world where everyone could read each others' minds. There would be no secrets—the very idea of embarrassment wouldn't exist.

Would such a world be a utopian dream? Or a nightmare?

I don't know. But I do know that in this world identification cards do exist—and personal information that, if discovered, can be used against you.

In this part of the book, you'll learn to protect your privacy against strangers and businesses ... and also friends and family. Because sometimes there are things you don't want to share with even the best of friends.

When They Think It's You, but It Isn't: Identity Theft

You might be wondering—what does identity theft have to do with you? After all, what can you possible have that would make someone want to steal your identity?[1]

And in a sense, you'd be right. Identity theft is a much greater problem for adults than for teenagers.

However, consider the following discussion:

Your friend: Hey, why did you call me an idiot on IM last night?

You: What? I wasn't online.

Your friend: You were calling me all sorts of stuff.

Your friend: And you were telling OtherFriend99 that she was a big fat stinking slob. She was really pissed.

You: No way! I was grounded from the computer yesterday.

Your friend: Yeah, sure . . . she's gonna believe that.

You may already have guessed what happened here. "You" in this case left an instant messenger program installed on a computer configured in a way that it automatically logged on under "your" account. Perhaps it was at a friend's house or public computer. Anyway, someone came along, found an active instant messenger screen, and started chatting with people on "your" buddy list.

Yes, it might just be a practical joke. But it can also be socially devastating. And things are worse if someone can change your IM or e-mail password and continue to pretend to be you. It can take days or weeks to notice the problem, not to mention clean up the mess.

---

[1] *If you're an adult reading this book, the answer is a lot easier . . . bank accounts and credit cards are obvious, but there are other risks, as you'll soon see.*

So surprise—teens do suffer from identity theft. And it happens all the time. In this chapter and the ones that follow, you're going to learn the basic precautions to prevent this kind of problem.[2]

And guess what? Many teens do have bank accounts, and though they usually aren't quite big enough to justify a determined assault, if you make it easy enough someone might just slip in and clean out what you do have. And someone trying to commit fraud or a crime and frame someone for it may not care if it's an adult or teen identification they steal for that purpose. Oh, and one more thing: The things you learn and habits you form in this chapter will help you for the rest of your life. They'll help you prevent identity theft later, when an attack can cost you thousands of dollars and take years to clean up.

NOTE How big a problem is identity theft?

In a Federal Trade Commission survey dated September 2003,[3] 1.5 percent of respondents experienced a major fraud incident, with an average loss of $10,200 (of which the victim ended up losing an average of $1,200). Another 2.4 percent of respondents experienced some sort of credit card fraud. When asked, an astonishing 12.7 percent of respondents experienced some kind of identity theft in the past five years, and spent an average of $500 and 30 hours cleaning up the mess. Note, however, that in most of these cases the information used for the identity theft was obtained through old-fashioned methods—stolen mail or credit card receipts—and not through the Internet. Visit http://www.ftc.gov for more details.

What Identity Thieves Want

Ultimately, what thieves want is the ability to pretend to be you. They want to be able to buy things on a victim's credit cards, to pull money out of their bank accounts, and even to commit crimes and have the victim take the blame.

One way they can do this is by calling up an institution (bank, credit card company, etc.) and pretend to be you. These companies verify your identity by asking personal questions that supposedly only you would know. If the thief has that information, they can successfully pretend to be you and give instructions to the institution that they will follow, assuming they are talking to the correct person.

It's a bit like the classic case of a student calling the school office while pretending to be a parent, and trying to explain why they aren't in school that day—except it's much more extreme and the stakes are higher.

---

[2] You'll find details on disabling automatic logon for instant messenger programs in Chapter 11.

[3] Prepared by Synovate Research. See http://www.ftc.gov for the complete survey.

Who Are You?

To steal your identity, a thief needs information about you. And some information is more dangerous than others. The following list is roughly in order from least to most dangerous with regards to identity theft.

Name and Address

This information is actually more important to protecting yourself (Part III) than protecting your identity. You should only give this information to a web site when you are asking them to send you something by mail (either information, or when you are buying something). It's generally safe to use your first name on web sites, but you should not give out your last name unless you have good cause. Name and address alone is not generally enough to steal someone's identity,[4] so shopping online and requesting information be mailed to you is reasonably safe.

> ⚡ **CAUTION** While your name and address is not high-risk information in regards to identity theft, it is extremely high-risk information to give out in a public chat room or otherwise post in a public forum. Be sure to read more about this in Chapter 14.

Phone Number

Your phone number is also a relatively low-risk piece of information to give out—as long as your number is unlisted. If it is listed in a phone book with an address, it is possible to use a reverse directory to obtain the address given the phone number. One quick way to find out if this applies to you: Go to Google.com and enter your phone number in the search window. If it pops up with your address, you should use extra caution in posting your phone number.

Credit Card Numbers

While most teens don't have credit cards, they routinely use their parents' cards for online shopping. And in fact, that's pretty much the only time you want to enter your credit card onto a web site—when making a purchase on a secure web site.

Curiously enough, credit cards are the safest way to make purchases online because they have the strongest fraud protection. If you buy something by credit card, and it never arrives, the credit card company will refund your money and charge the seller.[5]

---

[4] *However, many cases of identity theft occur not from the Internet, but from the more primitive approach of mail theft. And if someone knows where you live . . .*

[5] *Protection for debit cards is more limited, as you'll see later in this chapter.*

Driver's License Number

As a form of identification, it's fairly dangerous—the last thing you want is somebody else creating a fake driver's license with their picture, and your personal information.

Never give this information out online.

Birth Date

Your birth date is a key piece of information that can be used to identify you. Never give it out unless you are on a secure connection (which you'll read about shortly), and you absolutely trust the security of the web site.

Some sites will ask for your birth date—they want this information because your age is one of the most useful pieces of marketing information a site can have when trying to sell you things. In cases like this, you should seriously consider not registering with the site at all—any site that requires you to provide personal information should be considered suspect. If you want to register anyway, consider creating a fake birth date for use online.[6] If you want them to know how old you are, keep the year the same, just change the month and day. As long as it doesn't match your birth date on official records, you're reasonably safe.[7]

Social Security Number

This one is worse than the birth date. Never give it out—period. Any site that asks for your Social Security number is almost certainly pulling a scam.[8] Don't use a fake Social Security number either—that's just plain against the law. Plus, you run the risk of choosing a real one, which can cause grief to someone else.

Mother's Maiden Name (or Secret Word)

Historically, most banks and similar institutions would use your mother's maiden name (that's her last name before she got married) to help identify you, under the assumption that it's the kind of information only close family would know.

Nowadays most institutions will accept any password as an alternative.

Treat this information as you would your Social Security number. Never give this information out online.[9]

---

[6] *I'll talk more about lying online in Chapter 11. There are cases where you can get into trouble for lying—if you are attempting fraud or agreeing to a document where you assert that everything you're saying is truthful. But for surveys and routine registration on web sites (where they are just collecting marketing information), it's generally OK.*

[7] *I say reasonably safe, because banks and financial institutions do make mistakes.*

[8] *There are a few exceptions to this—when dealing with some financial institutions and insurance companies with which you already have an account, or when applying for credit. Some colleges use it for identification purposes as well.*

[9] *The same exceptions apply here as with Social Security numbers.*

Online Account ID and Passwords

If you really want to make it truly easy for people to steal from you or impersonate you, the best thing you can do is give out an online ID or passwords. That saves thieves the trouble of trying to obtain the information by pretending to be you and allows them to go directly to the account in question and do whatever they want.

Never give out your password. If you do give it out, or you receive a password reminder or temporary password via e-mail, change it immediately.

Your password is more critical than your online ID (the login or user name you use on various sites). That's because many sites use your e-mail as the user name, and that is generally considered public information anyway.

I'll talk more about passwords in Chapter 11.

Permanent vs. Temporary Information

These warnings may seem extreme—especially given that many of you don't have dealings with financial institutions at all. But it really is important to get into good habits now. That's because some of the information here—like your Social Security number and birth date—are going to be with you for the rest of your life. The last thing you want is an entry like this somewhere on a web site:

Jan Somebody

123 Someplace Lane

SomeCity, California 95151

SSN 123-45-6789

DOB: 1/1/1990

Once archived by search engines, it may be impossible to ever remove this information from the Internet—meaning you will spend the rest of your life potentially at risk of identity theft from anyone who stumbles on this information—or who even does a search based on your name!

How They Get It

There are three main ways that outsiders can get at your personal information using the Internet:

1. They can steal it off your system using Trojans, worms, or viruses, or by physically accessing your computer.[10]

2. They can steal it right off the Internet itself.

3. You can give it to them yourself by being tricked into entering it into a malicious or fake web site.

In Part I of this book you learned how to protect yourself from the first of these attacks, and you'll learn more in the chapters that follow, where I cover privacy on public computers and on a local network.

The second and third of these will be covered in this section.

Packet Sniffers

When you communicate on the Internet, whether it is by browsing the web or sending and receiving e-mails, the data is split up into smaller blocks of data called *packets*. Those packets of data are generally transferred exactly as you see them. Those packets can go through many different computers on the way to their destination.[11] That means it is possible for each one of those computers to examine the data and read whatever information you sent.

A device called a *packet sniffer* is used to read packets of data as they move through the Internet. If someone has managed to attach a packet sniffer to a computer, or chooses to examine packets moving through their machine, they can use software that seeks out certain keywords to try to collect personal information.

The answer to packet sniffers is to use a protocol called *SSL* or *Secure Sockets Layer*. This causes the data being transferred to be encrypted. Nowadays almost everyone uses 128-bit encryption, which is very secure.[12] A web site or web page that uses SSL is called a secure site or page. It uses a protocol called *HTTPS*, so you'll often see the web URL in the form https://www . . . instead of http://www . . .

You should always make sure you are connected to a secure web page when transferring any personal information. You can tell a page is secure because you will see an indication in the browser window. In Internet Explorer it is a small lock at the bottom right part of the page as shown in Figure 10-1.

---

[10] Breaking into your house and logging in, examining leftover information on a system you've sold or given away, or seeing what you've left behind on a public computer

[11] If you'd like to see how many, bring up a command window and type in the command **tracert url**, where url is the address of a web site—for example, tracert www.AlwaysUseProtection.com. Each line in the results shows you a computer that handled the data as it traveled between your computer, and the web site.

[12] 40-bit encryption, which was common a few years back, is virtually useless against any but the most casual attack.

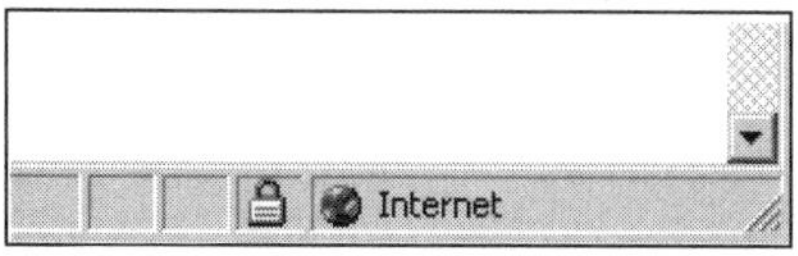

Figure 10-1 The lock indicates a page is secure.

It is also possible to secure both instant messenger communication and e-mail messages. However, these are still fairly uncommon even in the business world, and I have yet to meet any home user who does either.

You should therefore assume that anything you send or receive via e-mail or instant messenger is insecure. That includes information sent when using an IM direct connection between computers.

Does this mean you should never send any personal information by e-mail or IM?

Well, it all comes down to the amount of risk you are willing to take. Personally, I will use e-mail or IM to send friends my phone number, or directions to my home. The risk of these being intercepted is fairly low, and even if they are—this information isn't exactly top secret.

Never ever send your Social Security number, mother's maiden name, driver's license, or account ID and password through e-mail or instant messenger.

Server Vulnerabilities

In Part I of this book you read about many different ways that a computer can be attacked. You also learned about the reasons for those attacks, and that one of those reasons is so people can steal information from your computer.

You may have just written off that particular reason as unimportant. Your biggest concern might be the proper operation of your system, or preventing loss of data. You may be concerned about your computer being used to attack others, or to host illegal web sites. You may even be most concerned about attacks that might reduce your available bandwidth for online gaming.

But I'd like to turn this around for a moment and ask you to look at the problem of computer attacks not in terms of how it affects your system, but how it affects the web sites you visit.

After all, you now know that a web site is nothing more than a computer somewhere on the Internet that is running a program called a web server. And that computer is also subject to being attacked.

Now, many of the people who run major commercial web sites put a lot of money into securing their sites. They not only use antivirus software and perform system updates, they also use very expensive security hardware (think of them as firewalls on steroids), and constantly monitor their systems.

Nevertheless, if there's one thing you've learned, it's that no security is perfect. Not only is there always a window of vulnerability to new attacks, there's always the chance of human error.

So what happens when a web server gets attacked?[13] What if it's a web server that contains some of your personal information?

Well, the thieves can end up stealing that information—along with the personal information of a few hundred thousand of your closest friends.

So, it's not enough for you to see the lock that indicates that a web site is secure. All that tells you is that your communication with that web site is secure. It tells you nothing about how well the computer that hosts the web site protects any information it collects.

And there's no real way for you to know. It's not uncommon to hear news stories about institutions such as banks or major online stores who report the theft of information from their servers.[14]

There are ways you can limit your risk.

- The larger sites are more likely to invest heavily in security, so be more cautious with the information you give to smaller sites or companies.

- Use multiple passwords. That way if a password is stolen from one site, it won't compromise your security on others.

- Always buy online using a credit card. If the number is stolen and fraud occurs, the loss should almost always be covered by the credit card company and not by you.[15]

Speaking of Credit Cards

It may seem odd to talk about credit cards in a book intended for teens—since relatively few teens have their own credit cards. But the fact is that online shopping really does require credit cards, especially if you want to protect yourself from fraud. So here is some basic information about credit cards that you should know, which might actually help you when it comes to getting your parents to let you use a credit card or (if older) to obtain one yourself.

Credit Cards vs. Debit Cards

When you charge something to a credit card, you are borrowing money. Once a month a credit card bill arrives in which you either pay back the loan or part of it along with interest. A debit card looks like a credit card, but is not. When you charge something to a debit card, the money is immediately withdrawn from the checking account linked to the card.

---

[13] *These kind of sites aren't just subject to Internet attacks. What happens when a disgruntled employee decides to burn a CD with a few thousand credit card numbers before they resign? They need good internal security as well.*

[14] *Or from other sources. In November 2003, a laptop was stolen from the offices of a contractor working for Wells Fargo. It contained the personal information of thousands of customers. It was recovered successfully and, by all accounts, Wells Fargo did an excellent job of notifying customers and handling the situation in a responsible manner.*

[15] *Read the card agreement and follow their instructions. Be sure to report any suspicious charges as soon as you know about them.*

Now, here's the most important thing to know about these cards:

For various legal reasons that don't necessarily make any sense, credit cards provide you a great deal of protection if anything goes wrong with a purchase, but debit cards do not.[16]

With a credit card, if a product never arrives, you probably won't have to pay for it. If the card is stolen, your maximum loss is usually limited to about $50. If you have a problem with the company that sold you the product, the credit card company will often refund you the money and then go back and get it from the company.

With debit cards, if you're a victim of fraud or have problems with a purchase, you're usually out of luck. By the way, **ATM cards are debit cards.**

So, when you are making purchases online (whether with your card or your parents'), be sure you're using a credit card and not a debit card.

Getting Your Own Card

Once you turn 18, if you're holding a job, it's not terribly hard to get a credit card. If your parents are willing to cosign,[17] it will be easy. Financial institutions love to get people hooked on credit and into debt as young as possible.

It is possible to get a credit card when you're under 18 if your parents cosign it, or give you one on their account.

Single-Use Card Numbers

The best deal around for both preventing fraud and for convincing parents to let you use their card is a feature offered by some credit card companies in which they give you a new card number that is attached to your credit card, but can only be used once, or for a limited time. In other words, let's say you have a card with the number 1234-5678-9012. Rather than entering this into an online store, you ask the card company for a temporary card number—they don't actually give you a physical card, just a number. Let's say they give you 1111-2222-3333, which you use to make the purchase. The charge shows up under your main account, but this temporary card number soon expires. This approach serves two purposes:

1. You don't have to worry about the merchant storing the credit card number. If the web site is attacked and the number stolen, it won't matter as it will probably have long since expired.

---

[16] *To be specific: Credit cards are covered by Federal law under the Fair Billing Credit Act, which provides significant protection against fraud. Debit cards only offer the protection that the company that issued the card is willing to give you, which is rarely as good.*

[17] *Guarantee repayment if you don't*

2. Your parents don't have to worry about you somehow reusing the number without their knowledge. They can give you a new number for each purchase.

Contact the credit card company to see if your card supports this feature. Some cards that include this feature are

- *American Express:* Look for "private payments" on their web site or see `http://www.americanexpress.com/privatepayments`.[18]

- *Discover card:* Look for a feature called "DeskShop" on their web site, `http://www.discovercard.com`.

Microsoft Passport

If you have a Hotmail account, or use Windows Messenger, or have Windows XP and followed their instructions that literally beg you to create a Passport account, you have an account on Microsoft Passport.

The idea of Passport is that you can have one account name and password that can be used on many different sites. When you log in to a site, rather than it keeping track of your user name and password, it redirects you to the Passport login site. You then log in to Passport, and the Passport site tells the other site you came from that you are logged in, and gives it some information so it knows who you are.

This presents two huge advantages to you. First, it allows you to limit the number of account names and passwords you have—using the same one on multiple sites. Second, it reduces the risk of attacks on other sites compromising your security—because they don't store your user name and password. It's all kept on the Passport site.

However, this also presents two huge disadvantages to you. First, if your Passport account and password is compromised, people will suddenly have access to your account on every system that uses Passport. This includes the ability to hijack them all at once by changing your passport address (so they can impersonate you on Hotmail, Windows Messenger, etc.).

Second, you run into the same kind of effect as you have with viruses—people write viruses primarily for Windows because everyone uses Windows—it's a big target. As Passport acquires more and more accounts, it becomes a bigger target, and more and more attackers try to find vulnerabilities either in the way it works or on the Passport computers themselves.

---

[18] *One nice thing about American Express private payments is it runs entirely off the web—you don't need any desktop software.*

And there have been some cases where those vulnerabilities have been exploited,[19] including one where just opening a message in Hotmail could give a person access to someone else's personal information on Passport.[20] That vulnerability has long since been closed, and Microsoft has invested a great deal of effort on securing Passport, but reports of new vulnerabilities do appear periodically

If you have a Passport account, you should sign on to the account directly at http://www.passport.com, log in, and review and edit your profile. Try your Hotmail or MSN Messenger account ID and password to log in.

At the bottom of the profile page appears a list of options on which types of data Passport can share with other sites. The most sensitive piece of information Passport keeps at this time is your birth date. I prefer to leave them all unchecked (instructing Passport to keep my information confidential). You may also wish to delete or edit your birth date, since that is the most critical piece of information that could be lost if Passport itself is compromised.

Fake Web Sites

Packet sniffers and server attacks are both technological means of getting your private information. But why go to all that work if they can just con you into giving it to them directly?

Figure 10-2 shows an example of a typical spam e-mail message that looks very official. In this case, it comes from someone who claims to be from eBay.

```
▽   Subject: Official Notice for all E-Bay users
       From:  ebay <user-support8@ebay.com>
   Reply-To:  ebay <user-support1@ebay.com>
       Date:  12:28 AM
         To:  Dan

Dear eBay User,

During our regular update and verification of the accounts, we
couldn't verify your current information. Either your information
has changed or it is incomplete.

As a result, your access to bid or buy on eBay has been
restricted. To start using your eBay account fully, please update
and verify your information by clicking below :

https://scgi.ebay.com/saw-cgi/eBayISAPI.dll?VerifyInformation

Regards,
eBay


**Please Do Not Reply To This E-Mail As You Will Not Receive A Response**
```

Figure 10-2 E-mail claiming to be from eBay

Now everything about this e-mail looks legitimate, even the link, which appears to be a secure URL on eBay's web site.

---

[19] *Do a Google search on "Passport vulnerabilities" or "Microsoft Passport" and "security" for a variety of articles and news reports on Passport.*

[20] *At the time, Passport included an "express purchase service" also known as Passport Wallet in which Passport stored credit card numbers so you wouldn't have to reenter them when purchasing at different sites. This particular security vulnerability allowed people to steal those credit card numbers. The Passport Wallet had been discontinued as of the time this book was printed.*

However, in HTML it is easy for a page to lie about where a link will actually take you. If you actually were to click this link, you would get to the page in Figure 10-3.

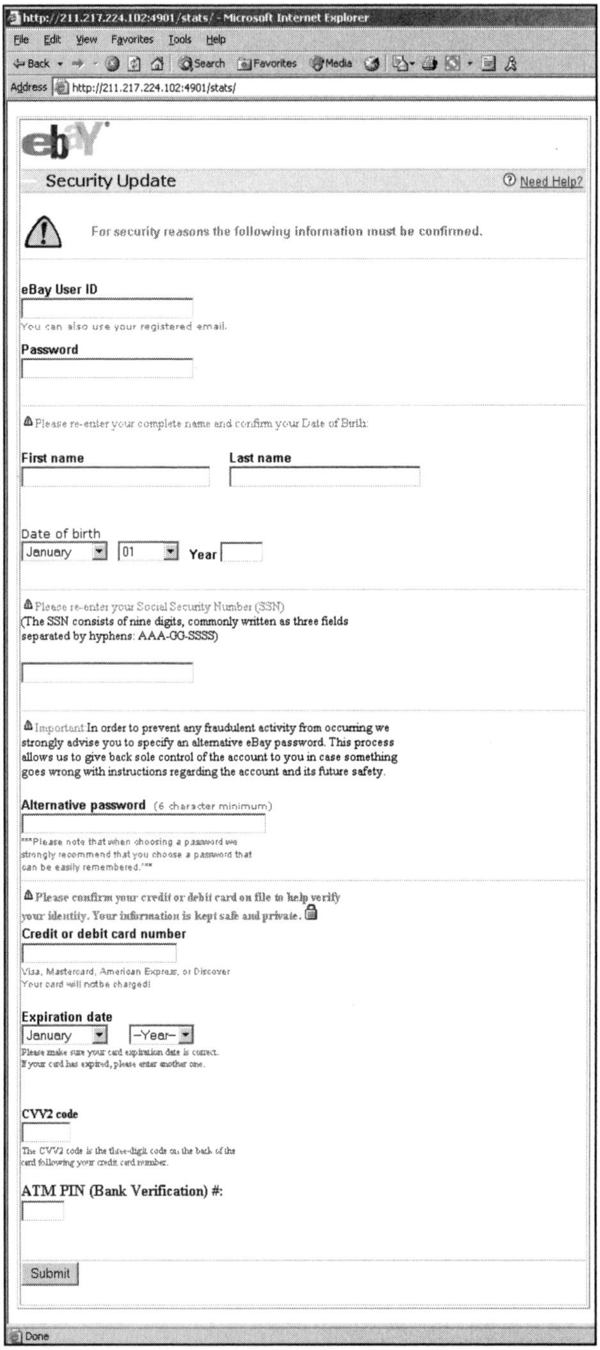

Figure 10-3 Is it eBay, or not?

You have to give them credit for nerve—they not only want your credit card information and Social Security number, they even want your ATM code!

So here's the deal:

Both e-mail and web sites can lie. It's remarkably easy for one web site to look just like another. Fortunately, it's not hard to protect yourself. Here are a few simple rules:

- Always double-check the URL that appears in the address window of your browser. If it doesn't match that for the site where you think you are, you may be on a fraudulent site.

- It is always safest to get to a site by typing in the URL rather than clicking a link. For example, to be sure you really are on eBay, just type in **http://www.ebay.com**.[21]

- Never trust e-mail or click a link in an e-mail message unless you are absolutely certain it is safe. One common exception is verification links that some sites use to make sure your e-mail address is valid. For example, if you sign up for an e-mail list, a web site will usually send you an initial e-mail with a link in it that you must click to confirm that you want to join the list. But only click the link if you have requested to join the list, and you recognize the sender.

- Legitimate companies should never send you an e-mail requesting you to provide this kind of information—they got what they needed when you registered the first time.

How Honest Is Spam?

You know that spam e-mail messages lie, but here are some numbers from an April 2003 FTC report.[22]

33 percent of all e-mail lies about who it's from: half of those claim to be from someone you know.

22 percent contain subject lines that have nothing to do with the contents of the message.

40 percent of the messages contain content that is typical of known cons, scams, or fraud.

Overall, 66 percent of spam lies to you in some way.

And here's another fun one: 63 percent of requests to remove your e-mail from a list are simply ignored.

---

[21] *You should still double-check the URL after you've reached the page. Some viruses and worms are designed to redirect your browser to fake sites, so an infected system can be the first step towards identity theft.*

[22] *The report is titled "False Claims in Spam: A Report by the FTC's Division of Marketing Practices,"* dated April 30, 2003. Visit http://www.ftc.gov *for the full text.*

Public Records

In Orwell's book *1984*, the government is able to watch everything you do. Back in 1984, the thought remained scary, but it still seemed a bit hypothetical—the cost to build that kind of database and monitor people to the extent described in Orwell's book was so high that it wasn't something most people were concerned about. In 2003, you can spend under $200 for a hard drive big enough to store all of the personal information (name, address, Social Security number, etc.) of every resident of the United States. For under $1,000, you could store that information for everyone in the world.

So it's not surprising that a great deal of personal information can appear on the Internet in ways you never expected.

Telephone directories, real estate transactions, and corporate records are among the public records where individuals can be listed, some of which are easily browsable through the Internet. Many sports events, including high school sports results, end up on the Internet—and that's one of the most common pieces of information that comes up for teenagers when you do a search on their names.[23]

For those of you who run your own web sites, if you obtain your own domain name, the information you provide also goes into the public record. Some registrars will register a domain under their name to help protect your privacy. Check with the registrar to see if that is possible.

The Things You Post

Every time you post to a discussion forum, or add content to a web site (whether a school site, a club site, or one you are writing yourself), that information is likely to be stored somewhere on one of the major search engines.

Try it for yourself. Do a search on your full name using Google or another search engine. You may be astonished with what comes up. Next try your parents—that might be even more interesting.

Once on the Internet, it's almost impossible to get rid of it. So you need to be very careful what you post.

- Never post your name and address and phone number on a discussion forum or include it on a web site, unless you don't mind it becoming public information. Don't allow your school or club to include a roster on their web site that contains that information.[24]

---

[23] Yes, if you participate in high school sports, there's a good chance that just by typing in your full name on Google, someone can find out what city you live in, what school you go to, and what grade you are in. See why even giving out your full name can be risky?

[24] Most school administrators are well aware of privacy issues and will be glad if you point out problems of this kind.

- Never post other personally identifiable information on a discussion forum or web site—especially critical information such as birth date (or a list of birthdays), Social Security numbers, and so on.

- Never post your real e-mail address on a discussion forum or web site unless you really want to receive tons of spam.[25]

I Browse, Therefore I Exist

Identity theft may not be as serious a problem for teens as adults by some measures, but it does occur and can be just as painful to the victim. In this chapter, you learned the kinds of information that you should keep private, and some of the ways that people can obtain that information—both technological and through fraud and trickery.[26]

We've just begun our exploration of privacy issues. For example, I really haven't discussed how to prevent someone from taking over your IM account (which is how this chapter started). But fear not, the answers to those problems come next.

---

[25] There are tricks you can use to post an e-mail address so that spammers can't easily pick them up with automatic tools. If your e-mail is myname@someplace.com, you could enter "myname at someplace dotcom" or use mynameNoSpam@someplace.com and instruct people to just remove the NoSpam.

[26] One of my reviewers commented that he found this chapter very scary. Frankly, I was at a loss to reassure him. Identity theft is a big problem, and it's probably going to get worse before it gets better. The best I can say is that if you get in the habit of taking precautions now, you will dramatically reduce the chance of suffering identity theft in the long run.

CHAPTER

11

Passwords: Your Key to the Internet

In Chapter 10, you learned about identity theft and the various pieces of information that can be used to identify you. Of all the information mentioned, the one used most often to identify you on the Internet is your user name and password.

Your user name can vary depending on the type of site. Some web sites use e-mail addresses. Some, like instant messenger services, ask you to create your own user name. Some financial institutions use account numbers. Few use your real name.

In almost every case, the user name is considered the "public" information—it's the way they address you, and it may appear on the web page, or on a discussion forum, or as your name in a chat room. In order to verify that you actually are who you say you are,[1] these sites and services use a secret password.

Which brings us to the most important thing to remember about passwords:

> **Since computers confirm who you are by using a password, if someone else has your password, they can pretend to be you.**

So good password management is a key part of preventing identity theft.

Password Strategies

Most people do a terrible job managing their passwords.
Here are a couple of common approaches.

---

[1] *The technical term for verifying that you are who you say you are is **authentication**.*

159

Scenario 1

You create a password that is easy to remember. Maybe it's the name of your pet, a random word, your birthday, or your name.

You then use that password on every web site, for e-mail, for your instant messenger program, and as your computer password.

One day someone figures out your password (maybe by guessing, or by looking over your shoulder as you typed it in, or because you were sharing files on a network and they needed it to access your hard drive).

That person logs on to your e-mail account, and sends your teacher an incredibly nasty message. They also use your IM account to send crazy-sounding messages to your friends, and post messages from you on your favorite discussion forums in which you advocate making drinking of Coca Cola a felony.

Your teacher, concerned, refers you to an endless series of counselors and psychologists who refuse to believe that you had nothing to do with the messages (since they clearly came from your accounts). You flunk out of school and find yourself living the rest of your life in a van down by the river.

Scenario 2

You carefully follow the recommendations of security experts, creating very secure passwords that mix case and contain punctuation and numbers. Passwords like Yk3&z89W(&q.

You make sure to use a different password and user ID for each web site you register with, each e-mail account, your instant messenger accounts, and your computer. That way, even if someone was able to figure out one password, they would only gain access to one account, minimizing the possible damage.

The good news is nobody can guess your passwords, and your accounts are secure.

The bad news is you can't remember your passwords, so your accounts are inaccessible.

You therefore can't check your e-mail, and you miss the message from your teacher about that four-year scholarship with a $100,000 signing bonus. In despair, having missed that opportunity, you see an endless series of counselors and psychologists, but they help little. You flunk out of school and find yourself living the rest of your life in a van down by the river.

OK, you're right. Most people don't follow the advice of security experts with regards to creating strong passwords and using different passwords (and changing them frequently). That's because normal human beings can't remember strong passwords.

The problem is, most people really do follow scenario #1—they use a single password that is easy to remember (and therefore easy to crack).

So I'm not going to tell you how to use passwords properly. I'm not going to repeat to you the best recommendations of security experts. I realize that this will cause many security experts to criticize me and this book.[2] I don't care. The best advice in the world is useless if people won't follow it.

Instead, I'm going to teach you a password strategy that is pretty good. More important, it's one that is easy to make into a habit and to follow.

How Many Passwords Do You Really Need?

One password is never enough. That's because some web sites are downright careless with your password.

Most web sites have a way to recover a lost password based on a secret hint or question that you provide. For example, when you register, they might ask you to choose a question, like "What city were you born in?" or "What is the name of a favorite pet?" If you can answer it correctly, they will usually do one of two things:

- Issue you a new temporary password by sending it to your e-mail account.

- E-mail your actual password to you.

Those that issue you a temporary password are doing things correctly—you can then log in and change the password to something you will remember.

Those that e-mail your password to you have compromised your password—because it can be read by any packet sniffer on the Internet.

If that's the one password you use everywhere, you now face the need to either take a chance that nobody saw it, or change all of your accounts to a new password.

I would suggest that the minimum number of passwords you really need is three.

Your Three Passwords

You need one very secure password to use on sites that you believe are trustworthy, and that protect information you really care about (like credit card numbers or other personal information). This is the password you use for things like online shopping. You should only use this password on web pages that are secure (check the lock icon at the lower right of the window as described in Chapter 10).

You need a second password for use on sites where you won't suffer terribly if it is compromised. Use this for discussion forums, e-mail, and instant messenger. You can use this password on web sites that aren't secure. You

---

[2] *Probably in endless personal attacks (called **flames**) on various discussion forums*

should still protect this password (as I'll describe later), but the idea is that you're not protecting anything so critical that someone with a packet sniffer will go through the hassle of following through with an attack. Most individuals aren't subject to the kind of attacks that a business may face (with lots of money on the line).

You need a third password for your computer. There are two reasons for this:

1. You may want to give out this password for file sharing, or to let someone use your system. You wouldn't want them to also gain access to your online accounts.

2. Windows 95/98/ME does not store computer passwords securely. In fact, there are programs readily available that will display the user names and passwords of every account on a Windows 95/98/ME computer. So if you use your one password on those machines, anyone sitting down in front of your computer can within minutes find the password and use it elsewhere.

If a web site is suspicious in any way, consider creating a "throwaway" user ID and password just for that one site. That way if it is a scam or fake web site (trying to grab account information to use elsewhere), you won't compromise your three main accounts.

Creating a Strong Password

Experts will tell you that a password should be at least seven characters long, should contain both upper- and lowercase characters, and should include numbers and punctuation. The result is typically a password that is impossible to crack, and equally impossible to remember.

How Passwords Are Cracked

There are four main approaches for cracking passwords:

1. A program or hacker guesses based on what they know about you. Names of family members, birth dates, etc., are often used as passwords. This is called an *intelligent guessing attack*.

2. A program just tries every word in a dictionary including common names. This is called a *dictionary attack*.

3. A program tries every possible combination of letters, numbers, and punctuation. This is a *brute force attack*.

4. Someone breaks into your house, looks at your desk, and finds the Post-it note on which you've written your account IDs and passwords. This is called *breaking and entering*.

So what should you do?

I'm not going to tell you. Because if I gave a formula for you to use, it might become popular and then easy for other people to guess.

But I'll tell you some basic ideas that can help you create your own memorable password, and avoid creating one that's too easy to crack.

- Try for seven characters, but never less than five. Your secure password should always be at least seven characters.[3]

- Avoid the obvious. Don't use something people can figure out about you, such as a name of a family member, a driver's license number or license plate, birth date, or the city where you were born or live.

- Pick a word that you will remember. It should have nothing to do with you whatsoever. Even better, pick two and string them together.

- Add some numbers. Best is to put them inside the word somewhere. Don't use obvious numbers like your area code, zip code, phone number prefix, or birth date. Please don't use your ATM number! Yes, I know, remembering random numbers is painful, but you only have to do it once.[4]

You can do some mixing and matching—like using the same number but different words for each of your passwords. It's not ideal, but it does reduce the risk of you forgetting without a great increase in risk.

Your computer password doesn't need to be very secure if you're behind a firewall unless you're concerned about a serious attack from someone on your local network.

> **NOTE** These recommendations provide decent security for individual and home use. Businesses have very different issues both in terms of the size of the local network, the more complex network configurations, and the potential costs of unauthorized access. In other words, for business applications, listen to the security experts, not the advice I offer here.

---

[3] *Between upper- and lowercase letters and numbers, you have 62 characters. A 4-character password has about 15 million possible combinations, which is far too many to test if you were doing so by hand, but no trouble at all for a computer attack. 5 characters brings the count up to a billion possibilities, which is better. 7 characters results in over three trillion possibilities, which might not slow down the NSA, but is fine for most purposes.*

[4] *One of my reviewers suggested I offer a list of possible ways to create passwords, like using anagrams or reversing words. The reason I am not doing so is simple: Any "system" I offer to create passwords may end up being used by many people who read this book. As a result, attackers (who can also read) will design attacks specifically to counter those suggestions—which would result in the rules that I offer to make passwords more secure actually having the reverse effect!*

Cycling Passwords

Experts will recommend that you change your passwords every 30 to 60 days. Business networks often require this. Some schools require it.

But unless it's required, you probably won't do it. So don't worry about it.

Change your password any time it is compromised. And consider changing them all once a year just to be safe.

Writing Down Passwords

Experts will recommend that you never write down your password.

But you probably will anyway.

So here's the strategy. Write it down just in case, but store it somewhere that has nothing to do with your computer. Not on your desk. Not on a Post-it note. Not on a file in your computer. Hide it somewhere you'll remember in case you forget your password. (Remember, you just went to a lot of trouble to make up a password that you would remember, right? So you should never need this.)

Should you keep a list of which web sites use which password? Not really. Since you only have a few passwords, you can just try them when you visit a site until you find the right one.

Giving out Your Password

You may find yourself giving out a password in order to let people connect to a shared drive on your hard drive. That is the only password you should ever give out.

NEVER, NEVER, NEVER give anyone your password to a web site, e-mail account, or IM account. If a web site sends you an e-mail with a link asking you to confirm your account information or password, it's a scam. If someone calls you asking for your account information and password, it's a scam.

If you're sharing files on a local network, it's OK to give out the password to your shared drive. That's why you gave it a different password from the one you use online.

Passwords and the Evils of Automatic Login

Software developers know that passwords are a necessary evil, so many applications (including Internet Explorer and instant messenger applications) offer a convenient feature called *automatic login*. You'll sometimes see this feature referred to as *automatic logon*, *automatic sign-in*, or *sign in automatically*. The idea is that your computer can remember the user account and password for you, and automatically log you on to a web site or instant messenger service as soon as you access the site or launch the application.

As long as you're absolutely certain that you're the only person who will use your computer (or your account on a Windows 2000/XP computer), automatic login can be a huge convenience.[5]

The problem with automatic login is simple—if anyone has access to your computer, your accounts and password can be stolen.

OK, part of this is obvious. Sure, if someone uses your computer, they'll be able to log on to web sites or use instant messenger or read your e-mail without knowing your password.

But it's worse.

In order to log on to a web site or service, your computer has to store the password. There are programs that can retrieve those passwords from a computer. Which means that if someone hacks into your system, they can retrieve that information as well. In other words, if your computer is a victim of a virus or Trojan, your passwords can be stolen and used even if the hacker doesn't have access to your computer.[6]

And of course, if your computer is stolen or sold, those passwords will be available to the new owner. And more and more teens (especially college students) are using laptop computers, which are more vulnerable to theft than desktops.[7]

This is all bad, but there's more:

If you turn on automatic login when on a friend's computer or public computer, anyone who uses that computer afterwards will have access to that account, and possibly be able to figure out your password (and since you almost certainly use that password for other accounts, that represents a huge security breach).

This is how most identity theft happens with teenagers—they visit a friend's house, log in to their instant messenger account, and leave automatic login turned on. Next time their friend uses the computer, they find it logged in to an IM session, and proceed to do with it whatever they want.[8]

That may not be very scary, but there are also cases of "friends" doing some creative shopping online using stored user names, passwords, and credit card numbers. And if you're on a public computer, and you've entered any

---

[5] *Automatic login settings are unique for each user account on a computer. So if your account is password protected, and you're using Windows 2000 or XP, you have some extra protection, as long as you don't let someone sit down and use your computer while it's logged in to your account.*

[6] *One of my teen reviewers made this comment: "I always take precautions ever since my computer was hacked 3 years ago. They (the hackers) told all my friends stuff about me, and swore at them, and they sent me a virus and changed my passwords ... I'm hella cautious now." (submitted by A.R.).*

[7] *Safeware, a major PC insurance company, estimates there were over 600,000 computers stolen in the U.S. in 2002. Visit* http://www.safeware.com *if you're interested in insuring your computer—they're the leader in the field.*

[8] *I mentioned earlier how I sometimes host LAN parties. You wouldn't believe the number of times I turn on one of my computers to find it automatically signing on to one of my guest's IM accounts.*

personal information, it becomes available to the next person to sit down at that computer.

So here's the deal. Now you understand the risks—and if you are truly confident that your computer is secure, go ahead and use automatic login. But it is my personal opinion that automatic login is evil, and you should never allow a computer to remember your password for you—even your home system.

So now I'm going to tell you how to turn it off.

> **NOTE** While the instructions that follow are for just a few products, the concepts apply to many kinds of software and future versions of these products. So the instructions shown here should give you a good idea of what to look for on whatever browser, e-mail program, or instant messaging service you use. Visit AlwaysUseProtection.com for updates and instructions for other software.

Turning off Automatic Login for Internet Explorer

To turn off automatic login for Internet Explorer, start by choosing the Tools ➤ Internet Options menu command from Internet Explorer. You can also choose Internet Options from the Control Panel.

Next, select the Content tab as shown in Figure 11-1.

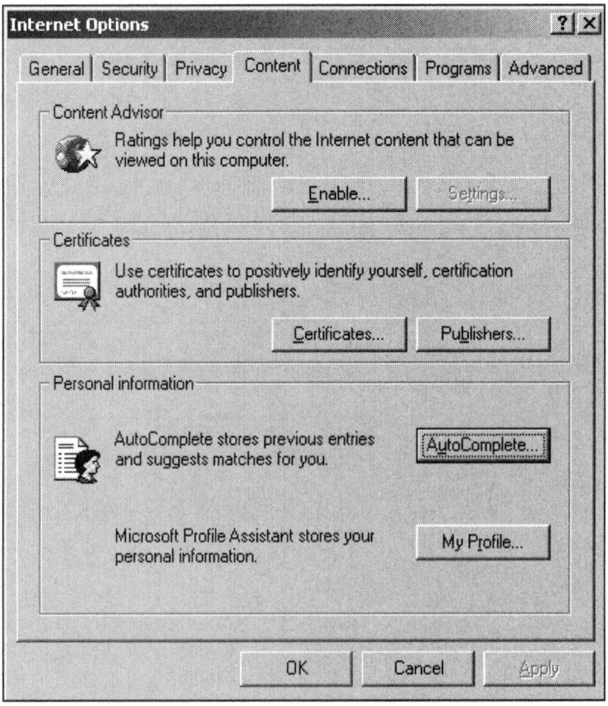

Figure 11-1 The Internet Options content dialog box

By default, the Microsoft Profile Assistant isn't enabled, and most people don't use it, so I won't go into it here. However, the AutoComplete feature is enabled by default. AutoComplete is a feature that remembers how you fill out a form on a web page. Anytime you return to that page, it can fill in the form with the same information you used last time—which can be great for tasks like online shopping, since you won't need to retype your name, address, and so on each time you visit. Click the AutoComplete button and you will see the dialog box shown in Figure 11-2.

AutoComplete Settings ?×

AutoComplete lists possible matches from entries you've typed before.

Use AutoComplete for
- ☑ Web addresses
- ☐ Forms
- ☑ User names and passwords on forms
  - ☐ Prompt me to save passwords

Clear AutoComplete history

[Clear Forms]   [Clear Passwords]

To clear Web address entries, on the General tab in Internet Options, click Clear History.

[OK]   [Cancel]

Figure 11-2 The AutoComplete Settings dialog box

The settings shown in this figure are my recommended settings.

- The "Web addresses" setting allows Internet Explorer to guess which site you want when you start entering a web address. Though this might be a privacy issue (a subject for the next chapter), it's a minor one, and certainly isn't a security issue.

- The "Forms" setting allows Internet Explorer to store entries when you fill out online forms. Since this can include personal information, I recommend you turn it off.

- The "User names and passwords on forms" and "Prompt me to save passwords" settings store user names and passwords when you log in to web sites. By default, Internet Explorer will prompt you to save passwords. However, most people when they see the prompt will by default turn it on and store the password, not realizing that's what they've done. The settings shown here (with the "User names and passwords on forms" check box checked, and the "Prompt me to save passwords" check box unchecked) allows Internet Explorer to store user names but never store passwords. This is a reasonable choice—the convenience of having the browser remember your user name outweighs the security risk—as long as the password is not stored as well.

Before closing the dialog box, click the Clear Passwords button to erase any passwords that had been previously stored.

Turning off Automatic Login for Outlook Express

If your e-mail program has automatic login to your e-mail server, anyone using your computer can read your e-mail. For those of you who use Outlook Express, it's easy to turn off this feature.

Open Outlook Express, and choose the Tools ➤ Accounts menu command. Next, choose the Mail tab and select your e-mail account by clicking it. Next, click the Properties command button.

Choose the Servers tab, and you'll see the dialog box shown in Figure 11-3.

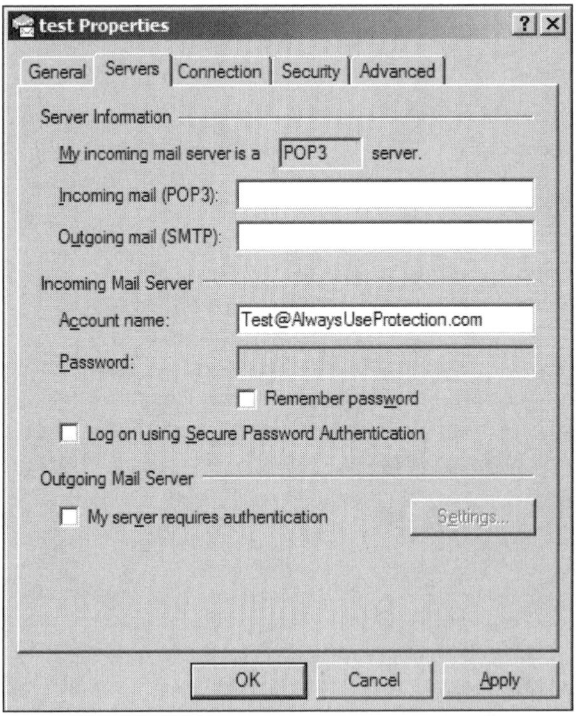

Figure 11-3 Clearing passwords on Outlook Express

Uncheck the "Remember password" check box to prevent automatic login to the e-mail account.

Turning off Automatic Login for AOL Instant Messenger

I like AOL Instant Messenger (AIM), but AOL really should be ashamed of themselves—making automatic login the default. This is apparent from one of the first dialog boxes you see during installation as shown in Figure 11-4.

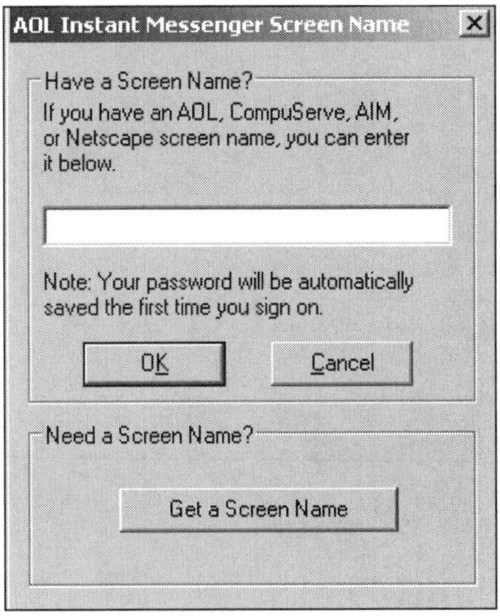

Figure 11-4 The AIM sign-up dialog box

There it is in plain text: "Your password will be automatically saved the first time you sign on."

Do you ever remember reading that message? Probably not. I've installed AIM on dozens of computers and I didn't remember that message when I did the installation to generate the screen shots for this chapter.

And there's nothing here to turn it off. That's left for the actual sign-on, shown in Figure 11-5.

You should always uncheck the "Save password" check box.

But what if you forgot to do so? You won't see this logon dialog box again, because the computer will just go ahead and sign you on. The answer is to use your Buddy list window, and select the My AIM ➤ Edit Options ➤ Edit Preferences menu command (or just press the F3 function key when the Buddy list window is active). You'll see the dialog box shown in Figure 11-6.

Figure 11-5 AIM Sign On dialog box

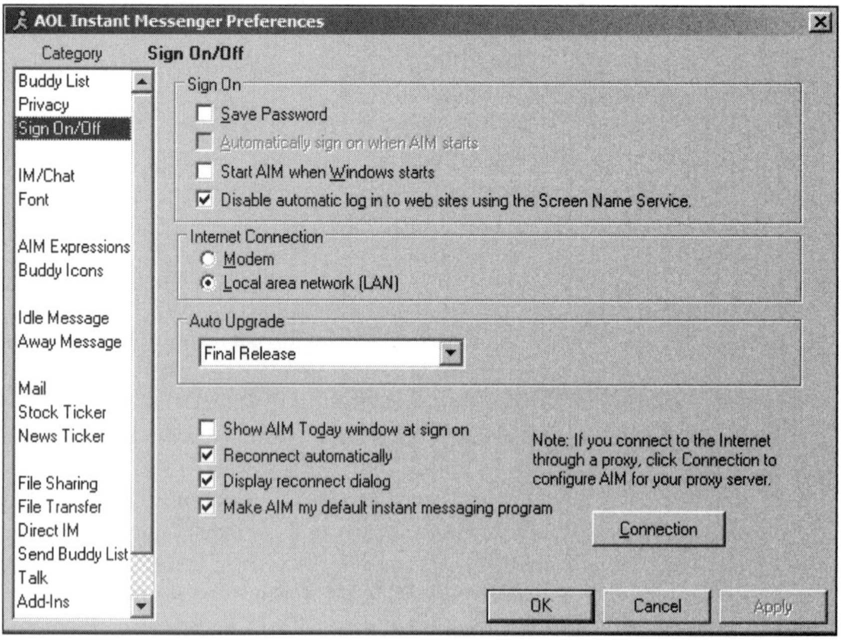

Figure 11-6 Disabling automatic login in AIM

Click Sign On/Off in the category window on the left. You should uncheck the Save Password check box.

Turning off Automatic Login for the .NET Messenger Service and MSN Messenger

Kudos to Microsoft on this one: By default, automatic login is turned off for current versions of the .NET Messenger and the closely related MSN Messenger.

However, if you have the misfortune to log in once with the "Sign me in automatically" check box shown in Figure 11-7 enabled, the ability to turn off the automatic login for .NET Messenger is well hidden and poorly documented.

Figure 11-7 The .NET Messenger Service sign-in dialog box

Here are Microsoft's instructions for clearing automatic login:
You can do either of the following:

1. If you are not already signed out of Windows Messenger, on the **File** menu, click **Sign Out**.

2. In the main window, click **To sign in with a different account, click here**.

3. In the **Sign in to .NET Messenger Service** dialog box, clear the **Remember my name and password on this computer** check box.

or

1. Go to User Accounts in the Windows XP Control Panel (to open Control Panel, click **Start**, and then click **Control Panel**, then click User Accounts).

2. On the **Advanced** tab, click **Manage Passwords**.

3. In **Stored User Names and Passwords**, click **Passport.Net***, and then click **Remove**.

This does not delete your Passport, but removes its connection with your computer.

4. Click **Close**, and then click **OK**.

What they don't tell you is, if you're using Windows XP, you must choose the second approach. The first option alone won't work.[9]

Better not to choose automatic login the first time around.

If you are using the MSN Messenger client, you can disable automatic login by going to the Tools ➤ Options menu command, choosing the General Tab, and unchecking the check box labeled "Allow automatic sign in when connected to the Internet". **However, clearing this check box is not enough to clear any passwords stored on your computer if you've already used automatic login.** You must also clear your stored password as described earlier.

Beyond Passwords

In Chapter 10, you learned about identity theft. In this chapter, you learned that one of the ways you are most vulnerable to identity theft can be the information you leave on computers, both your own and those of friends (not to mention public Internet computers).

In fact, this is the first chapter that really focused on the idea that information on your computer can compromise your privacy. But there is more to protecting your privacy than identity theft and more things that can be found on your computer than passwords—as the next chapter will show.

---

[9] *This may be winner of the least intuitive user setting ever. Making you go to a Control Panel applet to disable automatic login of an IM application is absurd.*

The Traces You Leave Behind: What Your Machine Says About You

I started this section of the book on privacy talking about identity theft. There's a reason for that. Most everybody you meet will agree that identity theft is a bad thing.[1]

That's probably where agreement on privacy issues ends.

Many of the most significant issues our society faces hinge on privacy rights. Should a company interviewing you for a job have the right to see your school records? Should the college you are applying for be allowed to check your driving record along with your grades? Can insurance companies look at your private medical records before granting you insurance? The pervasive use of security cameras may protect stores and help police ticket speeders, but the vast majority of people whose activities are captured and recorded are innocent of any wrongdoing. How much privacy do we give up in return for how much additional security?

And of course, there's the age old argument: If you have nothing to hide, why would you care if you have no privacy?

This book is intended to teach you about how your privacy can be invaded, and how to protect it—to whatever degree you wish. If you really don't care about your privacy beyond preventing identity theft, you really don't need to read this chapter or the one that follows.

The next chapter will discuss the traces you leave behind as you browse the Internet. This chapter will focus on the traces you leave behind on your machine.

Footprints on Your Machine

Think back for a moment to a time when you visited the house of a new friend for the first time. Remember when you first entered their room?

You can learn a lot about someone from their room.

What kinds of books do they read? Do they have any hobbies? Trophies may be a sign of interest in sports. Posters might indicate a favorite band, or a particular political viewpoint. A report card or honors certificate might give an idea of how they are doing in school. A CD collection demonstrates taste in music (or lack thereof). Are they organized to a fault, or total slobs?

What could a person learn about you by visiting your computer?

- Web sites you've visited

- Actual pages from web sites you've visited

- E-mail you've sent and received

- Records of instant message conversations

- Product recommendations based on items you've bought or looked at in the past

- Contents of any files (letters, homework assignments, downloaded files)

- Contents of any files or programs you've downloaded

Now, you might be thinking, "Why should I worry about what can be found on my computer?" After all—it's *your* computer, right? Well, consider all the cases where someone might have access to a computer that you have used:

- Anyone who sits down at your computer, including friends, parents, and siblings, will have access to that information.

- If you're on a local network, anyone else on the local network may have access to your computer. If it's an unsecured wireless network, anyone driving by may have access.

- If you've used a computer at a friend's house, or a public computer, whoever uses it after you can find traces of your visit.

- If you've been hacked by a Trojan, the attacker will have access.

- If you sell or give away your computer, you'll be giving away all that information if you don't take precautions to clean it up.[2]

- If you send your computer to a store for repairs, the people working on it have access to your information.

- And, of course, if your computer is stolen, the thief will have access to everything on your machine.

---

[2] One time I was helping set up a computer that a friend had obtained from a nonprofit organization—one they no longer needed. It had all sorts of leftover information including donor lists and employee records.

If you're sharing a computer, you've probably already thought about these issues. But as you can see, even if you have your own computer and you're the only person who normally uses it, you might want to spend a few minutes thinking about the traces you leave behind on your machine.

Browser Footprints and How to Erase Them

Just as the books on your bookshelf help visitors to your room learn your interests, people visiting your computer can learn your interests based on the web sites you visit.

It may seem odd that just looking at a web page is comparable to buying a book and putting it on your shelf. In fact, the web site is much more obvious. Visiting a web page is more like putting a book on your shelf, stapling a poster about the book on your wall, leaving a calendar with the dates when you read the book, and leaving photocopies of many of the pages lying around in plain site.

> **NOTE** The instructions that follow are only for Microsoft Internet Explorer, because that is currently the most popular browser. However, other browsers (Netscape, Mozilla, Opera) have comparable features. Refer to your browser documentation for details.

Browser History

The most obvious way guests can determine which pages you visit is by looking at the history log of your browser. This feature allows you to quickly review pages you visited—a great convenience when it comes to navigating the web (especially when it comes to remembering that site you visited just the other day).

To delete your browser history, start by using the Tools ➤ Internet Options menu command from Internet Explorer.[3] Be sure the General tab is selected. You'll see the dialog box shown in Figure 12-1.

Click the Clear History button to clear your browser history. This will also clear the list of recently visited sites in the address bar of your browser.

---

[3] Remember, the Internet Options tab only controls Internet Explorer. Refer to your browser documentation if you use a different browser.

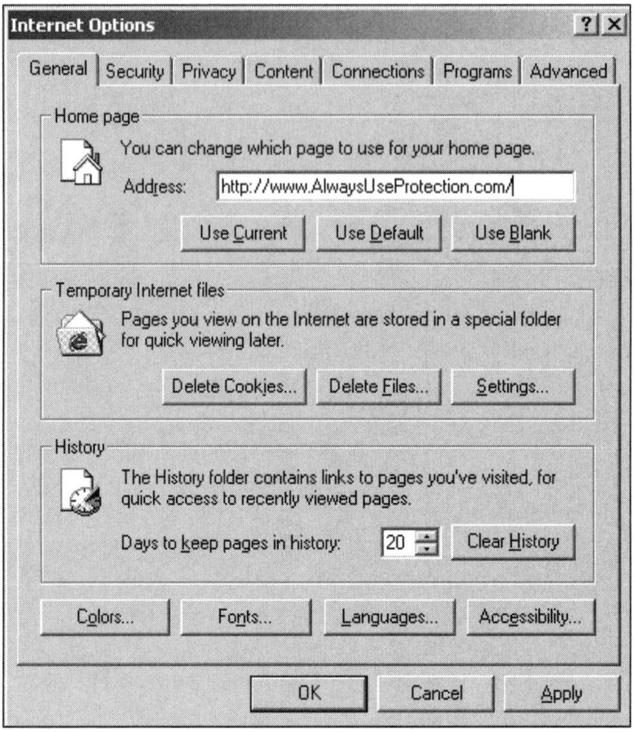

Figure 12-1 Internet Options dialog box (General tab)

Cookies Part I

Cookies have gotten a lot of bad press. In fact, cookies themselves are not the problem—it's how some sites use them that can be a problem.

What's a Cookie?

Every time you access a web site, what really happens is that your computer connects to the web server computer and requests some information. The web server computer obviously knows the IP address[4] of your computer—because if it didn't, it wouldn't be able to send the information back to you.

The problem that web sites face is this: Each request is completely independent. It's not like a phone call—where you keep talking back and forth. Instead, imagine a phone call where every time the person you were calling answered you, they hung up, and you had to call back . . .

---

[4] IP addresses were covered in Chapter 5 (for those of you who may have skipped right to this chapter).

Ring, ring . . . Hello?

Hi, it's Dan. What's up?

Nothing much . . . Click.

Ring, ring . . . Hello?

So, did you want to go out Saturday?

Sure, sounds great! . . . Click.

Wait, who was it I just agreed to go out with?

You see, the only way a phone conversation like that would work is if every time you called back, you started out by saying who you are.

That's all a cookie is. When your computer contacts a web site, the site can request of your computer, "Next time you come to this site, please tell me who you are by sending back the following information with your request." That information your computer includes with the request is called the *cookie*. It allows the web site to know who you are by examining the cookie information that it sent your computer earlier.

If you want to see what a cookie looks like, open your Explorer window (the file manager, not the browser). On Windows 2000/XP, navigate to the Document and Settings directory on the drive that holds your operating system. Select the directory with your user name. You should see a folder named Cookies.[5] On Windows 98/ME, look for the Cookies directory under your Windows directory.

The Cookies directory contains a bunch of text files. If you open one, you might see something that looks like this:

```
PREF
ID=428c71b47f0abbdc:TM=1043926063:LM=1264348905:TB=2:S=326SavWsbdgREfMs
google.com/
1024
2317858231
12915624
2324444869
39893231
*
```

This is a cookie for Google.com.[6] So anytime this computer connects to Google.com, it will send this information with the request.

What does this information actually mean?

---

[5] *This is how you view cookies stored by Internet Explorer. Other browsers store cookies in different ways. For example, the Netscape browser stores cookies in a file named cookies.txt in the directory where it stores user configuration data.*

[6] *Actually, it just looks like one. I randomly changed most of the numbers and letters to protect my own privacy.*

I have no idea. Most of the information in a cookie only has meaning to the web site that set the cookie—it's how the web site figures out who you are. That doesn't mean it has to make any sense to you.

How Do Cookies Affect Privacy?

There are actually two types of cookies: session cookies and permanent cookies. A session cookie is kept on your system for a limited amount of time (called a *session*). This kind of cookie is very important: When you're buying concert tickets online, if the web site couldn't remember you from one page to the next, you could easily end up with somebody else's tickets.

Permanent cookies are stored on your system for longer periods. For example, let's say you browse Amazon.com for fantasy books. Next time you visit Amazon.com from that machine, you might find that the home page includes a fantasy book, popular fantasy book lists, and a section that reviews which books you looked at on your last visit!

So you see, it's not the cookies on your machine that pose the greatest privacy risks. It's the chance someone will sit down in front of your computer, and, upon visiting the sites you've visited, be able to see recommendations that are based on things you've purchased or information you've provided in the past.[7]

I'll have a lot to say about cookies and marketing in the next chapter, and I'll talk more about Amazon.com. But I want to point out something nice that Amazon.com does with regards to privacy. They allow you to edit the items that influence their recommendations. Just log on to your account, click the Your Account button, and scroll down to the section named "Recommendations". You'll see a link called "Improve your recommendations", which will allow you to edit recommendations based on past purchases, ratings, and even areas you've visited on Amazon.[8]

Third-Party Cookies

When you browse to a particular site, it may include images or content from other web sites. When one of those sites (one you didn't browse to directly) tries to set a cookie, it's called a *third-party cookie*. Third-party cookies come in two forms: Some are used by online stores to process payment information,

---

[7] One of my reviewers challenged this statement. He wondered, What if the cookie contains your Social Security number? Well, it is, of course, possible that a really stupid web site would actually put your Social Security number in the cookie—but I've never seen this happen. The cookie itself rarely contains any useful or personal information by itself—the cookie is best thought of as an index into a database on the web server itself. Your private information is stored in that database, and the cookie is used to find it.

[8] Of course, the intent of offering these options is that they want you to give them more information on what you like so they can offer better recommendations and sell more books. But the flip side works too—by telling them not to recommend books on certain topics or based on past purchases, people using your computer will no longer see recommendations that are based on information you would rather keep private.

others are used by advertisements to track you online. You'll read more about third-party cookies (especially the second kind) in the next chapter.

Controlling Cookies

Internet Explorer provides good control over the use of cookies. You can decide if cookies are allowed or blocked, or if you want to see a prompt each time a web site wants to use a cookie. You can control these for both session and permanent cookies. You can also allow or disallow third-party cookies.

Bring up the Internet Options dialog box again, but this time choose the Privacy tab. You'll see the dialog box shown in Figure 12-2.

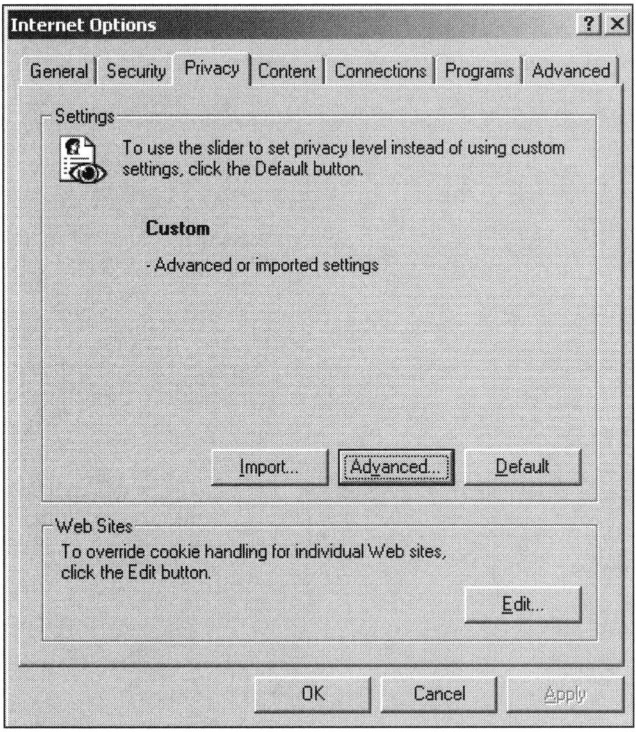

Figure 12-2 Internet Options dialog box (Privacy tab)

Click the Advanced button and you'll see the Advanced Privacy Options dialog box shown in Figure 12-3.

The settings shown here are the ones I prefer. I allow session cookies. I want to be prompted for first-party cookies (those coming from the site I explicitly navigated to), so I can block those I don't want to keep. And I also prompt for third-party cookies, though you may prefer to just routinely block these. Be aware that there are some sites that won't work properly if you block first-party cookies. Most sites will work properly if you block third-party cookies.

Figure 12-3 Advanced Privacy Settings dialog box

If you click the Edit button in the Internet Options dialog box (Privacy tab) shown in Figure 12-2, you'll find a list of all of the web sites for which Internet Explorer has records. You can set those to block or allow cookies, or remove them from the list so you'll be prompted next time you visit the site.

Keep in mind that this list represents another place people can go to find out what sites you may have visited.

Clearing Cookies

The General tab of the Internet Options dialog box (shown earlier in Figure 12-1) also contains a Delete Cookies button. This button allows you to simply remove all the cookies on a system. But be sure to read the section later in this chapter called "The Files That Wouldn't Die" for instructions on how to make sure the cleared cookies are really cleared.

The Cache (Temporary Internet Files)

Downloading pages takes time—especially on slower Internet connections. One way performance is improved is by using a technique called *caching*: storing downloaded information on your computer in case it will be needed later. Let's say a page you are viewing has ten images. When you come back to the page a week later, your browser looks to see if those images have already been downloaded. Finding them in the cache, it displays the images from the cache instead of downloading new copies. Internet Explorer will cache entire web pages so you can view them after you've disconnected from the Internet—they refer to these pages as *offline content*.

Caching can dramatically improve performance, but one side effect is that the actual content of many of the web pages you view can be found on your computer.

Deleting the cache is easy.[9] The General tab of the Internet Options dialog box (shown earlier in Figure 12-1) also contains a Delete Files button. This button brings up the Delete Files dialog box shown in Figure 12-4.

Figure 12-4 The Delete Files dialog box

Select the "Delete all offline content" check box and then click OK to clear the cache. But, be sure to read the next section for instructions on how to make sure the temporary files you delete are truly deleted.

The Files That Wouldn't Die

You can delete your browser history. You can delete cookies. You can delete files from your cache. You can delete other files from your system.

But guess what? In all the time you've used your computer, you may never have actually deleted anything.

In fact, it's quite difficult to delete information from your system.

What Happens When You Delete a File?

You've just finished working on a school project. It's in a binder and ready to turn in. The next morning you can't find it.

Is it deleted? Of course not. You can probably recover it if you work hard enough at searching for it.

Unfortunately, your dog found it, and dutifully (being a neat dog), grabbed it and dropped it into a trash can. It then got thrown out.

Is it deleted? Not at all. True, you might have to dig through a lot of trash to find it, but it still exists. And somebody wandering through the dump could find it as well.

---

[9] *Each browser you use will have its own cache. The instructions here will only clear the cache used by Internet Explorer.*

If you actually wanted to delete your school report, you would probably need to run it through a really good shredder.

The Recycle Bin

When you "delete" files using the Windows Explorer, you'll usually see a prompt asking if you want to move the file to the Recycle Bin. This is a lot like losing the school project—except it isn't even lost. All you're really doing is changing the directory on your computer so the file seems to be in a different location—a special folder called the Recycle Bin.

Figure 12-5 is a very rough illustration of how files are stored on a disk drive.

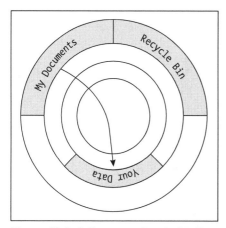

Figure 12-5 A file is stored in the My Documents folder. The folder points to the location of Your Data on the hard drive.

The My Documents folder is in reality a special file on your disk called a *directory*. This directory points to the location on the disk that contains the actual file (in this example, the file called Your Data).

When you move a file to the Recycle Bin, the data itself rarely moves. Instead, the entry for Your Data is removed from the My Documents directory folder, and an entry is added to the directory called Recycle Bin as shown in Figure 12-6.

You can clear the contents of the Recycle Bin by right-clicking the drive letter in the Windows Explorer, choosing Properties, and clicking the button named Disk Cleanup. This will give you the option of clearing the Recycle Bin. You can also right-click the Recycle Bin itself and choose Empty.

But this does not delete the file.

Instead, it removes the pointer to the file from the Recycle Bin, resulting in the situation shown in Figure 12-7.

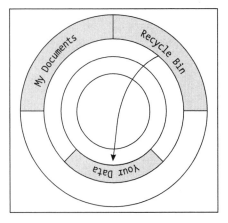

Figure 12-6 A file is moved to the Recycle Bin by removing the pointer from the My Documents folder and instead pointing to Your Data from the Recycle Bin folder.

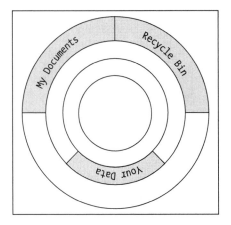

Figure 12-7 A file after "deletion": Though there are no pointers to Your Data, the data still exists on the hard drive.

As you can see, while the system can no longer find the file, the data in the file is still on disk. In fact, even formatting a drive won't necessarily erase the data on your drive!

It goes without saying that there exists software that can examine your drive and seek out and reconstruct data, even after it has supposedly been deleted.

Deleting Files—for Real

When you delete a file, or remove it from the Recycle Bin, you are doing the computer equivalent of throwing something into the trash and carting it off to the dump. The file is not destroyed—it's just lost.

To really delete a file—to actually *destroy* a file—you need a file shredding program. This is a program that, before deleting a file, finds out exactly where it is located on your hard drive. It then writes over the data—recording over it much as you would record over a cassette or a CD-RW.[10]

In fact, the good ones write over the old data multiple times to eliminate any possible traces of the previous data.

And there's better news yet.

There's an excellent file shredder available for free. It's even open source for those of you who are programmers who want to see how it works.

It's called Eraser, and can be found from Heidi Computers Limited at `http://www.heidi.ie`. (They're an Irish company.) You can download it from their web site, or from `http://www.sourceforge.net`.[11]

It not only erases files that you specify, but more important, it can be set to simply write random data over unused space on your hard drive. That way, instead of having to list files to shred before deleting them, you can simply delete them as you normally would (including clearing cookies and the Internet cache using the techniques described earlier), then allow Eraser to scour the unused areas of your disk—those that now contain the leftover remnants of the files you deleted—to make sure that they are well and truly gone.

> ⚡ **CAUTION** As far as I know, Eraser is safe to use. However, as with any program that writes to disk, there are potential risks of data loss (especially if it aborts in the middle of an operation because of a system crash or power loss). As always, good backups are essential.

The Page File

Another place where scraps of information can remain on your system is a file called a *page file*. It's a large hidden file named pagefile.sys, typically found at the root level of the drive that contains your operating system.

The purpose of this file is to trick your software into thinking you have more memory installed than you actually have. Let's say you have 512MB of memory installed. Windows might create a 512MB page file on disk. Windows then acts as if it has 1024MB of memory, swapping data from real memory to and from the page file. For example, let's say you are using a video editing program that can benefit from having 700MB of memory. Well, it doesn't need all that memory at once, so Windows will put 512MB of it in real memory, and load the rest into the page file. Then, as the program runs, anytime it tries to access data or run code that isn't in real memory, Windows will load that data or code from the page file into memory, and swap something else out to the page file.

---

[10] *Technically speaking, the cassette is the better example, because hard drives, like cassettes, use magnetic recording.*

[11] *Visit AlwaysUseProtection.com to find the latest links in case changes have been made since this book went to press.*

This means, of course, that at any given time, copies of information from your computer's memory may be found in the page file.

If you're on Windows 2000/XP, you can instruct Windows to clear your page file when your system shuts down.[12] To do this, go to the Control Panel, select Administrative tools, and then choose Local Security Policy. You'll see a dialog box such as that shown in Figure 12-8.

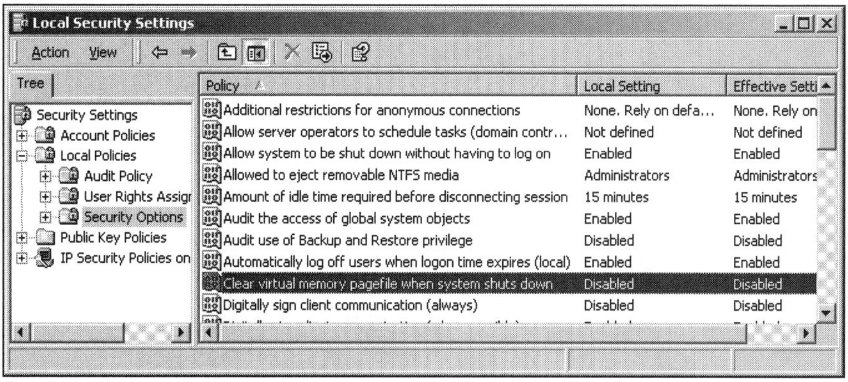

Figure 12-8 Local Security Settings dialog box

In the left pane, click Security Options, and then choose "Clear virtual memory page file when system shuts down". Double-click this line and change the setting to Enabled.

The Hibernation File

Laptop computers by default often have a feature called *hibernation* enabled. Hibernation allows a computer to store the entire contents of memory in a file so that your computer can continue from where it leaves off. It's a lot like standby, except that it will keep your data even if your battery goes completely empty (since the data is stored on disk, not just in memory).

Of course, your hibernation file will contain whatever information was in your computer's memory when it last went into hibernation.

You can configure your hibernation settings by going to the Control Panel and selecting Power Options, which brings up the dialog box in Figure 12-9.

You can disable hibernation by unchecking the "Enable hibernate support" check box on the Hibernate tab. Disabling hibernation should also delete the hibernation file on your system, thus reclaiming a substantial amount of disk space.

---

[12] *Sorry, I don't know of any way to clear the page file on a Windows 95/98/ME machine.*

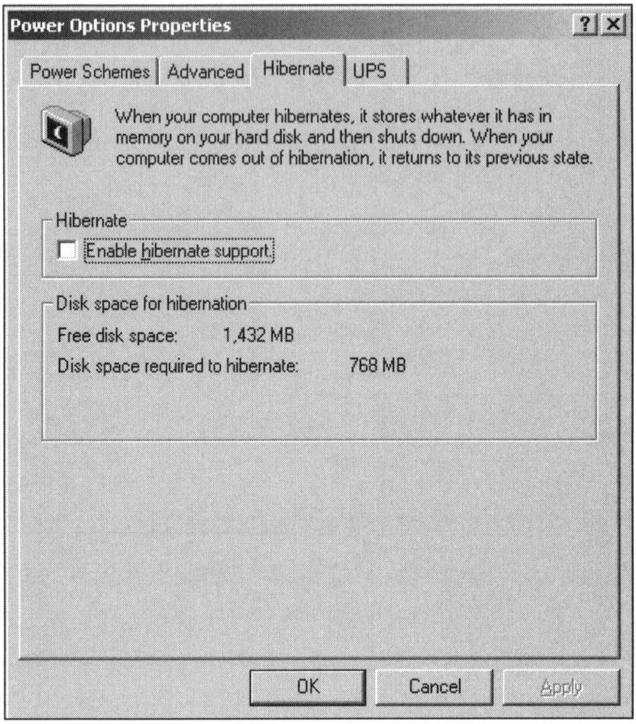

Figure 12-9 Hibernation settings

How Secure Do You Need to Be?

Privacy, like other aspects of security, is never an absolute. And at some time you reach a point of diminishing returns—where you're spending so much time trying to guarantee your privacy that you don't have time to do anything else.

The techniques you've learned in this chapter will allow you to reach a level of privacy that will be good enough for most people. It protects you from casual visitors and provides limited protection from malicious guests and experts.

But don't expect it to protect you from a visit from the NSA.[13]

---

[13] *National Security Agency, or the FBI, CIA, or similar organizations. Their computer security experts are **good,** and the steps taught here will still leave scraps of information that they can find— for example, fragments of old files left over in unused space within the disk space used by an existing file.*

Privacy Software

There are a number of companies that sell software that is designed to help you protect your privacy. These programs can be helpful, in that they can warn you about privacy issues and provide varying degrees of automatic protection. However, you don't need to spend money on privacy software to achieve a high degree of privacy. Most of what these programs do is perform tasks that you can do for yourself—those described in this chapter.

I tend to prefer the techniques described in this chapter for a number of reasons:

- Except for file shredding, you don't need to install another piece of software to use these techniques. That means they work on any machine (including public terminals).

- Software bundles often include features you don't want, and some of their components may have side effects.

- Everything described in this chapter can be done for free.

But there is no doubt that some of the available applications can provide additional privacy and automate the tasks described in this chapter.

Dozens of these programs are available. Here are a few of the more popular:

Webroot Privacy Software	`http://www.webroot.com`
Acronis Privacy Expert	`http://www.acronis.com`
McAfee Internet Security Suite	`http://www.mcafee.com`
Norton Internet Security	`http://www.symantec.com`

Visit AlwaysUseProtection.com for additional recommendations and reviews as they become available.

Encryption: Privacy for Data You Want to Keep

Everything you've read so far in this chapter relies on your deleting information in order to keep it private. After all, if information is truly deleted, nobody else can find it. What about information you want to keep that you don't want others to see?

The answer is to encrypt the files. This scrambles the files on your disk so that only people who know a password can read them.

There are dozens (hundreds?) of file encryption programs available (do a Google.com search under "File encryption" for a list or visit `http://www.sofotex.com/download/Security/File_Encryption`).[14]

Many of these are shareware products in the $20–$70 range, and I am reluctant to recommend one—not because they are shareware (I have no problem with shareware), but because I do not have enough experience with any one to recommend it over another. Nor, based on reviews and information I have available, does one seem to stand out over the others. So I'd suggest if you really are interested in file encryption that you download some of the trial versions and see what you like.

Built-in Encryption: Windows 2000 and XP

Windows 2000 and XP have support for file encryption built into the operating system. However, instead of encrypting each file with a password, they encrypt files and directories using a private key associated with a particular user (Windows creates the key for you and stores it in a safe place on the disk—you don't get to specify your own password).

As long as the user account is protected with a password, any files encrypted by that user can only be viewed by that user, because the hidden key that Windows created for you can only be used by a person logged on with this user account.

If you take this approach, be sure to export a copy of the private key and save it somewhere (on a floppy disk or CD). That's because

> **If the private key associated with the user is ever lost,
> you yourself will never[15] be able to read those files.**

And yes—a private key can be lost in many ways:

- Accidentally or intentionally deleting the user account (or if a virus or Trojan does so).

- If you have to restore, repair, or reinstall your operating system, it is possible that user account data, including the private key, can be lost.

- Bugs in applications can cause the private key to be changed, making existing encrypted files unreadable.

Be sure your computer has 128-bit encryption installed. The default 56-bit encryption is not very secure.

You can read about this built-in encryption in Windows help if you're interested. It will explain how to save your key to a floppy disk.

---

[14] Visit AlwaysUseProtection.com for updated links—these are subject to change.

[15] Never, when it comes to 128-bit encryption, means there is no practical way to ever recover the information—even if your best friend has a bunch of supercomputers at hand.

I personally do not recommend this approach. I prefer password-based schemes—they provide good security with less risk of accidentally losing all your information.

Laptop Encryption

Laptop theft is a much greater problem than computer theft in general (both because laptops are so much easier to steal, and because desktop computers are so cheap that it's hardly worth the trouble). To protect your privacy, many laptop manufacturers have built-in password-based encryption.

Review the documentation for your laptop to find out if it supports this feature.

Stepping Out

In this chapter, you learned how to protect your privacy by obscuring the tracks you leave behind on your computer. But this is only the first step. After all, once you start using the Internet, every time your computer interacts with another computer, you start leaving traces behind on that computer as well.

What form those traces can take, and what people can do with them, may astonish you.

But that's a subject for the next chapter.

Every Move You Make, They'll Be Watching You

In 1975, an author named John Brunner published an astonishing science fiction book titled *The Shockwave Rider*. In it, he made a number of predictions that have largely come true with regards to the Internet and its impact on society. Other predictions have not come true—but it's still early.[1]

One of the major issues in this book is the tension between privacy and utility.

Put your contact information on the Net—so people will be able to reach you via phone, fax, e-mail, pager, or IM regardless of where you go.

So now they can trace your movements.

Put your medical information online, so if you're ill or in an accident, doctors can get your records quickly and help you.

So now they can deny you employment or insurance based on those records. Maybe someday they won't allow you on a ride at an amusement park because your medical record suggests you may not be able to handle it.

Put your school records online so potential employers or colleges can get your records and make decisions quickly.

Should a disciplinary incident when you were a high school freshman really be on your record for the rest of your life? Or public information if there is a security breach? This adds new meaning to the term permanent record.

Put your relationship preferences online, and the Net will help you make new friends. List your friends online to help you make new friends. Use recommendations on online stores to let your friends get discounts on products you think they'll like. Store your buddy lists and address book online so you can contact your friends easily.

Now they know who your friends are also.

---

[1] Recently the Defense Advanced Research Projects Agency (DARPA) discontinued an experimental program due to political pressure. This program would have allowed people to gamble on the likelihood of future terrorist events—a sort of futures market of politics. The theory is that such a market would help predict the likelihood of such events, making it easier to prevent them. I won't bet they got the idea from this book, but it wouldn't surprise me—it's there in black and white.

Sure, the various web sites you visit promise varying degrees of confidentiality—but if there's one thing you know having read this book, it's that even the best of these sites are vulnerable. So even if a web site isn't intentionally selling what they know about you to everyone in sight, it's still possible that the information you give them will get out.

Convenience and utility versus privacy. It's a tough problem.

Hypermarketing

So who are "they"—those folks who can use the Internet to track your movements, your interests, your friends?

Well, that depends on a lot of things, including your own personal level of paranoia. If you're a Libertarian or antigovernment survivalist, "they" might refer to the government. "They" becomes *1984*'s [2] "Big Brother"—the all-invasive government that watches your every move.

For some of you, "they" refers to the RIAA, [3] an organization that is spending a great deal of money to track down what files you download and share with others under the theory that the best way to ensure the loyalty and support of customers is to sue them.

But there is one "they" that applies to virtually everyone who uses the Internet.

"They" are companies who are trying to sell you something.

These companies work hard to accumulate as much information as they possibly can about you so they can figure out better ways to sell you stuff. Their methods range from helpful (product recommendations), to annoying (spam and pop-ups), to downright invasive (adware, spyware, and hijacking your browser).

In the rest of this chapter, you'll learn more about the ways "they" collect information and track you online, and the things you can do to maintain varying degrees of privacy.

But before getting further into the privacy issues, I'd like to invite you to join me on a visit to the site that I believe best demonstrates hypermarketing.

Amazon.com

If you want a taste of what Internet marketing is going to be like in the future, all you need to do is look at Amazon.com today. They are, without a doubt, the most innovative marketers on the Internet.

---

[2] *1984 is George Orwell's classic book, whose predictions, thankfully, haven't come quite as true as those in Brunner's **The Shockwave Rider**—but it's still early.*

[3] *Recording Industry Association of America, for those of you who have been living in the wilderness for the past few years*

Think of some of the things they do already:

- They keep track of what you buy and what you view, in order to offer you recommendations for other products that might interest you.

- They examine buying patterns of large groups of customers to generate recommendations. For example, if many people who buy this book also end up buying one of my other books, *How Computer Programming Works*, people who look at this book will see a note like "People who bought *Always Use Protection* also bought *How Computer Programming Works*." They'll also offer package deals—allowing you to buy both at a discount.

- They have buying circles, allowing you to find out what members of a group are buying. For example, what books or videos are popular among Microsoft employees? What books are popular in New York City?

- When you buy from Amazon.com, they allow you to forward recommendations to friends, offering them a discount in the process (and helping them determine who your friends are).

- They have an affiliate program, allowing anyone with a web site to make money by promoting sales on Amazon.com.

- They allow readers to offer feedback and customer reviews, making it easier for people to figure out which books are best for their needs.[4]

- They have recently added the capability of searching through the text of books, making it easier to find books if you don't know the title.

Now, make no mistake, I am a huge fan of Amazon.com.[5] I've found the site incredibly helpful in finding books and DVDs I like. Their product recommendations, since they are based on information from thousands of customers, have often introduced me to books, authors, and films that I would never have found otherwise, and ended up liking a great deal.

But what about the privacy issues?

I encourage all of you to visit Amazon.com's section on privacy. You can find it by going to the help department and selecting the link for privacy and security.

In this section, you'll learn how to update and remove recommendations, and how to be sure you've "logged out" of Amazon.com so the computer you're on won't assume you're a returning visitor. You'll also be able to read in

---

[4] By the way, those reviews are important to authors—so if you do like the book, I would be incredibly grateful if you would post your comments on Amazon.com, or other review sites. If you don't like the book, obviously I'd prefer you keep your mouth shut—but hey, it's still a free country (for those of you who live in free countries), so I'll respect your choice either way.

[5] And not just because I made a few thousand dollars on their stock, of which, for the record, I still own about 150 shares at the time I'm writing this

detail Amazon.com's policies regarding information they obtain, and how and when they might share it and use it.

So, there only remain two questions:

1. Do you believe what they say?

2. Do you trust that they can keep their own systems secure?

For what it's worth, I do believe their privacy statement. This is for two reasons:

1. The privacy statement is so thorough and specific that it's clear they've invested a great deal of thought in the problem.

2. If they start violating their privacy policies, sooner or later someone will find that out and it will become public. That would be a public relations disaster that I don't believe Amazon.com would want to risk, not to mention an invitation for numerous lawsuits.

As to whether they are able to keep their systems secure—well, you should know by now that no system is absolutely secure. So, if you truly want to buy something anonymously, you may be better off going to a store where nobody knows you and paying cash (of course, many stores nowadays have cameras monitoring customers, so there is a limit to privacy there as well).

The Children's Online Privacy Protection Act

The Federal government enforces a law called *COPPA*—the *Children's Online Privacy Protection Act*. This law imposes specific requirements on any web site that either targets children or knowingly welcomes children to visit. These requirements apply to the kinds of information the site can collect and the way it collects that information, and requires the site implement a way to obtain parental consent before obtaining information. There are additional requirements relating to when and how a site can sell or distribute the information it collects.

Oh, by the way, a "child" for the purposes of COPPA is anyone under 13. That's why many mainstream web sites require people using the site to be 13 or older. By stating that only those 13 or older may participate, these sites don't have to comply with the restrictive COPPA requirements.

So, if you're 13 or older, you're an adult as far as this particular law is concerned. And since this book is intended primarily for teens and older, this is the last I'll be saying about COPPA. Those of you who are teens with younger siblings or parents of younger children can read more about COPPA at http://www.ftc.gov/privacy.

How They Track You, and What You Can Do to Prevent It

The first step to understanding how to protect your privacy online is to understand the various ways that you can be tracked.

Cookies Revisited

In the last chapter, you learned what cookies are, and how they let a web server recognize that two different requests come from the same computer.

Now, I'd like to take this idea one step further. Take a look at the partial web page shown in Figure 13-1.

Figure 13-1 Web page example from Bayarea.com

This is a page header for Bayarea.com—home of the *San Jose Mercury News* (my local newspaper). Take a look at the banner on the upper right. This banner is an image. But where did the image come from?

When a browser requests a web page, it first retrieves all of the text on the page. Then it needs to make separate requests for each image. And those images don't have to be on the same site that hosts the text. In this case, the banner comes from the following URL:

```
http://m3.doubleclick.net/viewad/827910/4-468x60_newredcopy.gif
```

What is the *San Jose Mercury News* web site doing linking to an image on DoubleClick.net?

DoubleClick is an Internet marketing company that provides advertising services to many web sites. There are many such companies. When you browse to a web site that uses DoubleClick, your browser makes a separate request for the image from the DoubleClick.net web site. This allows DoubleClick to record information about the request, and to place a Double-Click cookie on your computer.

When you browse to one site, but it contains links to images on other sites that try to set a cookie, those cookies from other sites are called *third-party cookies.*[6] When third-party cookies are used to track your movement and build up a database of the sites you visit, they are often called *tracking cookies*.

Imagine an advertising web site called AdServer.com.[7] Let's say AdServer.com has contracted with three other companies to do their advertising—a car company (trying to sell a car), a movie production company (trying to sell a movie), and a magazine publisher (trying to sell a magazine).

Meanwhile, two different local newspapers have contracted with AdServer.com to provide banner advertising. To understand the finances, here's how the money flows:

- The car company pays AdServer.com to advertise a car.

- The movie company pays AdServer.com to advertise a movie.

- The magazine publisher pays AdServer.com to advertise a news magazine.

- Meanwhile, the local newspaper web sites (in this example NewsWebsite1.com and NewsWebsite2.com) are paid by AdServer.com for displaying the ads.[8]

So let's follow the sequence of what happens (numbers refer to the numbered arrows in Figure 13-2).

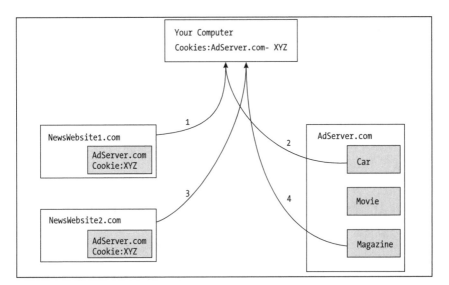

Figure 13-2 How ad servers work

<hr />

[6] *Depending on your perspective, either you or the site you're visiting is the first party—the other is the second party. The sites they link to, that you didn't explicitly browse to, are the third parties.*

[7] *There is such a company, and they do the kind of thing described here—but for this example I'm not referring to the specific company but rather to any company that does online ad serving.*

[8] *This is a bit of a simplification. In practice, the sites are often paid only when someone clicks the ads.*

1. First you visit NewsWebsite1.com. Your browser downloads the text, and then sees an image link to AdServer.com.

2. Your browser then requests the image from AdServer.com. Because this is your first visit to AdServer.com, they request your computer store a cookie on your machine. Let's call this third-party cookie XYZ. AdServer.com then sends a random image (because they don't know anything about you yet). In this example, they send the car ad, which you then see on the web page. AdServer.com records in their database the fact that cookie XYZ came from someone who visited NewsWebsite1.com.

3. Later on, you visit NewsWebsite2.com. Your browser downloads the text, and then sees an image link to AdServer.com.

4. Your browser then requests the image from AdServer.com. Seeing a cookie for AdServer.com, it sends the XYZ cookie with the request. AdServer.com sees the cookie and looks it up in its database. It notices that you had previously visited NewsWebsite1.com, and concludes that you're interested in the news. It then looks in its lists of ads and discovers that one of its advertisers is trying to sell a news magazine—a perfect match for your interests. So this time it sends the image of the news magazine to your browser.

As you browse more and more sites, advertising services can build a very sophisticated picture of who you are and what you are interested in—based on the sites you visit. The more ethical advertising servers don't keep personally identifiable information (i.e., they only know who you are based on the cookie they see when you request an ad—they don't know your name and e-mail address).[9] However, once you provide personal information to a site (by logging in or registering), it becomes possible for a less ethical company or advertiser to track who you are. Next thing you know you may be getting calls or e-mails that have an eerie knowledge of your interests.

Fortunately, it's quite easy to protect your privacy from this type of tracking. The techniques for blocking cookies (described in the previous chapter) work just fine. Be sure you specify the Prompt or Block option for all third-party cookies, and if set to Prompt, just deny permission to any that aren't obviously important for what you want to do.

Also, some spyware and adware prevention software can detect and remove tracking cookies as well. You'll read more about that later in this chapter.

---

[9] *Which advertisers are ethical? Well, if you visit the DoubleClick.net web site, you can read their privacy policy and decide for yourself. I'm willing to give them the benefit of the doubt—at least they have a privacy policy.*

Log Files

Anytime a request comes in from a web browser, the web server receives information that it can save for future reference. Among the information it can log is

- Your computer's IP address
- Your computer's host and domain name (if it has one)
- The type and version of browser that you're using
- Any information you filled out on a form when you made the request
- In some cases, the URL of the referring site (the one you clicked from to get to the site filling the request)
- Any cookies set by the site
- And, of course, the time, date, and page being requested

This information is typically used by web masters to calculate statistics on the numbers of visitors. Some of these are obvious (time, date, page, and information on a form). But some raise privacy issues as well. An important one is your IP address—which we'll look at in the next section.

Your Browser

The type and version of browser is most often used to allow web sites to send the correct information to your browser. For one thing, different browsers support different features. For example, if a site is using an ActiveX control, they might first make sure you're using Internet Explorer—because ActiveX controls won't work on other browsers. If you're using an older browser version, a web site might send a simpler version of a web page, avoiding newer features that could cause the page to display incorrectly.

The URL of the Referring Site

When you click a web link, the site you visit also typically receives the URL of the site that contains the link. In other words, a web site can find out where you're coming from and log that information. This can provide valuable marketing information to a site (if they see that many visitors are coming for a particular search engine, they might increase their advertising on that search engine). There isn't much you can do about this, but it's not a particularly serious issue for most people.

Information You Provide

It's sort of obvious—if you provide any information to a web site, they will store it. They may then use it for marketing purposes, or it might be stolen from them (if the web site is hacked), or they may sell it. Later in this chapter you'll read more about strategies for limiting the amount of personal information you give.

Privacy and Your IP Address

You already know that your IP address is the "phone number" of your computer—it uniquely identifies your computer on the Internet at any given time. A web site has to have your IP address—without it, the page will never find its way back to your computer.

Marketers rarely use a computer's IP address to identify you. That's for two reasons:

1. Computers that dial up to the Internet and many DSL lines use dynamic IP addresses. That means that each time you dial up, you get a different IP address.

2. Just as a NAT-based router allows an IP address to be shared among many computers, companies often use something called a *proxy server* to allow potentially hundreds of computers to share an IP address.

Because IP addresses are often shared, they can't be used reliably to identify a computer over time—they are only good for identifying a computer during a particular request. Cookies are much better for identifying computers, because they are stored on the computer.

Marketers can sometimes use IP addresses, however, to identify what country you're connecting from or what Internet service provider you're using. For example, if they see a request coming from a block of IP addresses that belong to AOL, they can conclude that you're an AOL customer. Another Internet service provider might pay an advertising company to deliver ads to current AOL customers using this information.

Tracing an IP Address

Just because marketers rarely use IP addresses to keep track of you doesn't mean that it isn't possible to do.

- If you have a fixed IP address (common with some DSL, cable modem, and T1 connections), the IP address can reliably identify your computer or local network.

- Some routers and proxy servers (devices that allow sharing of an IP address among different machines) create logs that could allow specific Internet requests to be traced back to a particular computer.

- Internet service providers that allocate IP addresses dynamically can log each time an IP address is allocated to a user, meaning that given an IP address and date, an Internet request can be tracked back to a particular user.

Ultimately this means that if someone gives your Internet service provider an IP address and time and date, there is an excellent chance they'll be able to tell which machine is at that IP address and who owns the account used—for example, your AOL or MSN account information.

Because only your ISP has easy access to this information, the risks to your privacy come from two sources:

1. Your ISP may choose to monitor the sites you visit to build their own database of marketing information. This is a particularly invasive kind of monitoring because they not only know what web sites you're visiting, they also have all your personal information that you used when you created the account. Check the privacy policy of your ISP to see if they use this information for marketing purposes.

2. Government agencies can obtain this information by using the judicial system. The Digital Millennium Copyright Act (DMCA) makes it easy for corporations to subpoena ISPs for information that connects IP addresses to user accounts. This is a major tool that the RIAA is using to develop lists of people to sue for file sharing.

Anonymous Surfing

There are services that provide anonymous surfing. The way they do this is quite simple in principle. They have a network of anonymous servers. You contact them, and they forward your web page request to the site you specify, and return the result back to you. They don't create any log files, so ultimately the IP request stored on the final destination site is that of the anonymous server, and not yours. As long as you trust the service to not create any log files, you have a high degree of privacy.

Check out `http://www.anonymizer.com` for information on anonymous web surfing.[10]

Hidden Image Tracking

Hidden images are used to track e-mail messages. In Chapter 3, you learned about HTML e-mail, and how it can in some cases allow attacks against a system. You also know that HTML can contain image links, and those image links cause a browser to make a separate request to download the image.

So here's what spammers do.

They include in an e-mail message a tiny picture—one only 1 pixel in size—so small you won't even see it. The image URL points to a web site belonging to the spammer, and they add to each image request additional tracking information that identifies the original e-mail.

---

[10] *Watch for more information on this topic on AlwaysUseProtection.com.*

When you read the e-mail, your e-mail reader requests the hidden image. It also sends along as part of the request a code that identifies the original e-mail address to which the message was sent. The spammer detects the request and logs the information. What information?

- They know your e-mail address, and that the e-mail address is good (since you've just read the message). So they will probably keep sending you spam.

- They have a chance to try to place a cookie on your system (when your browser requests the image, the web site containing the image can store a cookie on your system if you're allowing third-party cookies).

- They know your IP address.

They can then sell this information to other spammers or to marketing firms.

A spam filter will generally allow you to preview messages without downloading hidden images, and this is actually one of the best reasons to use a spam filter (even beyond filtering out the spam messages).

Spyware and Adware

Way back in Chapter 2, you learned about spyware and adware. In that chapter, you read about the security aspects of spyware and adware. You discovered that

- Spyware can monitor your keyboard activity, potentially sending everything you type (including account names and passwords) to an attacker.

- Web page trackers can monitor your browsing activity, sending a record of the sites you visit to an attacker.

- Spyware and adware can eat up your Internet bandwidth, slowing download speeds and causing severe lag or dropouts when playing online games.

- Spyware and adware can download and bring up annoying pop-up ads—regardless of the web page you're visiting—and sometimes even when you aren't browsing the Internet.

- When you agree to download adware, you probably won't read the license agreements. But if you do, you'll be astonished at what you're agreeing to. For example, you may be allowing them to update the software—meaning they can run any program they want on your computer. You may be agreeing to not remove or disable their software.

- Spyware can watch your online activity and bring up ads or special offers based on sites you visit. Sometimes these can be quite aggressive. For example, a hypothetical computer company called Joe's Computers could plant spyware on your system, and bring up an ad for their computers anytime you visit another computer company's site. A bookseller could detect when you're visiting Amazon.com and try to redirect you to their site instead.

Spyware can intercept your web requests, placing their affiliate code in the requests to try to make money off your shopping. Here's how it works:

- Many web sites (like Amazon.com) offer referral fees. This means that anytime someone reaches that web site through a referral from another site, the owner of the referring site makes a small commission on each sale.

- In many cases, you can benefit from this. For example, if your school is signed up through Schoolpop.com, anytime you shop using a link from Schoolpop.com, Schoolpop.com receives the affiliate fee and gives part of it to your school.

- Some spyware attempts to bypass this by sneaking their own affiliate code into the request. This can prevent the referring site from receiving the commission. In this case, it could prevent your school from receiving benefits from your purchase.

Now, here's where things get into a gray area. Schoolpop.com itself had a program called the *Schoolpop Shopping Buddy*,[11] which it described thus:

> Schoolpop Shopping Buddy is a memory tool that ensures more of your online shopping supports your school. By downloading Schoolpop Shopping Buddy any purchase you make with a School-pop online merchant will generate a rebate to your school, even when you forget to shop through `http://www.schoolpop.com`. You'll also have easy access to Schoolpop merchants, and your school and account information.

Hmm . . . a tool that watches where you're shopping, and makes sure that your Schoolpop.com affiliate code is automatically inserted when you shop at certain sites. Sure sounds like spyware to me! But you see, not all spyware and adware is necessarily bad. Like many tools, the techniques employed by spyware can be used for both good and evil. It's up to you to decide which of these you'll allow on your system.

---

[11] At the time this book was published, the Schoolpop Shopping Buddy was no longer available for download. According to their site, this is because of the difficulty of supporting the program over the many different versions of operating systems and browsers now commonly in use.

Stopping Spyware and Adware

Before you can decide what spyware and adware you wish to allow on a system, you need to know what spyware and adware is actually installed on your system.

Antivirus software isn't the right tool for this job. You see, antivirus software is designed to eradicate viruses. There's no gray area here—if it's a virus, you want to kill it. Period.

But spyware and adware fall into a gray area. Sometimes such programs are useful—making it easier to donate money to a cause, or helping you find a cheaper price when shopping online.

Generally speaking, the antivirus companies target spyware that is known to be malicious—the kind that spreads itself like a virus. They don't generally target spyware and adware that you yourself install.

But in many cases, you might install programs without realizing you're doing so.

Fortunately, a number of programs are available that can help you track down not only spyware and adware, but also identify and remove common tracking cookies from ad server companies.

One of the best is a program called Ad-aware, whose basic version (adequate for home use) is free. Visit `http://www.lavasoftusa.com` or `http://www.lavasoft.nu` for more information and download instructions. Ad-aware works much like an antivirus program, except that it reports programs and cookies that are privacy risks rather than viruses.

Another popular antispyware program is Spybot Search and Destroy, which is also free. Visit `http://www.safer-networking.org` for more information.

Also, unlike antivirus programs, these programs don't use active scanning (they generally scan only when you ask them to), so it's usually safe to have them both installed on the same system at once. One may catch spyware that the other misses.

Note that like antivirus programs, there is a risk that some of your applications will stop working after using these tools. It's possible, though unlikely, that they will damage your system software as well, so you should use the same backup precautions you use with antivirus software.

P2P Clients

Like most of you reading this, I am what would traditionally be called a "law-abiding citizen." Sometimes the laws can be quite perplexing—especially when it comes to the problem of P2P[12] networks such as Kazaa, Grokster, etc.

I mean, what does one make of a law that routinely turns tens of millions of people into criminals?

---

[12] P2P stands for **peer-to-peer**. In a P2P network, different computers communicate directly with each other, without going through a central server. For example, when you download a file from Kazaa, your computer is connected through the Internet directly to the computer from which you're downloading the file.

Seriously, right now our society is engaged in a major conflict—the kind that will provide no end of annoyance to history students 50 years from now when they study how it was resolved.[13] How much is content such as music, video, and software worth? What are the rights of developers of content? What are the rights of those using the content? How much control will individuals have over their personal information? It's corporations versus individuals. It's government versus both corporation and individuals. It's Microsoft versus Linux and open source.

I'm much better at asking the questions than offering answers.

But because I am a law-abiding citizen, I've tried to follow the principle in this book of not encouraging or showing readers how to break the law. I mean, this book is about protecting yourself from lawbreakers, right?

So I'm going to follow that principle as best I can, and leave it for you to figure out how to apply what I say to your individual situation and values.[14]

Kazaa

You can't talk about spyware and adware without talking about Kazaa. My own surveys show about 90 percent of the teens I polled have it and use it (or Grokster, which is comparable).

Kazaa and Grokster come in two flavors. The free one is adware. For $20 or $30, you can buy an ad-free version.

Figure 13-3 shows the main Ad-aware window display after a scan on a system immediately after the free version of Kazaa is installed (before the scan, the system was checked out completely clean).

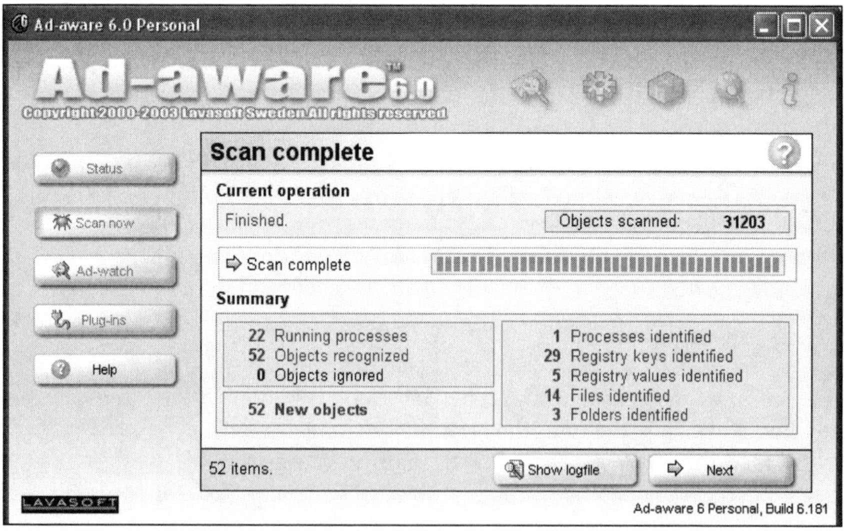

Figure 13-3 The main Ad-aware screen

---

[13] Assuming they still have the freedom to do so

[14] For the record, as a software developer and author, I've had a lot of my work stolen over the years. It's quite annoying (to say the least).

Oh my, 52 potentially troublesome objects. Figure 13-4 shows the screen after you click the Next button.

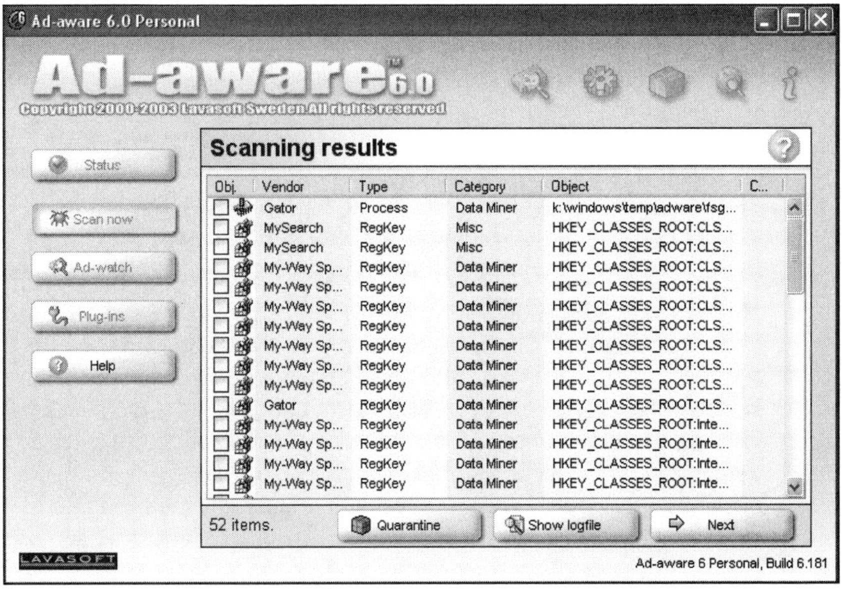

Figure 13-4 Detailed display of Ad-aware after a Kazaa installation

You can click each of these to find out the details. Note, though, the first one. It's our good friend Gator from Chapter 3! Figure 13-5 shows what Ad-aware has to say about this particular piece of software.

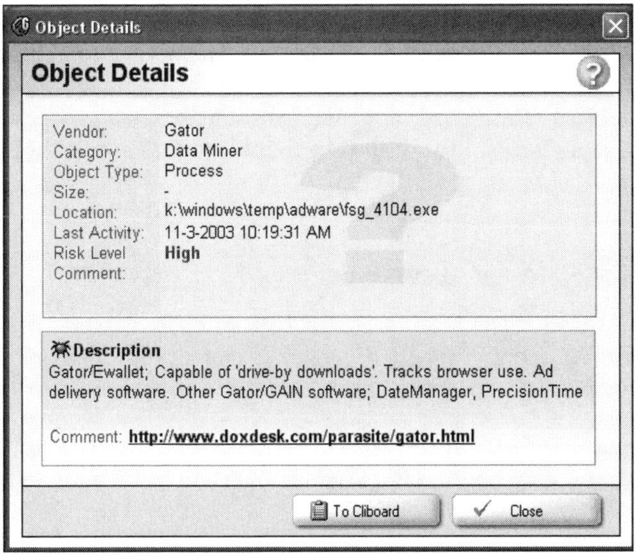

Figure 13-5 The Ad-aware view of the Gator object

So, here's the deal: If you've installed Kazaa or Grokster, you have just seriously compromised your privacy. Based on the experiences of friends of mine, you've also slowed your system down for general Internet use and online gaming. And while turning off Kazaa will help, it won't eliminate the problem. The spyware and adware continues to run even when Kazaa doesn't.

Being a law-abiding citizen, let me tell you what you can't do.

- You can't just use Ad-aware to disable the spyware. First, when you downloaded Kazaa, you agreed not to do so. (Remember those license agreements you didn't bother to read?) Second, Kazaa will detect wholesale deletion of the spyware and will stop working.

- You also can't download one of the free Kazaa-compatible clients such as Kazaa-Lite (also known as KLite or Kazaa Lite K++). Even though it's fully compatible with the Kazaa network, and is completely ad free, it violates the Kazaa license and is illegal to use (it says so in the license agreement that comes with the software). Because of the ongoing legal disputes (which seem to change daily and go from country to country), it's not clear how long it will remain available, or where you can find it. However, various search engines would undoubtedly help you find a download site should it ever become legal for you to download and use the software.

You can, however, purchase an ad-free version of Kazaa or Grokster directly from them. You can also check out other P2P communities—the popularity of different networks varies, and both the technology and the latest legal escapades change weekly.

By the way, should you decide to uninstall Kazaa, be sure to run Ad-aware or a similar program after you do the uninstall and delete the spyware and cookies that it leaves behind.

Also, remember that if you leave file sharing on[15] and allow your computer to act as a supernode, you increase your risks of being sued by the RIAA.[16] You can visit the Electronic Frontier Foundation's web site at `http://www.eff.org` for further information on how not to get sued by the RIAA (I'll have links to this on AlwaysUseProtection.com as well).

Parental and Employer Controls

Another form of useful spyware is parental control software. It's software that is used by some parents to monitor their kids' behavior online. This software

---

[15] *If your client doesn't allow you to turn off file sharing, simply delete files from your shared files folder.*

[16] *As of the publication date of this book, the RIAA was only suing people who share music for others to download. However, downloading is also illegal, so they could choose to sue people who download music as well—assuming they can find them.*

(sometimes called *nannyware*) monitors web activity and e-mail, filters the content of web pages, and blocks access to inappropriate web sites.

Now, frankly I don't know any teenagers who like the idea of parental control software. I know very few who have it.

But I'm also not going to get in the middle of an argument on this particular issue. The use of parental control software is a matter of discussion between teens and their parents. If it's there, it's presumably there with the agreement of both sides, and thus qualifies as spyware that is installed intentionally.[17]

Some businesses have this kind of software installed on their employees' computers as well. This is likely to be a condition of employment and not subject to discussion.

It's OK to Lie: Web Sites and Newsgroups

Cookies and spyware represent technological means that marketers and others have of tracking you and finding out about you. But nothing is better (from a marketer's viewpoint) than information you give to them voluntarily.

Just as spammers use tempting e-mail to try to get you to open and respond to their message, marketers try to tempt you to respond and give them information that will help them sell to you.

What kind of things do they want?

- Your name and address, of course

- Your e-mail address and phone number

- Your age

- Your gender

- Your hobbies or interests

- Your income level

You would be astonished at the level of detail they can go into. They build models of what people are likely to buy. For example, they might know that

---

[17] *Parents, I have more to say on this subject in Appendix C.*

16- to 18-year-old guys who live in a certain neighborhood in a particular city are likely to buy a specific album from a new hip-hop artist. So when they find out that you're one of those people, you'll suddenly start seeing web site ads and spam trying to sell you that album. And you know what—there's a good chance it will work. Then you'll become part of their online database used to help sell something to the next person. And so on.

In Chapter 10, you learned about the tricks that can be used to try to obtain your personal information. Here the issue is much more simple: What information should you provide to legitimate sites when they ask for it?

They'll Take What You Give Them

Generally speaking, there are four major ways that legitimate web sites try to obtain marketing information:

- They ask for it during registration to the site.

- They ask for it when you request information (perhaps you're requesting information on a product, or sending a request for online help, or signing up for an online newsletter).

- They ask for it by getting you to sign up for contests.

- They ask for it in the form of surveys.

Let's briefly look at each of these.

Site Registration or Requesting Information

Most web sites where you register request more information than they need. The best web sites will label which information is required and which is optional. It's up to you which optional information you provide. The more you provide, the more likely it is they will market products to you that interest you—and you might actually want that.

You might want to check their privacy policy first, to see what they do with that information.

Free Services

A number of web sites offer a variety of free services, such as online calendars, greeting cards, and so forth. Before you use them, be sure to check their privacy policy.

For example, I once received a greeting card e-mail from a friend. Upon further research, I discovered (by reading their license and privacy statement) that in order to see the card, I would have to download their greeting card software (including an ActiveX control) that would leave spyware permanently installed on my system.

I sent an e-mail to my friend thanking her for the card, but explaining why I would not be able to view it.

Greeting cards and discount referral programs can be especially risky, because not only might they capture your e-mail address—they capture your friends' addresses as well.

Contests

Companies don't run contests because they like giving things away. They run contests because it's the cheapest way for them to get the information they want. They expect to make far more money using that information than the contest costs them.

Remember, entering a contest gives them a lot of information. They know you're interested in the contest, the site that hosts the contest, and probably the prize. They have your contact information, often name, address, phone number, and e-mail (required to notify you if you win). They may have your age and birth date. That's a lot of information they can use or sell.

So, before entering a contest, check out what they say they'll do with the information, decide if you trust them, and then enter or not as you see fit.

Polls and Surveys

Many people participate in various online polls and surveys. They don't seem to pose much risk, since they are anonymous, right?

True, you usually don't give them contact information. But remember: They do know what site you came from, they do get your IP address, and they may have a cookie set on your machine.

So they do have enough information to add you to an ad tracking system. They do potentially have the information needed to trace the entry back to your machine via IP address. And, it's certainly possible to cross-reference other databases and potentially tie your contact information to the other information they just acquired.

However, polls and surveys from reputable sites (like news organizations) are low risk. They are more interested in your opinion than in selling you something (because what they are selling is the statistics that you help generate—not your individual opinion).

Little White Lies

As you learned in Chapter 10, some information is more important than other. A good web site will request the absolute minimum information needed to support the web site's features. For example, if you're asking to join a mailing list, all they need is your e-mail address. If you want information by mail, they should allow you to specify your mailing address without your phone number.

Unfortunately, many sites ask for more information than they really need. In those cases, you may want to lie in order to protect your privacy. Be sure not to lie in any place where you're stating in an agreement that you have told the truth (such as credit applications, job applications, etc.).

Birth Date

If a site is offering a gift or prize on your birthday, you should give them your birth date—as long as you really trust that they will keep that information secure and not sell it. Otherwise, pick a different date but keep the same birth year. That way you keep the age correct, but don't give away the personal information that can be used later for identity theft if it gets out.

E-Mail Address

Unless you're joining an e-mail list, or specifically want to receive e-mail from a site, feel free to give them a fake e-mail address. Be aware that some sites will use e-mail addresses to send you password reminder information if you forget your login—so if you're registering for a site that you intend to use regularly, give them a valid e-mail address.

Some people use names like nospam@nospam.com or other random names. Some people create free e-mail accounts on Hotmail or Yahoo and then use those as "throwaway" e-mail addresses.

Never, never, never post your real e-mail account on a public newsgroup or forum. That's like begging spammers to target you. They use automatic programs that check the Web and newsgroups, searching for e-mail addresses that they can mail to.

If you must post your e-mail to a forum or newsgroup, don't post it in standard format—write it out. For example, Joe at somedomain dot com. Spammers have a harder time finding this type of format (though it's not impossible).

Phone and Fax Numbers

When lying about phone or fax numbers, choose an area code and then use the prefix 555 (just like they do on TV and movies). For example: 415-555-8396 is a nice random number.[18]

The prefix 555 is reserved for "throwaway" numbers that are never assigned. Don't use 555-1212 though—that's directory assistance.[19]

---

[18] *This information obviously applies to readers in the U.S. and Canada. I'll post fake numbers for other countries on AlwaysUseProtection.com as I find out about them. If you know the numbers for your country, please let me know by visiting the feedback section on the web site.*

[19] *In the U.S., you can dial 411 for information—but that only gets you information for your local area code. If you want information for another area code, you can dial that area code followed by 555-1212.*

Social Security Number

Any site that requests this, unless you're registering for your classes at college or applying for credit, insurance, or a bank account, is probably not legitimate. So don't provide it. Don't make up a fake Social Security number—that's illegal. Your best bet if someone asks for it: Leave—you don't want any dealings with that site.

Let Freedom Ring

If you're interested in learning more about maintaining your privacy online, and privacy issues in general, there is probably no better organization than the Electronic Frontier Foundation. Visit `http://www.eff.org` for the latest news and legal cases relating to privacy issues.

This concludes the part of this book that talks about protecting your privacy. These risks are great, and unfortunately are likely to increase over time. But if you adopt some commonsense habits now, you can maintain a fair amount of privacy. Or at least as much as is possible given the nature of our society.

Now it's time to move on to what is in some ways the most important part of the book, even though it's one of the easiest problems to deal with—protecting yourself.

PROTECTING YOURSELF

You've learned to protect your computer from attack. You've learned to protect your identity and privacy. But it's sad to say that there are people out there who, given the opportunity, will go after you personally. Don't worry, though—these are usually the easiest problems to avoid with just a bit of attention and common sense.

Chat Rooms, Public and Private

"Dangerous sexual predator arrested while waiting to meet teenager he contacted first in an online chat room—News at 11!"

How often have you heard stories like that? Come to think of it, every day we are exposed to TV messages along the lines of the following:

> You (member of a community, group, gender, age, etc.) are in great danger from (someone, something, faulty product, criminal element, negligent doctor, health risk, etc.)—News at 11!

Let's face it. Sex sells. Scary stories sell. Scary stories about sex sell really well.

Scary stories about sexual predators who meet teens on the Internet and then manipulate them into meeting and then kidnap or assault them—well, there's just about nothing that sells better than that. Next to a war maybe.

Yes, there are real dangers out there. And yes, some teens have been hurt. But exactly how scared should you be?

Let's Look at Some Statistics

Mark Twain said, "There are lies, damn lies, and statistics."[1] Statistics have a remarkable ability to be twisted into saying all sorts of things. The best numbers currently available are from a report called "Online Victimization: A Report on the Nation's Youth," released in June 2000 and funded by a grant from the U.S. Congress. Because this report was published by the National Center for Missing & Exploited Children, it's safe to assume that the numbers are accurate.

Now, the National Center for Missing & Exploited Children is a reputable organization with an important and worthwhile goal. At the same time, every

---

[1] He attributed this to British Prime Minister Benjamin Disraeli, but there is nothing in Disraeli's writing that provides evidence that he originated the phrase.

organization also has the goal to perpetuate itself, and let's face it—there is at least the potential for bias in interpreting the results, given that the scarier the results are, the easier it will be for the organization to convince people to give it more money to do its work.[2]

The Numbers

Here, then, are some numbers. Decide for yourself what they mean:

> **When asked, 19 percent of respondents received an unwanted sexual solicitation or approach in the past year.**

The report trumpets one in five youth as receiving such a solicitation. Another way of looking at this is that 81 percent of respondents didn't receive an unwanted sexual solicitation or approach.

Personally, given the amount of such junk out there, it's astonishing that it's so low. One reason, I suspect, is that most teenagers don't waste time on public chat rooms!

What's really interesting about this is another number:

48 percent of those making the solicitation were under 18!

Only 24 percent were known to be 18 or over, and only 4 percent older than 25.

> **5 percent of respondents received a solicitation experience in which they were very or extremely upset or afraid.**

So if 19 percent received a solicitation, and only 5 percent were extremely upset or afraid, it suggests that 14 percent were able to handle the situation with a reasonable degree of comfort.

3 percent of respondents reported a solicitation that included an attempt to contact the person, either in person, over the phone, or by mail. The report calls these *aggressive solicitations*.

Since 34 percent of those aggressive solicitations were by adults, that says that about 1 percent of the respondents had to deal with an adult attempting to contact them.

Curiously, the report didn't ask another question: How many of the youth were pretending to be an adult at the time? A rather important piece of information, don't you think? My own informal surveys show that most teens who spend any time on chat rooms do lie about their age or gender.

---

[2] *I really mean no offense to this organization—I'm just stating the obvious.*

So, How Much Danger Are You Really in?

In this particular survey of 1,501 kids and teens, there were no cases of actual sexual assault, though one incident was particularly suspicious. While these statistics do show the potential for real risk, they also show that the vast majority of teens use the Internet—even online chat rooms—safely.

In the rest of this chapter, I'll lay out some basic, commonsense precautions that, if followed, will make sure you never become the tagline for a "News at 11" promotion.

Chat Rooms

There are two main types of chat rooms: public and private. Public chat rooms are those you find on major networks like AOL.[3] They are usually divided by subject—you search for a chat room on a subject that interests you. In most cases, you arrive and discover that it is incredibly boring.

Private Chat Rooms

Private chat rooms are chat rooms in which you invite friends to chat together. These are typically run by instant messenger systems or online gaming services.

The nature of the risks differs considerably between the two chat rooms. In public chat rooms you are dealing with strangers. In private chat rooms you are usually dealing with people you already know personally, or people that have been introduced to you by friends.

Obviously, private chat rooms are a lot less dangerous (assuming, of course, that your friends are safe to talk to).

So I'm going to focus entirely on public chat rooms, but you should definitely apply the precautions I describe to any strangers whom you allow to join a private chat.

Don't Give out Your Contact Information!

If you don't tell them who you are, they can't find you. Don't give out your last name, address, or phone number. If you want to exchange e-mail, create a separate e-mail address just for use on chat rooms.

This is the modern equivalent of "Don't talk to strangers," or at least don't tell them where you live.

---

[3] Recently MSN dropped their public chat rooms, claiming this was to protect the safety of children online. They will continue to provide monitored chat rooms to paid subscribers. Was it a sincere effort to protect children? Or was it an excuse to dump an unprofitable free service and try to move people to paid subscriptions? You decide.

It's sort of obvious, but really—this is the single most important thing you can do to protect yourself.

Don't Visit Adult Chat Rooms Unless You Want to Receive Sexual Solicitations

If you go to a public chat room that has an adult or sexual theme, you will get approached. That's why people go to those rooms in the first place. Staying away from them is another simple and obvious way to avoid that kind of thing.

Everybody Lies

We're taught when young that lying is bad. When older, we sort of learn that "little white lies" are alright. Well, guess what—when it comes to online chat rooms, lots of people lie. They lie about their age. They lie about their gender. They lie about themselves.

This isn't necessarily a bad thing. Especially as a teen, lying online can give you a chance to experiment with different personalities—perhaps a safer way than doing so in person where a mistake might damage some important relationships with friends, teachers, and parents. Also as a teen, the anonymity of online chat rooms can allow you to be treated as an adult—but in a good way. It's an unfortunate truth that many adults will dismiss what a teen says just because of their age—before even listening to the content. I've known a number of teens who have found themselves being treated with levels of respect online that they were unable to achieve in person just because of their age.[4]

Just remember that the person you're talking to, no matter how nice or sympathetic they sound, may be putting on an act. And no matter how nice they may sound, they may have ulterior motives.

Instant Messenger Programs

Instant messenger programs are one of the most popular tools around. In most cases you will be communicating with people on your Buddy list or Friends list. So you're usually not really dealing with strangers. There are a couple of issues to keep in mind, though.

---

[4] Orson Scott Card's outstanding novel Ender's Game *includes a storyline in which two children successfully establish themselves as influential writers, with nobody realizing how young they are. I've seen real-life cases that are similar.*

- Don't automatically assume the person you're chatting with is the person you think they are. You read in Chapter 11 that IM accounts are among the easiest accounts to steal (mostly because of automatic logon). So double-check that your buddy is really who they say they are before sharing anything personal.

- Be quick to block people not on your Buddy or Friends list.

I will sometimes accept an IM from a stranger—as long as it doesn't have an obscene name (obviously IM spam). I'll usually ask who they are and what they want before sharing any personal information. If the response is annoying or obscene, they get permanently blocked. If it's someone I know, as soon as I iden-tify them I put them on my Buddy list for future reference. If it's a pleasant stranger, I might engage in a brief conversation, but won't share any personal information (a request for personal information leads to an immediate block).

If you are facing ongoing harassment through IM, there are things you can do. I'll discuss them in the section "When Trouble Strikes" later in this chapter.

If You Have to Meet Someone You Met Online

Some people who meet online end up forming close friendships. The Internet use report referenced earlier states that 16 percent of the youth using the Internet meet people online who they considered close friends (even though few actually met in person). Most of these were other youth.

So here's the deal. If you do decide to meet someone in person, use some commonsense precautions.

- Ideally, you should talk to your parents before arranging to meet. Especially if you're younger.

- Don't give out your personal information. Instead, always meet for the first time in a public, safe, well-supervised place. Be sure to let friends or family know about the meeting—just in case.

- Don't meet the other person alone. Bring your parents or at least a friend.

Look at it this way: If the person you're meeting is not totally comfortable with the precautions you want to take, that's a very clear warning that some-thing isn't right. If someone warns you not to tell friends or parents about the friendship, that's awfully suspicious as well.

When Trouble Strikes

One of the surprising things about the Internet use report is how few teens reported problems that did occur. One teen I know explained his theory—teens don't report incidents because they're afraid their parents' response will be to simply disconnect the Internet or take away their computer. And you know what? In some cases I believe they are right—because let's face it, in many cases teens understand both the nature and risks of the Internet better than parents do.

So here's the deal. If you feel threatened online, if someone is harassing you or stalking you, there are things you can do.

Talk to your parents if you can. Show them the following paragraph I've addressed to parents if you think that may help:

> **NOTE TO PARENTS** Surveys show that most teens who run into uncomfortable or scary situations online don't tell their parents. There are many reasons for this, including fear that you will restrict their Internet use, or embarrassment over what they were doing. I strongly encourage you to discuss this issue with your son or daughter and to make it clear to them that they can come to you when problems occur without fear of punishment. It is possible to use online chat rooms safely, and if your teen is showing you this paragraph, chances are good they already know what precautions to take. You can make it safer yet by making sure your teen can talk to you without fear that you'll overreact.

You can call the police. One nice thing about all the media hype about the dangers of online chat rooms is that the police and FBI do take reports seriously. And go ahead and tell the person that you will be calling the FBI. This alone may be enough to scare them off. Police departments in larger cities often have cybercrime units that will understand exactly what you are talking about, and will be able to offer good advice as to how to proceed.

Copy every message you receive (including IM and chat messages) into a text file or print them out. Note the time and date of each one.[5]

In most cases, access to chat rooms requires an account on the chat room service. It's often possible for law enforcement officers to trace chat room names back to the individual who owns the account, or at least the originating machine.

Block any instant message sender who annoys you. If necessary, create a new screen name and abandon the old one.

---

[5] *If you are sent child pornography, do NOT store a copy—delete it immediately. It is illegal to possess, even to use as evidence. Instead, record the URL of the image if you have it.*

If you are in trouble, and you need someone to talk to, check your phone book for teen crises hotlines or runaway hotlines. Or you can call the national runaway hotline at 1-800-621-4000. **Remember—no matter how sympathetic your online friends are, no matter how well you think you know them, they are still strangers and may be lying about who they are.**

Are We Safe Yet?

This is a short chapter. Because the truth is that you already know what you need to do to remain safe. Your parents taught it to you when you were very young. Don't talk to strangers. Don't wander off with a stranger. Don't take candy from strangers. Don't tell a stranger your name and where you live.

The Internet is NOT a dangerous wilderness where teens are being constantly stalked by evildoers.[6] The miracle of the Internet is that for the first time it is actually possible for you to meet strangers, engage in conversation, and form friendships with them safely—just by following a few simple precautions that keep your online identity separate from your real one.

---

[6] *It is a dangerous wilderness where computer viruses breed. As you can probably tell, your computer is at significantly greater risk of being successfully attacked than you are!*

Scams

Dan

I can't even begin to tell you what a great month it's been. Since getting that new e-mail account I've received opportunities that you wouldn't believe-it's like a whole new world opening up to me. First, I lost 10 pounds with that new Phentermine and Adipex stuff. I look great. And guess what? I'm getting younger, and burning fat, with absolutely no dieting or exercising! I'm also feeling pretty relaxed thanks to the low cost Valium I got through another offer.

Oh, and you know that student loan I had outstanding? I got the rate lowered to 1.625% - my payment was down by 70%! Financially business is good. I got rid of all my debts and didn't even have to declare bankruptcy. A small investment has been bringing in $10,000 a week-I'm reaching 52 million people with my infomercial, and there's no work involved! I'm making another $5,000 a week with a new technology marketing system. I saved thousands on that property I was buying and got a fast mortgage approval as well. And I've invested in several new OTC companies that have shot through the roof.

I just got a free classic games CD-ROM for the kids. And a free digital camera.

And socially, you should see the dates I've been getting. And at no charge! And with unlimited supplies of Viagra I ⎯⎯⎯

Dear Mr. Appleman

We regret to inform you of the sudden passing of your friend. We found this last letter addressed to you and are forwarding it. The doctors say his death was due to sudden drop in blood pressure that occured when all blood in his body rushed to an extremity that had mysteriously grown from six inches to nearly 85 inches in length.

Regretfully yours
The Law Offices of Spammer and Spammer

The preceding letters are based on a selection of the spam I received in one 12-hour period.

TANSTAAFL

TANSTAAFL is short for "There ain't no such thing as a free lunch."[1] It's a fancy way of saying that nothing is really free—you pay for it in one way or another. And if an offer seems too good to be true, chances are it isn't true.

Scams appeal to your natural instinct to trust people.[2] They appeal to your greed. They appeal to your desires (whatever they may be). And sometimes they can be hard to resist.

Let me tell you the dirty secret about scams (whether delivered through spam or through the web).

The reason there's so much of it out there is because so much of it works.

That's right—people wouldn't send spam if it weren't for the fact that they do make money at it. All that pornography exists not because businesses love porn—it's because people are willing to buy it. And scams exist because scams work.

Yes, I know many of you might be thinking to yourself, "No way—I'm too smart to be taken." But let me tell you—those people are very good at what they do. Even the smartest, most vigilant people sometimes get tricked.

Top Scams

One of the best sites for reading about the latest scams belongs to the Federal Trade Commission (http://www.ftc.gov).[3] Another great resource is Scam-Busters at http://www.scambusters.org. Here are some of the top scams:

---

[1] *The acronym was coined by Robert A. Heinlein in his book* The Moon Is a Harsh Mistress. *If you aren't familiar with Heinlein's science fiction, run, do not walk, to your favorite bookstore (online or real) or library and start reading. The Moon Is a Harsh Mistress is a fine start. Stranger in a Strange Land is perhaps his best known. But you can't really go wrong with any of them.*

[2] *The term* **con artist** *comes from the word* **confidence**—*people who rip you off by first gaining your trust.*

[3] *You might have noticed I refer to this site in a number of places in this book. It's a good site, and if you're in the U.S., you or your parents are paying for it anyway with tax dollars, so you might as well take advantage of it. If you're not in the U.S., think of it as a gift from the U.S. government.*

Internet Auctions

I know several teens who have been ripped off on eBay—often to the tune of hundreds of dollars. For any major purchase, always pay by credit card (not debit card). As you learned in Chapter 10, credit cards provide significant protection in cases of fraud. That includes cases where the product you are buying is defective, misrepresented, or never arrives.

If the auction site offers an escrow service, be sure to request it.[4] If the seller isn't willing to use an escrow service or accept credit cards, you should be concerned.

Credit Card Fraud

Once a company has your credit card number, they can try to run up the charges—even if you gave it to them just to identify yourself as being 18 or over. Your liability is limited to $50 (if it's a credit card), but it can be a real hassle. Especially if you're under 18 and trying to explain to your parents why there are a string of charges from "Hilda's House of Porn."

Business Opportunities

Anything that promises you hundreds or thousands of dollars a day or week for doing nothing is a con—most likely a pyramid scheme, where the people who start the scheme make off with your money and leave you hoping to profit from the gullibility of someone else.

Pyramid schemes take many forms, but they are all illegal. The classic pyramid scheme is one where you are supposed to recruit others to sell something or invest. Then you (or your recruits) send all or part of that money or investment to the person who recruited you. Someday, when your recruits find their own recruits, those people are supposed to send you money and you'll be rich. The problem with these schemes (aside from the legality) is that you and your recruits run out of stupid friends before you actually make any money.

Work-at-home schemes often end up being little more than scams—where you invest money on a "work-at-home marketing kit." This kit teaches you how to try to sell "work-at-home marketing kits" to other people.

---

[4] With an escrow service, you send your money to the escrow service. The escrow service notifies the seller that it has the money and instructs them to ship the product. Once you notify the escrow service that you've received the product in good condition, the escrow service releases the money to the seller. This reduces the chance of fraud, because there is a trusted third party (the escrow service) making sure everyone does their part.

Bulk E-Mail

These folks either want to turn you into spammers (which is liable to cause you to lose your Internet account through most ISPs), or to sell you useless mailing lists so that you can presumably make money through sending spam.

Health and Diet Scams

These are the modern equivalent of the old patent medicine show, where a traveling salesperson mixes up some random ingredients and sells them to a crowd (usually after a partner, or "shill," pretends to be cured by the miraculous medicine).

Investment Opportunities

If you'd like to find out more about these, watch the movie *Boiler Room*, which shows an investment company using aggressive sales techniques to sell and manipulate the value of a company's stock. Yes, that kind of stuff actually happens. Even when legitimate, the smaller stocks pitched by these scams are highly subject to manipulation.

Vacation Prize Promotions

Even when a legitimate vacation is involved, the quality often turns out to be less than what you expect. Like that luxury cruise liner stateroom that turns out to be a rat-infested inside cabin.

The Nigerian Scam

This is one of my all-time favorites. You receive a desperate plea from an ex-government official (or their spouse) for a troubled African nation (usually but not necessarily Nigeria), explaining how they have millions of dollars hidden or locked away and only you can help get it out.

If you provide your bank account number and other personal information, they will deposit huge sums of money into your account, and let you keep most of it!

Amazingly enough, there are lots of people who actually believe that some total stranger will choose them to share millions of dollars with, and proceed to forward their bank account information, blank letterhead, and cash "to get things started."

Is It a Scam, or Isn't It?

Sometimes there seems to be a fine line between a scam and plain old-fashioned marketing spin. Like seeing a product with a "New and Improved" label on the box, only to discover that the only thing new and improved was the box.

Just the other day, a friend of mine told me about an FM antenna he was planning to buy for his stereo to improve reception. This amazing antenna had the ability to take the incoming electromagnetic radio wave and filter out the "bad" electrical part, keeping only the "good" magnetic part. Well, I admit, it's been a while since I got my degree in electronic engineering,[5] but last I heard, what an antenna does is take an electromagnetic wave and convert it into an electrical signal that can be amplified and played on your TV or radio. Now this may be a fine antenna, but if it is, why do they have to make up scientific nonsense to sell it? Won't the truth do?

Exaggerated and misleading advertisement is something we are exposed to every day, whether it's on TV or on the Internet. So remember to be skeptical, even when visiting legitimate sites.

Here are some of the more common techniques you'll see that may not be scams, but are at least misleading.

You Just Won!

What do you do when you see a message like this:

> Greetings,
>
> As part of our grand opening promotion of Portable-Paradise.com, we are running a prize drawing. Your e-mail address was selected from an e-mail marketing list, and you have actually won an amazing Apple iBook notebook computer!
> Your iBook features
>
> 800 MHz PowerPC G4 processor
>
> 12-inch TFT display with 1024×768 resolution
>
> 256MB RAM
>
> 30GB hard drive
>
> CD writer/DVD drive
>
> ATI Mobility Radeon 9200 with 32MB video memory
>
> Apple's latest OS X 10.3 "Panther" operating system
>
> To claim your prize, you may now visit our web site and enter in your details. Please note that this prize is only available to

---

[5] *I'm not being sarcastic—I actually have a degree in electronic engineering. One in computer science as well.*

people aged 18 years or over! If you are under 18, you must let an adult claim your prize for you. We have provided the following web link for you; it is temporary and expires in 72 hours. If you do not visit within this time, your prize shall unfortunately be returned to the prize pool. Here is your link!

`http://www.portable-paradise.com/cgi-bin/server.cgi?winner=`
`youremail@yourdomain.com&code=BMC733572011`[6]

On this page you will need to enter this pass code number to proceed: 25213.

This is very important. Do not lose that number! Provide us with your details, and we will simply send your iBook to you. We hope that you will enjoy your new Apple iBook.

Congratulations on winning.

When you click the link, you find yourself at what looks like a completely legitimate online store, complete with shopping card, privacy policy, online catalog—the works.

Is it legit, or not?

To tell you the truth, I can't absolutely tell you that it isn't. It's just barely possible that this is a real, honest promotion from a new online retailer.

I admit, I was intrigued enough to read this one, but after researching it further I found . . .

- Their site doesn't include a phone number to call for customer service.

- There is no "About" information that points to a physical mailing address.

- I have never signed up for a contest on this site, or ever heard of it before.

- A Google search on Portable-Paradise.com has no hits. Portable-Paradise.com combined with other keywords like "laptop" and "apple" show no relevant hits.

- However, a search on "You've won an Apple iBook" retrieved several hits on dslreports.com in their Spam and Scam Busters section, which shows that an identical message was sent from another domain in 2002. Readers on the forum concluded it was a scam then.

- There is information in the Whois database including an address and phone number, but nobody answers the phone (at least when I tried it).

Conclusion? If it's a scam (as I suspect), someone went to a great deal of trouble to make it look legitimate. It even made me think twice (though not enough to enter any personal information or credit card info).

---

[6] *Actual numbers and codes changed to protect **my** privacy*

Play the Game and Win!

You know those banners that ask you to click a monkey or target at the right time in order to win something? Trust me—it doesn't matter when you click them. You'll always "win."

But it's not necessarily a scam. Usually it's just a marketing gimmick trying to collect your personal information and sell you something.

Your Computer Is Vulnerable!

This is usually a pop-up window suggesting that a vulnerability has been detected on your computer. More often than not, it's from a company trying to sell you antivirus or privacy software. However, it can also be a scam—trying to convince you to install or run a program that, while claiming to protect your computer, will actually attack it.

Stay skeptical, and when in doubt—don't click the link.

Consumer Reports

Consumer Reports is a great organization when it comes to evaluating marketing claims. They don't accept advertisements and are a great source for objective product reviews. If you're undertaking a major purchase, a subscription to their web site or magazine can really save you a lot of grief, and probably some money as well. Visit `http://www.consumerreports.org` for more information.

How Not to Get Taken

Sorry, I can't offer a magic secret that will guarantee that you won't get conned. I can only offer some commonsense suggestions that should become habit.

- Don't trust e-mail solicitations. Since ⅔ of them are outright scams of one form or another, it's better to just delete them all. You won't be missing anything important.

- Don't click web banner ads just out of curiosity. If it's clear that the ad is promoting something you are interested in, and it's appearing on a legitimate site, go for it. But if it's just some mysterious teaser playing on your curiosity, don't give them the satisfaction.

- Never fill in a form that appears in an e-mail message. Never fill in a form on a web page linked to from an e-mail message unless you recognize the URL that appears in the address bar of your browser. Even if you do recognize the URL, don't enter any personal information into the form—instead, navigate on your own to the web site and use its account management tools.

- Anyone or any message that tries to scare you, warn you, or tempt you should be immediately suspect.

- Any message that asks for personal information, even if it seems to come from a legitimate site (such as PayPal, eBay, or Microsoft), is probably a scam. Remember—sites where you have an account already have your personal information. They certainly don't need to ask for it from you.

Urban Legends

Did you know the word *gullible* doesn't appear in any dictionary?

OK, so most of these aren't scams. And getting caught by them won't hurt you. However, they can be quite embarrassing when your friends and family discover that you have been tricked by one of them.

There are so many of these that I won't even bother listing them. Visit `http://www.urbanlegends.com` or `http://www.snopes.com`, sit back, relax, and enjoy two of the most fascinating sites on the web.

Parting Words

So here we are, at the end of the book. You've learned to protect your computer from viruses and hackers. You've learned to protect your privacy from strangers and friends. You've learned how to protect yourself from scams and stalkers. There are a couple of appendices after this that you might find useful, but those are more like bonus material. You now have a knowledge of computer security that, although it perhaps doesn't qualify you as an "expert," certainly takes you well past the beginner stage.

I hope you've enjoyed this journey. But before you leave (at least for the moment), I'd like to say a few parting words, and extend an invitation.

Believe it or not, most authors don't write for the money.[7] I mean, J. K. Rowling may be richer than the Queen of England, but I'm no J. K. Rowling, and the wizardry you've learned in this book is not quite as fantastic as that of Harry Potter[8] (though I dare say it is both more real and at times much more scary).

Authors write because they have a passion for their subject. I wrote this book because, more than anything else, I believe it is desperately needed and can make a difference. Viruses and privacy issues are huge problems, and no one person or even government can solve them alone. But, if I can help educate some people, help them protect their computers, preserve their privacy—even play games without long lag times—well, that's a great feeling. And if I pay a few grocery bills in the process—that would be nice too.

So I'd like to invite you to join me in spreading . . . a virus of a sort, if you will.

If you found that this book helped you, then chances are you'll agree that it will help your friends as well. So please, tell them about it. Tell them in person. Tell them online. Tell them in forums and newsgroups.

Because you see, if together we can get every single teen who uses a computer to follow the basic guidelines in this book, and convince them to protect their parents' computers as well, the number of viruses and amount of spam on the Internet will drop to nearly nothing. And if we can raise the awareness of privacy issues—and help people realize how vast the threat is to our privacy, then maybe we can elect representatives who will place a high value on individual rights.

We are really just at the beginning of the Internet age. And what we do together is going to shape it for decades to come. So help me spread the word.

Finally, I invite you to visit `http://www.AlwaysUseProtection.com`. That's where I'll be posting not only updates to the book, but also other information and links on security and privacy themes that I hope you will find of interest. I also want to hear your stories—and gradually turn the site into an ongoing resource for everyone who has read this book.

Thank you, and best of luck to you all.

Dan Appleman

---

[7] An author will typically see about $1 of a $15 book.

[8] No disrespect intended to J. K. Rowling. I confess—I love the Harry Potter books. And last I heard, she actually is richer than the Queen of England.

PART

IV

APPENDIXES

Everyday Security

Security is a big subject. In this book, I've tried to not only give you specific suggestions regarding computer security, but also teach you the how and why of security—to cover the concepts that will help you deal with not only today's risks, but tomorrow's as well.

But there's a lot of information in this book, and I also want to make sure you can get the information you need quickly. Yes, this book has a table of contents, and yes, this book has an index. But I wanted something else. Here, then, is a summary guide to everyday security tasks. Consider these the most important things you should do and be aware of every day. Obviously, it's simplified considerably from the text in the book, and I won't discuss the exceptions to the rules shown here. But as a quick reference, I hope you find it useful.

Protecting Your Computer

There are three things you need to secure your computer: an antivirus program, a firewall, and system updates.

Antivirus

- Keep your antivirus program active.
- Keep your subscription up to date.
- Be sure your antivirus program updates itself automatically.
- Use active scanning (the antivirus program monitors files as you use them).

Firewalls

- If you use a phone dial-up connection to the Internet, use a software firewall such as ZoneAlarm.

- If you use cable or DSL to connect, use a router that supports NAT (also called Internet Connection Sharing).

- Learn to open individual ports to allow access to services without taking down your entire firewall.

System Updates

- Back up key data before you perform a major update.

- Visit `http://windowsupdate.microsoft.com` and install all critical software updates.

- On XP, use automatic Windows Update.

Software and System Configuration

- Turn off automatic downloading of messages (Outlook and Outlook Express).

- Turn off JavaScript and ActiveX controls in e-mail viewers.

- Use a password on your system.

- Use encryption if you have a wireless network.

- Turn off unnecessary services.

- Set your cookie configuration to block or prompt on all third-party cookies. Consider using prompts on first-party cookies as well.

- Turn off automatic login and password storage for web sites.

Spyware and Adware Blockers

- Use spyware and adware removal tools to help protect your privacy.

Using Your Computer

Here is a summary of things you should always keep in mind while using your computer.

Checking E-Mail

- Don't open attachments.
- Don't click links inside e-mail messages.

Floppies and CDs

- Scan floppy disks and CDs from untrusted sources for viruses.
- Hold the Shift key down when inserting a suspect CD to prevent the autorun program from starting.

Browsing the Web

- Scan any downloaded files for viruses.
- Don't trust ActiveX controls unless you explicitly request one.
- Don't give out personal information unless you truly trust the site.
- Don't give out your Social Security number or birth date unless you are absolutely certain it is safe.
- Deny permission to set cookies to all but the most trusted sites.

Instant Messenger Programs

- Turn off automatic login.
- Block harassing messages.

Shopping Online

- Use credit cards, not cash or debit cards.
- Use credit cards or escrow services on auction sites.

Passwords

- Use at least three passwords: one for high security, one for moderate security, and one for your computer. Create "throwaway" passwords for sites you don't trust or plan to visit again.
- Avoid the obvious (birth dates, names, etc.).
- Mix some numbers in with the password.

P2P

- Avoid the adware/spyware versions of P2P software.
- Turn off file sharing if your client allows it, otherwise take files out of your shared file folder.
- Do not act as a supernode or share files.

Privacy

- Clear your history, file cache (offline content), and cookies after using a public computer.

Chat Rooms

- Don't give out any personally identifiable information to strangers, no matter how nice they seem.
- Remember—everybody lies online.

Links

Here is a summary of key sites referenced in this book.[1]

- http://www.AlwaysUseProtection.com: For updated links, book updates and corrections, and anything else I can think of that might be fun or useful

Browsers

- http://www.microsoft.com
- http://www.netscape.com
- http://www.mozilla.org
- http://www.opera.com

Antivirus

- http://www.symantec.com, http://www.mcafee.com: Antivirus software
- http://www.lavasoftusa.com, http://www.safer-networking.org: Adware removal software
- http://www.cert.org, http://securityresponse.symantec.com, http://vil.nai.com, http://www.virusbtn.com, http://netsecurity.about.com: General antivirus information

Visit AlwaysUseProtection.com for more recommendations.

Antispam

- http://spambayes.sourceforge.net
- http://www.sunbelt-software.com
- http://www.mcafee.com

---

[1] *There are many other sites with security information and companies that provide security products. These were chosen primarily based on popularity and familiarity. Additional sites and companies will be listed on AlwaysUseProtection.com based on visitor recommendations and ongoing experience—the Internet changes quickly, so be sure to check in for updates. No company paid to be included in this book. With the exception of Amazon.com, and of course, AlwaysUseProtection.com, I do not own any stock in any of the companies mentioned in this book.*

Visit AlwaysUseProtection.com for more recommendations.

Routers and Firewalls

- http://www.linksys.com, http://www.netgear.com, http://www.dlink.com, http://www.speedstream.com, http://www.3com.com, http://www.hawkingtech.com: Routers

- http://www.zonealarm.com: Firewall software

Visit AlwaysUseProtection.com for more recommendations.

Backup

- http://www.maxtor.com: External hard drive

- http://www.backup.com: Internet backup service

- http://www.apc.com: Backup power (UPS)

Privacy and Consumer Rights

- http://www.ftc.gov: Federal Trade Commission

- http://www.eff.org: Electronic Frontier Foundation—privacy rights advocate

- http://www.americanexpress.com: One-time use credit card numbers

- http://www.heidi.ie: Eraser (secure file erase—also see http://www.sourceforge.net)

- http://www.webroot.com, http://www.acronis.com, http://www.mcafee.com, http://www.symantec.com: Privacy software

- http://www.anonymizer.com: Anonymous web surfing

Scams and Fraud

- http://www.ftc.gov, http://www.scambusters.org, http://www.consumerreports.org: Fraud and scam information

- http://www.urbanlegends.com, http://www.snopes.com: Urban legends

Other

- `http://www.knoppix.com`: Linux distribution that runs off a CD
- `http://www.powerquest.com`: Partition manager
- `http://www.safeware.com`: Computer insurance

Registry Tricks

Your system registry is a database on your computer—a file that contains centralized information that controls every aspect of your system, from key system software to individual application settings.

How important is the registry? If every file on your system was left alone, and you scrambled your registry, your system would be dead. Nothing would run. It wouldn't even boot. Lose your registry and it's game over—you won't lose your data files, but you'll need to reinstall your system. That's why emergency repair disks and system save points save the registry—Windows does what it can to make sure that the registry information is recoverable if something goes wrong.

But there isn't much it can do if you damage your registry intentionally.

In this appendix, I'm going to show you how the experts edit the registry. Knowledge of how to edit the registry can help you manually disable many worms and Trojans.

> ⚡ **CAUTION** Anything you do here is entirely at your own risk. Registry editing is designed for expert-level system configuration—and even the experts have been known to damage their registries using these techniques. You can wipe out your system if you accidentally delete or modify the wrong entry.

Using the Registry Editor

Start the Registry Editor by going to the Start menu, choosing Run, and entering the command RegEdit. Figure B-1 shows the main window of the Registry Editor.

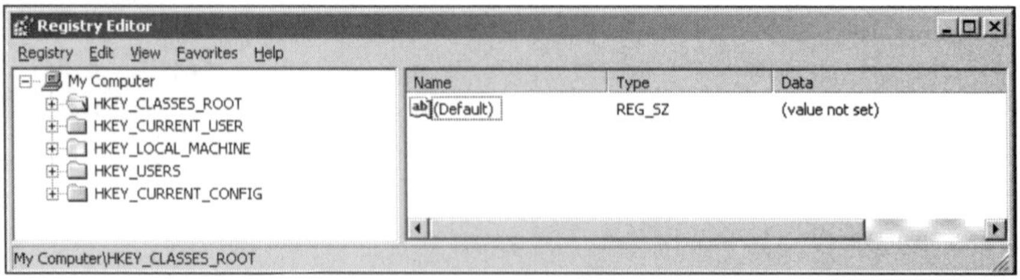

Figure B-1 The Registry Editor, main window

The Registry Editor window divides into two parts. The left-hand side contains objects called *keys*. Think of them like directory folders—containers that hold various values.

The right-hand side contains the values. Think of them a bit like files, except that they are individual numbers and strings that have names.

At the top level, your computer has five keys. Of these, the one we'll be most concerned with is named **HKEY_LOCAL_MACHINE**. That's the key that holds your machine configuration and settings.[1]

You can click on the little plus (+) symbol on the left to expand and collapse the subkeys (yep, keys contain other keys). Figure B-2 shows what happens when you expand the **HKEY_LOCAL_MACHINE** key, and then expand the **SOFTWARE** key.[2]

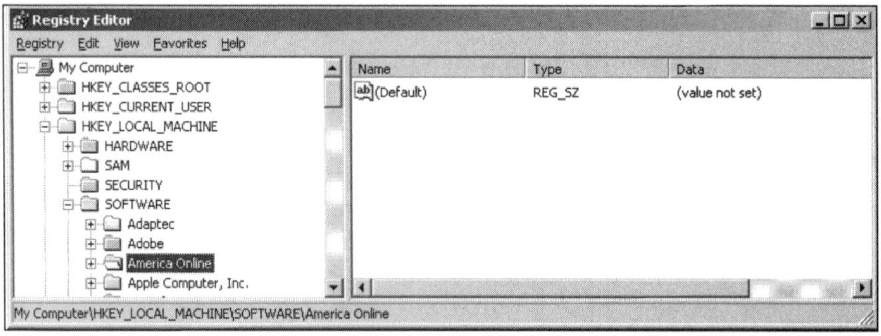

Figure B-2 Viewing subkeys in the Registry Editor

The highlighted key, America Online, would be referred to as

```
HKEY_LOCAL_MACHINE\SOFTWARE\America Online
```

[1] You may be wondering why I'm not bothering to explain the other keys. The thing is, people write entire books just about the registry. If I started trying to explain HKEY_CLASSES_ROOT, next thing I'd be trying to explain classes, COM, type libraries, AppIDs, GUIDs.... Anyway, you'd die of boredom long before we got to anything actually useful. So trust me, not only don't you need to know about the other keys—you don't want to know about them!

[2] The keys that appear under the SOFTWARE key on your system will probably differ, depending on what applications you have installed.

I'll continue to use that syntax to describe keys from here on.

As you can see, different applications can store their own software settings under the HKEY_LOCAL_MACHINE\SOFTWARE key. This is where applications will tend to store their machine settings. If you navigate to the HKEY_CURRENT_USER\SOFTWARE key, you'll see subkeys where different applications store settings that apply to the current user (some applications are able to keep different settings for each user on a machine—this is where they store those settings).

The key you'll be most interested in is is at

```
HKEY_LOCAL_MACHINE\SOFTWARE\Microsoft\Windows\CurrentVersion\Run
```

Figure B-3 shows the values located under this key on one of my systems.

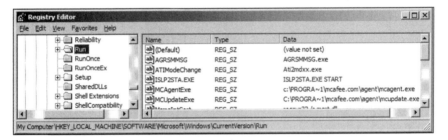

Figure B-3 Example of the contents of the Run key

Look in the right pane of the Registry Editor. Each line contains a value. The value is a text string (that's what the REG_SZ means), and the data is the command line to a program that should be run every time Windows starts.

Why is this important?

Because worms and Trojans love to install themselves in this key. That's what allows them to run automatically each time you start your machine.

If you find a worm or Trojan in this list, you can delete it by clicking it, and then either choosing the Edit ▸ Delete command from the menu or right-clicking and choosing Delete.

You should also check the following key:

```
HKEY_CURRENT_USER\SOFTWARE\Microsoft\Windows\CurrentVersion\Run
```

Programs under this key start automatically when this user (the one currently logged on) logs in again.

The RunOnce and RunOnceEx subkeys (under both the HKEY_CUR-RENT_MACHINE and HKEY_CURRENT_USER keys) may also be used by viruses, but this is uncommon, as Windows runs them once and then deletes them. They are used when you need to launch a program one time only the next time Windows starts.

Which Programs Are Viruses?

Figuring out which program should be deleted is where the real challenge lies. The safest way is to look at the manual removal instructions for the virus you have—the major antivirus sites include descriptions of known viruses and instructions on how to remove them manually (if possible—remember, some viruses prevent the Registry Editor from running).

You can sometimes figure it out for yourself. Each line consists of the path to the executable file. There are some tricks to be aware of though:

When you see a directory with a ~ character, you're looking at the shortened name of the directory. For example, C:\PROGRA~1 actually refers to C:\Program Files.

Sometimes the filename isn't at the start of the line. You may see a line like this:

```
RUNDLL.EXE SETUPX.DLL,InstallHinfSection 132 C:\WINDOWS\INF\SHELL.INF
```

In this case, RunDLL is a program that runs other programs or libraries (with the extension DLL). So if you see any filenames (files with the extension .exe, .dll, .bat, etc.) in the registry value, any of them might be a virus.

> ⚡ **CAUTION** Most of the files you find in this key aren't viruses, and are in fact required for your computer to work. So don't delete any entries from the registry unless you're certain they are viruses.

Once you've identified the filename, find it on your system using the Windows Explorer. It will usually be in your Windows or Windows\System directory. One way to do this is to just search for the filename.

Once you've found it, right-click it, select Properties, and then choose the Version tab.

In Figure B-3, the first program is something called AGRSMMSG.exe. What does that program do? Frankly, I had no idea when I first snapped that screen shot. But I found the file in the Windows directory, and looking at the version information saw the dialog box in Figure B-4.

I guess that's the program that runs my laptop's modem.

Worms and Trojans can lie about their version information, and files infected with viruses still have their original description. However, many virus authors just can't resist showing off, and will have missing or suspicious version information.[3]

I can't stress enough the risks of making a mistake here—if you delete a key or value that is critical to your system, it will stop working.

---

[3] Not every program with missing information is a virus, but it is awfully suspicious, as professional and commercial software developers all know how to set version information for a program.

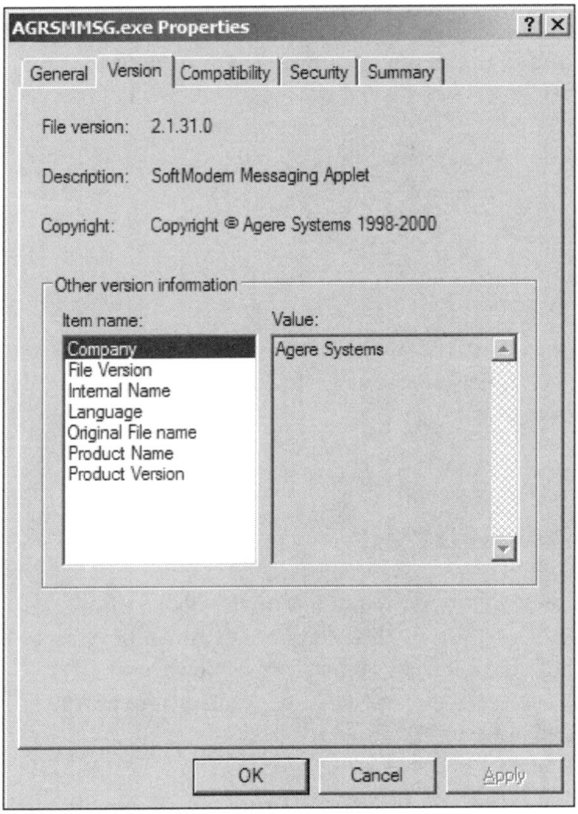

Figure B-4 Sample version information

Other Places to Look

There are a few other places where viruses can insert themselves so that they run automatically when a system starts.

Services

Occasionally a virus will install itself as a special kind of program called a *service*. A list of services can be found in the registry at the key

`HKEY_LOCAL_MACHINE\SYSTEM\CurrentControlSet\Services`

Each subkey is the name of a service. Look for the value ImagePath under the service's key to see the name of the program that is run when Windows starts up.

Win.ini

A long time ago, this file (found in the Windows directory) was used for system configuration (back before the registry was invented). It may not be used for much, but it still works.

You may find in the file a few lines that look like this:

```
[Windows]
Run=
Load=
```

The Run= and Load= lines instruct Windows to start and run (or load) the specified file when Windows starts. Viruses will often insert themselves both in the registry and in the win.ini file.

Disabling CD Autorun

Way back in Chapter 3, I promised to show you how to disable autorun for your CD drives. Autorun is actually a very low-risk operation—most viruses are spread nowadays through the Internet rather than via floppies or CDs. Nevertheless, if you do find yourself looking at CDs obtained from untrustworthy sources, it's a good idea to turn autorun off.

Figure B-5 shows you the contents of the HKEY_LOCAL_MACHINE\System\CurrentControlSet\Services\Cdrom key. As you can see, there is a value named Autorun, which by default is set to 1.

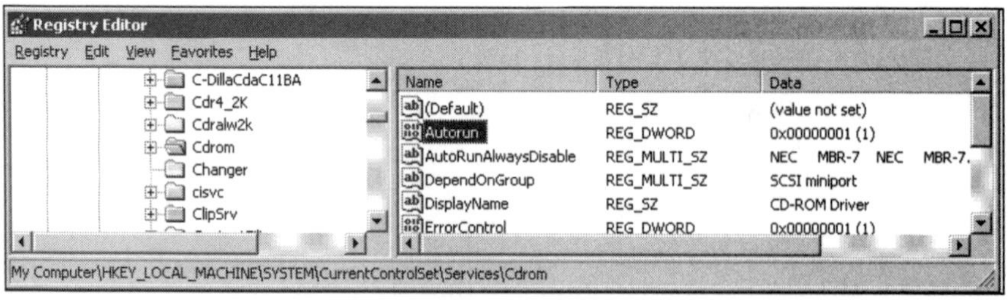

Figure B-5 Registry entry for the autorun feature

To turn off the autorun feature, double-click the Autorun value. You'll see the dialog box shown in Figure B-6.

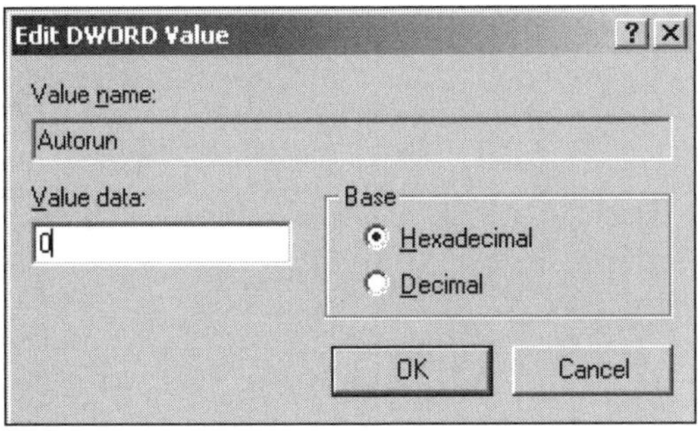

Figure B-6 Editing a numeric value in the registry

Change the number from 1 to 0, and click OK. Once you restart your system, the autorun feature is disabled.

A Note for Parents

The vast majority of parents of teenagers find the experience to be, how shall I put it, somewhat interesting. I've probably taught and worked with hundreds of teenagers, and if there's one thing I've learned, it's that it's both unfair and in fact impossible to lump them all into one group. The fact is, the stereotypes of teens that you see portrayed in the media do not reflect reality. And any advice I offer to you that addresses teens in general has to be interpreted in the context of your teenager and the relationship you share.

That made the material in this appendix some of the most challenging in the book to write. I've met teens who know next to nothing about their computers, and others who know more than I do in some areas. There are teens who discuss their online computer use with their parents and wouldn't dream of violating the rules they set, and others who secretly run their own porn web sites on a parent's computer with them none the wiser.[1]

This book is based on two fundamental truths: First, most teenagers today are perfectly capable of taking responsibility for their own computer and online security (whether they want to or choose to is another question, but they definitely have the ability). Second, most teenagers are fundamentally good people who, given the opportunity, will act in the best interests of themselves, their families, and their community.

With this in mind, and knowing you need to interpret what follows in the context of your own situation, I'd like to offer you a number of suggestions and observations that I believe will help you help your teen to keep your systems safe and protect yourselves and your privacy.

---

[1] *Good news: There are a lot more of the former than the latter.*

Teenagers Aren't Children

The *Children's Online Privacy Protection Act* (COPPA) makes it clear: As far as online privacy goes, teenagers aren't children. When I first started writing this book, I thought it would be for kids and teens, but I hadn't written one chapter before I realized that would be a mistake. You can't expect younger children to take responsibility for their own computer security. It requires patience and skills and an understanding of consequences that most younger kids don't have. So if you're a parent of younger children, this book can help— but it's up to you to read the book and apply the techniques you learn yourself. While a smart 11 or 12 year old might do well with this book, it really was designed for teenagers to help themselves.

The $99 Security Budget

I've done my best throughout the book to focus on security precautions that cost nothing to apply. However, there are some things you'll need that aren't free:

- An antivirus subscription
- A NAT-based router (for those who are on cable or DSL)
- This book (sorry, just couldn't resist)

Total cost: under $100, then maybe $30–$40/year afterwards.

My advice to you is simple: After reading this book, your teen will probably understand and care enough about security to pay for these things themselves. But I suggest that this is an expense that *you* should offer to cover. Don't take it out of their allowance. Don't make it a birthday or holiday gift. Don't make them pay for it with a part-time job. Think of this expense in the same category as healthy food, clothing, and medical care.[2] It may sound like a lot, but spending $40 or so to protect a $400 computer isn't so terrible, and a one-time expense of $50 on a DSL line that is costing you $20 per month isn't bad either. If money is tight, look for used routers on eBay—you don't need the latest and greatest to do a good job. Look for specials on antivirus software (they appear frequently). Borrow this book from a library if you can't afford it. But these are things you can't skimp on.

---

[2] *Of course, if you are one of those parents who makes their teens pay for these things, then you would have them pay for this as well.*

Grow Your Own IT Manager

Medium and large companies have people called Information Technology (IT) managers whose job it is to keep all their computers running properly and make sure the systems are kept up to date and secure. If you've read this book, you know that security for the home is not terribly complex, but setting it up (and cleaning up any problems) can be quite time consuming.

Consider letting your teenager be your household's IT manager. As long as they're already learning to protect their machine, why not let them protect yours as well? Scanning for viruses and backing up systems can be part of their monthly responsibilities—perhaps in place of less interesting chores. Even if you pay them for the work, it will be a lot less expensive than having your local computer shop do it for you (and a small investment in protecting your systems can save you a small fortune in cleanup costs).

Don't Expect Perfection

There is no such thing as perfect computer security. Even if your son or daughter memorizes this book, and studies every book and web site available on computer security and privacy, there is always the possibility that a problem will occur.

When problems do occur, don't overreact, and don't assume they did anything wrong. Give your teen a chance to deal with the problem. And try to avoid draconian punishments or restrictions. Remember—adults suffer from these problems as much or more than teens do.

Don't Rely on Technology to Teach Values

Lots of companies out there would be glad to sell you software that will monitor your teen's computer. They'll sell you filter software to control what your teen can see. They'll sell you monitoring software to let you see what they've browsed.

Frankly, I don't think much of these tools.

Oh, make no mistake—they have their place with younger children (and you should definitely consider this kind of software for them). But I do not recommend it for teens for several reasons:

- Most teens have the skills to bypass or disable this kind of software if they want to.

- While computer security problems are very common, they aren't generally dangerous. So if you're going to use more invasive forms of monitoring, use them for serious issues like preventing drug use, not computer issues.

- Let's face it, monitoring and filtering software carries the implicit message, "I don't trust your intentions" or "I don't trust your ability to protect yourself." Personally, I think it's better to start with trust and deal with the occasional disappointment than to start from a position of mistrust.

Instead of using monitoring and filtering software, I encourage you to discuss these issues with your teenager. Talk about your expectations and your values—what kinds of sites you expect them to visit or avoid. And check in now and then to see how things are going.

You'll get a lot further teaching your teens values by talking to them than by trying to find technology to do it for you.

Final Thoughts

If there's one thing I know about teens in general, it's this: They are capable of doing far more than most adults give them credit for. Computer security on home systems (or lack thereof) is a huge problem right now, and I wrote this book with the belief that not only can teens be a part of the overall solution to this problem, but they can also take the lead.

So I encourage you to sit back and give your teenager the opportunity to take charge of their own computer security, and maybe even yours. While I obviously can't make any guarantees, I am confident that the vast majority of you will be positively astonished by the results.

Index

forums.apress.com

JOIN THE APRESS FORUMS AND BE PART OF OUR COMMUNITY. You'll find discussions that cover topics of interest to IT professionals, programmers, and enthusiasts just like you. If you post a query to one of our forums, you can expect that some of the best minds in the business—especially Apress authors, who all write with *The Expert's Voice™*—will chime in to help you. Why not aim to become one of our most valuable participants (MVPs) and win cool stuff? Here's a sampling of what you'll find:

DATABASES
Data drives everything.

Share information, exchange ideas, and discuss any database programming or administration issues.

PROGRAMMING/BUSINESS
Unfortunately, it is.

Talk about the Apress line of books that cover software methodology, best practices, and how programmers interact with the "suits."

INTERNET TECHNOLOGIES AND NETWORKING
Try living without plumbing (and eventually IPv6).

Talk about networking topics including protocols, design, administration, wireless, wired, storage, backup, certifications, trends, and new technologies.

WEB DEVELOPMENT/DESIGN
Ugly doesn't cut it anymore, and CGI is absurd.

Help is in sight for your site. Find design solutions for your projects and get ideas for building an interactive Web site.

JAVA
We've come a long way from the old Oak tree.

Hang out and discuss Java in whatever flavor you choose: J2SE, J2EE, J2ME, Jakarta, and so on.

SECURITY
Lots of bad guys out there—the good guys need help.

Discuss computer and network security issues here. Just don't let anyone else know the answers!

MAC OS X
All about the Zen of OS X.

OS X is both the present and the future for Mac apps. Make suggestions, offer up ideas, or boast about your new hardware.

TECHNOLOGY IN ACTION
Cool things. Fun things.

It's after hours. It's time to play. Whether you're into LEGO® MINDSTORMS™ or turning an old PC into a DVR, this is where technology turns into fun.

OPEN SOURCE
Source code is good; understanding (open) source is better.

Discuss open source technologies and related topics such as PHP, MySQL, Linux, Perl, Apache, Python, and more.

WINDOWS
No defenestration here.

Ask questions about all aspects of Windows programming, get help on Microsoft technologies covered in Apress books, or provide feedback on any Apress Windows book.

HOW TO PARTICIPATE:
Go to the Apress Forums site at **http://forums.apress.com/**.
Click the New User link.